THE REFUGE

THE REFUGE

*A Look into the Future and the
Power of Living in a Christian Community*

JIM BAKKER
AND
KEN ABRAHAM

A
JANET
THOMA
BOOK

THOMAS NELSON PUBLISHERS
Nashville

Published in association with the literary agency of Alive Communications, 7680 Goddard Street, Suite 200, Colorado Springs, CO 80920.

Scripture quotations noted KJV are from the KING JAMES VERSION.

Scripture quotations noted NASB are from the NEW AMERICAN STANDARD BIBLE®, © Copyright The Lockman Foundation 1960, 1962, 1963, 1968, 1971, 1972, 1973, 1975, 1977. Used by permission.

Scripture quotations noted NIV are from the HOLY BIBLE: NEW INTERNATIONAL VERSION®. Copyright © 1973, 1978, 1984 by International Bible Society. Used by permission of Zondervan Publishing House. All rights reserved.

Scripture quotations noted NKJV are from THE NEW KING JAMES VERSION. Copyright © 1979, 1980, 1982, Thomas Nelson, Inc., Publishers.

Scripture quotations noted NRSV are from the NEW REVISED STANDARD VERSION of the Bible. Copyright © 1989 by the Division of Christian Education of the National Council of The Churches of Christ in the U.S.A. All rights reserved.

Scripture quotations noted TLB are from *The Living Bible,* copyright © 1971. Used by permission of Tyndale House Publishers, Inc., Wheaton, Illinois 60189. All rights reserved.

Library of Congress Cataloging-in-Publication Data

Bakker, Jim, 1940–
  The refuge : the joy of Christian community in a torn-apart world / Jim Bakker with Ken Abraham.
    p. cm.
  Includes bibliographical references (p.).
  ISBN 0-7852-7459-6
  1. Community—Religious aspects—Christianity. 2. Bakker, Jim, 1940– I. Abraham, Ken. II. Title.

  BV4517.5 .B35 2000
  262—dc21   00-028285
                                                                                    CIP

Published in Nashville, Tennessee, by Thomas Nelson, Inc.

Printed in the United States of America
1 2 3 4 5 6 7 8 9 10 BVG 09 08 07 06 05 04 03 02 01 00

To Lori Graham Bakker,

a precious gift from
God to me

CONTENTS

PART II:
LIVING OUT YOUR FAITH IN A COMMUNITY EXPERIENCE

PART I

LIVING IN THE
LIGHT
OF COMMUNITY

WHO YA GONNA CALL?

"HOW LONG DO YOU think the power will be out this time?" Christine asked pensively. "I'm afraid our food in the refrigerator is going to spoil."

"Hard to tell," Stan answered as he lit a candle. "The power has been out since early this morning, so please don't open the freezer any more than necessary. The ice cream is melting, but the meat should be okay for a while if we don't let any more cold air escape. Maybe we ought to go to the grocery store and buy some beans and other nonperishable food. We might be in for a long haul."

Stan stared out the window of the apartment he and Christine had been renting for the past six months. The couple had lived with Christine's parents for the first three years of their marriage, and although they were grateful for the family's hospitality, Stan and Christine were ecstatic when they could finally afford their own place. It was with a tremendous sense of achievement and freedom that they cut the invisible family ties that had connected them to Christine's parents. They had packed all their worldly possessions in the back of a U-Haul trailer and moved to a medium-priced apartment south of Los Angeles. They were not far from La Jolla, about an hour away from Christine's and Stan's families—far enough to have some privacy, but close enough that if they ever needed anything, some family member could come to their rescue.

"Free at last, free at last! Thank God we are free at last!" Stan had quipped playfully in his best Martin Luther King Jr. imitation, as they unloaded the last box containing their belongings.

"Yes, isn't it grand to finally be on our own?" Christine had commented.

✛ ✛ ✛

Now, six months later, in the aftermath of a stock market crash and shortages of almost everything, Stan wasn't so convinced that they had made the right move. *We're on our own, that's for sure,* he thought.

The normally well-lighted apartment complex looked almost sinister in the eerie darkness. The wind whipped up, swaying the trees, rustling the leaves, and making the ordinarily pastoral scene of the apartment complex's common areas appear somehow threatening. Adding to the surreal effect, here and there, Stan could see the flickering flames of candlelight dancing on the window shades of some of their fellow apartment dwellers. Many windows, however, were pitch black.

As Stan stared into the darkness, he heard a noise in the bedroom. Natalie, the couple's eighteen-month-old toddler, had roused from her sleep. "Maybe I better go to the store," Stan suggested, "and you can attend to Natalie." It wasn't Stan's disdain for changing dirty diapers so much as his concern for Christine's going out into the ominous-looking night that influenced Stan's decision.

"Okay, that will be fine," said Christine, already on her way to Natalie's room. "Try to get some bread and milk if you can. When I was at the store yesterday, the shelves were nearly bare. There wasn't a loaf of bread in the entire store. And I haven't been able to get milk for several days now. It's unbelievable the way people are reacting to this thing. I think people are stocking up as though it's a winter ice storm in Georgia."

"Well, you can't really blame them. Nobody wants to take any chances. Every time there is the least bit of bad weather or the slightest natural calamity, everyone converges on the banks and the grocery stores. I don't know when we will learn that the panic is more dangerous than the actual problem."

Stan pulled on a light jacket. The temperature had plummeted since the sun had gone down. It was unusually cold out that night, and with winter coming on, he'd soon need a heavy coat rather than the jacket. Worse yet, because the electricity was off in the apartment complex, not only were there no lights, there was no heat, either. "You may want to put a sweater on Natalie. It's getting chilly in here. I'll be back as soon as I can, honey," Stan called to his wife.

"I'm going to stop and put some gas in the car on the way to the store. No telling how long the lines will be at the pumps. But I'll try to hurry. If you need anything, just give me a call on the cellular phone. I love you, Christine. I love you, Natalie!"

"We love you, Stan," Christine called from Natalie's bedroom. "Please hurry if you can."

Stan closed and locked the door behind him as he headed toward his car. He put the key in the ignition, and the 1985 Chevy groaned until the engine reluctantly turned over. Stan cursed the blinking LED clock on the dash. No matter how often he reset the clock, it skipped back to 12:00 and continued blinking. For a while, the clock had bugged Stan so much that he had put a piece of duct tape over it, just so he would not have to be greeted by the irrepressible flashing green numbers every time he got in the car. But Christine said the tape looked stupid and, besides, they weren't the only ones with blinking lights in their cars these days. At least their car started.

Stan noted with concern that his gas gauge still worked accurately, as the indicator tilted far to the left, hovering precariously close to "E." He had planned to get gas anyhow, but he didn't realize they were so low. *This is no time to be out of gas,* Stan fumed, frustrated that Christine apparently hadn't filled up the last time she was out. *Why can't that woman get it through her head—gas isn't always available these days! We have to get it when we can.* Stan whipped the car out of the apartment area and headed toward his usual service station. Even at this hour, the roads leading toward L.A. were congested.

Sure enough, as the gas station came into sight, the right lane of traffic slowed to a crawl, then a stop. Cars lined the roadside for nearly half a mile, waiting for their turn at the pump. Stan's parents had told him that life now was reminiscent of the gas lines they had experienced during the Arab oil embargo in the early 1970s, when gas prices had skyrocketed while available supplies plummeted. This time, however, things were even worse. In an attempt to service as many customers as possible, many gas stations limited the amount of gasoline they sold to each customer. No more than ten dollars' worth could be purchased on good days, five dollars' worth when the station's supply was running out. Some days, a handwritten sign alerted customers to the bad news: NO GAS TODAY.

Just as Stan inched the Chevy across the gas station's property line, an attendant came out to the sidewalk and put up the dreaded sign: NO POWER, NO GAS. TRY TOMORROW. *Tomorrow!* Stan cringed. *I'll be lucky to make it home tonight! And I still have to get to the grocery store!*

Although the gas pumps were turned off, the snack bar and convenience store portion of the station remained open, lit by battery-powered emergency lighting. Stan couldn't help noticing the unusually large number of people congregating inside the store, in front of the food area. Many were buying whatever staple food items they could find on the shelves, but a large number of people were simply milling about as though shell-shocked. It looked to Stan as though they were gathered around a radio, listening. Some were crying; others sat dumbfounded outside on the sidewalk curb, as though they had been suddenly overtaken by a dizzy spell and had sought the first available place to sit down before they fell down.

Something strange is going on, Stan thought. Stan pulled his car over to the station parking area and turned off the ignition. He hopped out of the car and gingerly walked toward the crowd. The closer he got, the more he felt as though he had intruded on a funeral procession.

Everyone wore somber expressions. Many people wept openly. Others stared blankly into nothingness. Several women huddled together, arm in arm, swaying precariously, looking as though the entire group might tumble to the ground if even one of them let go.

A man and two teenage boys stood to the right of the store entryway. Stan noted with bewilderment that they were praying. *Praying at a gas station? For what? Asking God to miraculously send a fresh supply of gasoline? Ha!* Stan chuckled at the thought.

Stan walked past the praying fellows and entered the station. The interior of the convenience store section of the gas station was surprisingly quiet, especially considering the large number of people in the building. People pressed against a counter, focusing their attention on a small radio behind the counter.

"Turn it up!" a large disheveled-looking woman called from the aisle next to the darkened ice cream freezer.

"The volume is up as high as it will go," a man behind the counter replied. "My batteries are getting low. I'll replace them in a few minutes, but I don't want to miss anything right now. Just try to keep it down in here, and we'll all be able to hear."

Stan nudged a middle-aged fellow dressed in jeans and a sweatshirt. "What's going on?"

"They're about to give the latest death toll," the man replied sadly.

"Death toll? From what? Is something wrong? Was there an accident? A wreck on the freeway? People just need to slow down a bit when we have these brownouts . . ." Stan shook his head disgustedly.

"This is not just another brownout," replied the man in the sweatshirt.

"Oh?"

"Do you mean you haven't heard?"

"Heard what? What are you talking about? Our power has been out in our apartment complex, and I haven't seen a television or heard a radio broadcast all day. What's happened?"

"There was an earthquake in Los Angeles. A big one."

"So what's new?" Stan answered flippantly. He quickly sobered. He didn't mean to sound so callous, but earthquakes in California were nothing new, especially these days. According to recent reports, seismic activity was so rampant that the needles on the recording machines were having to be replaced regularly.

The man glared back at Stan as though he had insulted his mother. "Los Angeles is gone," he said icily.

"What? Gone! What do you mean, gone?"

"The entire downtown section . . . has been destroyed. It's gone. All the skyscrapers, the hotels, the banks, the insurance company buildings—everything just crumbled. From what they are saying on the news, it was unlike any earthquake L.A. has ever experienced before. The plates beneath the surface didn't just slide apart; they seemed to surge together, forcing each other into the air, and then buckled. It was as though all the pressure of the ages just blew the ground apart."

Stan could not believe it! He stood, mouth gaping, while the man continued.

"Thousands of people are dead; who can guess how many are injured? The quake hit right at rush hour, twisting the freeways that run through downtown into massive concrete and metal ribbons. Water lines are ruptured, electric lines are down, and gas mains are broken—all with no way to even get help into the city. Fires are burning out of control . . ."

"Shhhh!" A woman in front of Stan turned around, holding her index finger to her lips, quieting the man in the sweatshirt. "It's a news bulletin!"

An irritating but attention-capturing sound emitted from the boom box behind the counter. The sound repeated several more times before a voice could be heard. "Your attention, please. This is the Federal Emergency Management System. This is not a test. Repeat: this is not a test. The earthquake that struck Los Angeles earlier this afternoon is of massive proportions. We still have an extremely dangerous and unstable situation. Aftershocks are continuing to occur, and it is unsafe to go near the city. Repeat: do not, under any circumstances, attempt to enter the city. Those of you living between the Mammoth Lake area and Los Angeles should evacuate in an eastern or northern direction immediately. Do not go south; do not go west toward the sea. Do not attempt to pack your belongings. Take only enough food and water for your family and proceed immediately to the safe areas to which you will be directed. National Guard troops will assist you in the evacuation."

The moment the emergency management officer stopped speaking, the gas station crowd erupted into loud, frightened wails. Several people—men and women—fainted and slumped to the floor.

"I've got to get into the city," one man yelled. "My wife works in the Prudential Building."

"Are you crazy? Didn't you hear what the guy just said?"

"I don't care. I'm going to try!"

Just then, the man behind the counter began waving his arms up and down violently. "Quiet!" he screamed. "Quiet, everybody. Something's happening!"

The crowd calmed somewhat, and amid crackling static, Stan heard the frantic voice of a local radio broadcaster. "It's horrendous! This cannot be happening, yet even as I speak, the situation worsens. Tonight, approximately fifteen minutes ago, a gigantic fissure opened in the earth near Lake Crowley, otherwise known as the Long Valley Reservoir, in the Mammoth Lakes region of the eastern Sierra Nevada area. According to eyewitness reports from individuals who observed the lake from nearby higher ground, the lake seemed to heave into the air, virtually catapulting its contents out of the lake basin. Apparently coinciding with the earthquake—or perhaps causing it—is a volcanic eruption in the area, spewing lava, steam, and volcanic ash into the sky. According to the state's Department of Water and Power, increased volcanic activity has been detected for the past several years, and although seismic activity has recently increased in frequency and intensity, nobody could have predicted this sort of disaster.

"State emergency officials are warning people in Southern California not to drink your tap water. Repeat: do *not* drink the tap water. It has been contaminated. Lake Crowley formerly rested in a twenty-by-ten-mile crater that is thought to have been formed by a volcanic eruption seven hundred centuries ago. The lake is one of Southern California's main water supply sources, collecting mountain runoff, which flows hundreds of miles south by way of aqueducts to Los Angeles. But the catastrophic explosion caused massive amounts of toxic ash to fall into the water, thus contaminating the water supply. Adding to the problem, the volcano has caused rapid melting of snow in the mountains, and flash floods are ripping through the area even as I speak. The floodwater is teeming with potentially hazardous volcanic debris known as lahar. If at all possible, residents should avoid any unnecessary contact with the floodwater until its toxicity can be determined."

The announcer took a breath and then broke from his professional protocol. "It's awful," he gasped. "This is the worst disaster I have ever seen. There is no electricity throughout most of the state. Water is rushing through the valley like the Johnstown Flood, and our drinking water supply is contaminated. The earth is shaking beneath our feet, it's pitch black outside, getting colder by the hour, and we still have nine hours before sunrise. God help us all."

Stan stumbled to his car in a daze, trying to keep a grip on his emotions. *Think, Stan! Think!* he silently screamed to himself again and again. *What should I do? What can I do?*

For several minutes, Stan sat in the car in the dark. He didn't even bother to start the engine. Shock crept into the car with him. *Gone! Los Angeles is gone! It can't be! It must be a cruel, H. G. Wells type of joke. I can't take much more of this!* he thought. *What in the world is going on?* For the previous six months, nearly every time Stan had turned on the news, he had heard of another catastrophe. Hurricanes of enormous proportions, tornadoes, tidal waves, earthquakes in Turkey, massive mudslides burying people in Mexico. "It's a disaster of biblical proportions!" Stan and his buddies used to joke, as they laughed at the television commentators trying to outdo the other networks in their coverage of each new crisis.

Few people were laughing now.

And the calamities were, in fact, getting worse. It seemed almost as if there was a domino effect after the Japanese stock market crashed a year ago. Then came the horrendously devastating earthquake that rocked Japan, wreaking destruction not seen in that country since World War II, when two "small" atomic bombs had obliterated much of Hiroshima and Nagasaki, bringing the war in the Pacific to an abrupt halt.

When the U.S. stock market came crashing down, the toll was not simply in dollars and cents. Many leading businesspeople in New York had leaped from skyscrapers; the less imaginative had simply thrown themselves in front of the few subway trains that were still running. In the heartland, even farmers and "salt of the earth" types found the loss of their investments more than they could take. Sales of hunting rifles, shotguns, and pistols had been temporarily banned, not because of an attempt to control the game population, but to preserve the human population. Too many people, even some Bible-toting Christians, had used their weapons to take their own lives.

And in a time like this, we need our weapons, thought Stan. Just recalling the riots that took place after nearly every recent calamity sent shivers down Stan's spine. *How can you protect yourself against a mob of thugs who have no respect for life and aren't afraid to die themselves?* he asked himself. The riots used to take place in the ghetto areas; now the mobs surged through the upscale, suburban communities.

More frightening still was the increase in terrorist activity in the U.S., Russia, and around the world. Several times within the past few months, security officers at Los Angeles International Airport had intercepted nuclear devices that had been planted by terrorists. One brazen bomber had come right into Concourse A carrying a nuclear bomb the size of a football in a gym bag. Had he not bumped into a security guard—literally—the bomber might have made it out of the airport and into the community.

Terrorists had already brought down several airliners, and one cruise ship had already been sunk by a terrorist bomb, killing more than a thousand people and leaving more than five hundred others scarred for life. Deadly anthrax had shown up in several city water systems, and the word was out that terrorists had targeted more than 110 other cities to be hit with anthrax in a short period of time. So far, the authorities had been able to circumvent the terrorist plots, but Stan knew, as did the rest of the country, that sooner or later, somebody would slip up. The terrorists would succeed, and millions of people would die.

Betrayals were rampant, both on the national level and in personal relationships. Trust was a long-forgotten virtue. Nobody trusted anyone anymore.

Finally, Stan mustered enough of his faculties to pull his face out of his hands and start the car. He pushed the button indicating "heat" on the climate control panel, and soon warm air raised the temperature to the point he no longer noticed the chill. *Food!* He remembered the original reason for his venturing into the night. *I must get something to eat for Christine and Natalie . . . and I'd better hurry before all the groceries disappear from the shelves!*

He slammed the car into gear and roared out of the parking lot toward the grocery store. Arriving at the darkened store, Stan was surprised to see that there were no parking places available in the huge store lot. "Everyone in the county must have the same idea," Stan said to himself as he pulled the Chevy over the curb and parked on a well-manicured lawn.

I'd better let Christine know what's going on, he thought, reaching for his cellular telephone in the glove compartment. Stan switched on the phone, but there was no dial tone. "Now what?" he growled angrily. He checked the battery. It was fully charged. There was no reason why the phone should not be working . . . unless the entire cellular network was down. Stan threw the phone onto the seat and darted toward the grocery store door.

The automatic sliding doors were stuck in the open position, and the flow of people going in and out of the store seemed perpetual as Stan waited politely to slip inside. After waiting a few moments, he realized that most shoppers had long since discarded their manners as they made for the rapidly vanishing food supplies.

The large grocery store was dimly lit, as the juice dwindled in the battery-powered emergency lights dotting the walls. This store, like most modern grocery stores, drugstores, and department stores, had been built largely without windows to help prevent burglaries. It depended almost entirely on artificial interior lighting to brighten its aisles. Without electricity, the store became a huge, dark cave, with only the emergency spots providing any light at all.

Some people lit their way with flashlights as they attempted to find food, but most simply stumbled along in the dark, bumping from one person to the next, like a bizarre human pinball game. Several people tussled in the aisles, arguing over claims to foodstuffs. A few actually engaged in fistfights, throwing punches wildly, flailing at each other in the dim light. Civilization was deteriorating right between the canned goods and the macaroni and cheese. The store could not stay open much longer, but that mattered little; the food items most people were scouring the shelves for were all gone anyhow. More than a few brave souls purchased dog food in hopes that, if necessary, it would keep them alive until better sources of sustenance could be found. By now, Stan noted, even the dog food aisles were sparsely supplied.

The bread was gone; so was the milk. Empty egg cartons littered the dairy aisles. Most vegetable racks were vacant. The shelves where the canned foods were usually stocked were barren. Stan found a box of instant rice on the floor. Apparently someone had knocked it off a shelf and in the darkness, it had gone undiscovered. That and two dented cans of green beans were the extent of the food Stan carried as he made his way toward the long checkout lines.

"Oh, excuse me, ma'am," Stan said, more from habit than civility, as he bounced off a grandmotherly woman in front of him. She had actually been the one to bang into him, but assessing blame in these conditions was as foolish as someone complaining about an open window on the *Titanic* while it was sinking.

"Quite all right, young man. Are you finding any food?" the woman asked sprightly.

"No, ma'am," Stan replied. "Not much. And I have a wife and toddler at home. I don't know what we're going to feed our daughter."

"Well, take this." The woman handed a loaf of bread in Stan's direction.

"Oh, no! I couldn't take your bread," Stan replied, much to his amazement. "There's not another loaf to be found anywhere else in the store. Believe me, I've looked!"

"It's all right. Go ahead and take it," the woman said sweetly. "You need it more than I do."

"But what about you? What are you going to eat?"

"Don't worry about me. I'll be fine. My church is taking good care of me. I'm just here looking to find some food to help someone else. And I guess I found someone I could help."

"Your church?" Stan asked.

"Yes, for the past few years, our church has been stockpiling basic food supplies to help our congregation and other members of the community get through times of shortages. Many laughed at our pastor when Y2K was hardly a bump in the road, but he was not diverted from his belief in preparing ahead of time. As the Bible says in Proverbs, a wise man sees the need and prepares for it ahead of time. So our church stays ready for an awful storm, a flood, or even an earthquake." The woman paused for a moment, but it was long enough for Stan to notice the twinkle in her eye.

How can she be so calm in all of this? he wondered.

The woman's voice interrupted his thoughts. "Fortunately, we didn't need nearly as much food as the leaders of our congregation had prepared for," she said, "but it's a good thing the church thought ahead. No one is poking fun at our food pantry anymore."

"So your church is helping to feed you during these blackouts?" Stan asked, astonished.

"Oh, yes, the church provides food for about two hundred other people who live near our church property. We're not eating fancy restaurant cuisine, but we're surviving. A number of people are actually living in the church gymnasium. These stressful times have pulled our community together like never before."

"Yeah, I'll bet," said Stan as he accepted the bread from the woman. "Are you sure you are going to have enough?" he asked with genuine concern.

The woman smiled at him in the shadows as they inched closer to the parallel checkout counters. "Thank you for your concern, but it is unwarranted. I'll be fine. I have a good group of people around me. The church is just up the road from the grocery store." The woman reached into her purse and produced a church bulletin, complete with a picture of the church, an address, and a phone number. Stan recognized the church immediately. He had passed by it a thousand times before without giving it much thought.

"If you need help, please stop by," said the woman joyfully. "We can always stretch the soup a little further."

Stan was intrigued. Almost to his own surprise, he heard himself saying, "I'd really like to know more about your church."

"Well, I'm on my way there as soon as I leave the store. Why don't you come on over?"

"Maybe I will," Stan replied, as he thought of Christine and the baby at home in the cold, with nothing to eat. "Maybe we will."

WHERE YA
GONNA GO?

"NEXT IN LINE, PLEASE!" an exasperated voice somewhere up ahead of Stan called. "Come on, let's go. There are a lot of people waiting."

Stan thanked the elderly woman for the bread one more time, then stepped into the narrow lane in front of the cash register, while his benefactor waited in the line next to him. There were no scanners functioning at the checkouts, no calculators, computers, or working cash registers, so every transaction had to be calculated on paper. Purchases were cash only, and change could be made only to the nearest dollar or whatever coins were available. Anyone who balked at the inconvenience could leave empty-handed. Armed security guards patrolled the front of the grocery store, though no doubt, in the darkness and the confusion, some impatient customers simply walked out the open doors undetected, without paying for their treasures.

At the register opposite Stan, a belligerent fellow was giving the clerk a hard time. "This is ridiculous!" the man shouted. "Where's all the food? And why can't you people get some light in here?"

"I'm sorry, sir," the young man at the register tried to pacify the disgruntled customer.

"And why can't we use our credit cards?" the obnoxious fellow wanted to know. "The credit bureaus have all our financial information in their computers nowadays. If they're so smart, they should have a way they could read our bank account numbers without us having to carry cash or those cards. God knows there are muggers everywhere these days. I'll tell you what we really need," the man said to anybody who was listening. "We need a leader. I've been saying it all along. We need a worldwide leader, someone who can deal with all these problems, not those wimps we have. The world is falling apart; there's chaos everywhere. We need somebody who has some answers. My family is hungry. I have money in the bank, but I can't get to it. Somebody needs to get us back on the road to peace and prosperity!"

Stan noticed that the man's outburst had captured the attention of the people waiting in line. Frustrated at standing in the darkness for so long to check out what little provisions they could obtain at the grocery store, many of the listeners were glad for any diversion. Others listened intently and even nodded their heads in agreement with the oaf doing the talking. That only served to encourage him all the more.

"I'm tired of hearing about all these wars, too. We can't even defend our own shores anymore. What are we going to do? We need somebody who can bring some security into this situation. I've heard that there's some guy over there in the Middle East who has some answers, and I think it's high time we listen to him. So what if he has a few strange ideas? If he can get us out of this mess, I'd follow him anywhere!"

The maniacal bellowing had nearly mesmerized Stan. When he turned to see what sort of impact the rantings were having on the elderly woman who had given him her bread, he was surprised to see that she was gone. *That's interesting,* he thought. *She was farther behind in her line than I was. I wonder how she got through the checkout so quickly?*

Stan shuffled his way through the lines, exited the grocery store, and returned home. The Chevy's gas gauge now edged to the left of the "E." As he turned off the engine, Stan wondered whether the car would start again tomorrow with so little gas in the tank.

Christine and Natalie were wide awake on the sofa. "Stan! Where have you been? You've been gone for more than three hours . . . " It was then that Christine noticed the sparse amount of food Stan carried. "Simply to bring home some rice, bread, and beans? Stan, where in the world have you been? I've been worried about you. Our candles are getting low, and it's really getting damp and cold in this apartment without any heat. What's going on?"

Stan placed the meager groceries on the kitchen counter and returned to the living room. "Christine, please sit down," he said as calmly as possible. "We're in big trouble."

"Stan?"

He waved his hand as if to say, "Be quiet." Christine had rarely seen that sort of expression from her husband. She knew it must be something serious.

"There's very little food in the store," Stan began. "The electrical power is still out all over the area, the cellular phone system doesn't seem to work, and the gas stations are closed. But that's the least of our worries right now."

Christine's eyes widened, and she instinctively pulled Natalie closer to her. Stan continued soberly, "From what I heard on the news, there's been a major earthquake in L.A. and a series of other cataclysmic catastrophes that have hit California all the way from San Francisco to Los Angeles. We're talking volcanoes, toxic fumes, and that sort of thing. The water supply for most of the state has been contaminated. We have no food, no water, no electricity, no heat, no gas, and no way to get around anywhere."

Stan's body began to shake as his voice choked in his throat. Finally he whispered, "Christine, I'm scared."

Christine sobbed uncontrollably as Natalie stared at the tears streaming down her mother's face. "What are we going to do, Stan? Where can we turn?"

"I don't know. But I met a lady in the grocery store—she gave me the loaf of bread. She said that her church was providing her and a bunch of other people with food and shelter. I laughed at all those church people who spent so much time, energy, and money storing food and water and all that for Y2K, and then nothing happened. Now, it's not so funny."

Christine nodded and brushed her tears away.

Stan spoke quietly, "We don't have much gasoline in the car, but we can't stay here. There's only one place to go—the church. They used to say that the church was a refuge, a safe harbor in the time of a storm. Let's go see if we can find that woman's church, and let's pray to God that there is someone there who can help us."

"Okay, Stan. It will take me just a few minutes to get some things together."

Christine and Stan quickly assembled an "overnight" bag filled with a change of clothing, some basic hygiene items, and a few necessities for Natalie. On the way out the door, Stan paused long enough to grab the church bulletin the woman at the store had given him, and the meager groceries he had brought home, including the loaf of bread. "Somebody might need this," he said to Christine.

As they clambered into the car, Stan worried whether it would even start. The gas tank had to be nearly empty. Beyond that, if the car cranked, could they make it to the church? And if they did, would they really find a group of people like those the woman had described? A group that truly loved and cared for each other? A group that would take them in, as well?

Stan shoved the key into the ignition, turned the switch, and the car roared to life.

"It's a miracle!" Christine gushed.

Stan looked over at her and scowled. "Just because it started doesn't mean we have enough gas to get there," he was about to grouse, but then thought better of it and held his tongue. He had to admit, miracle or not, his heart had leaped when the car had started. *Maybe it's a sign,* Stan thought. He eased the car out of the parking space, careful not to use any more gas than necessary. He retraced the route back to the grocery store and drove a short distance beyond it, where he caught sight of the church. Just as Stan pulled the car into the church parking lot, the engine gasped and clunked to a stop. "Looks like we're going to be here for a while," Stan said to Christine, as he quickly turned off the ignition to conserve what he could of the battery.

The church wasn't a fancy building. From the outside, it looked more like a school, complete with a gymnasium, than it did a cathedral. Stan gathered his family's belongings, and Christine hoisted Natalie onto her shoulder. They walked to the side door of the sanctuary and stepped inside. Although the electricity was still off in the area, the interior of the building was well lit by dozens of candles and kerosene lamps, flames flickering against the lightly painted walls, giving the large room a warm and cozy feeling. It reminded Stan of the Christmas Eve candlelight services he had attended as a boy.

The room was filled with bustling people, some bearing backpacks, others carrying sleeping bags, still others toting boxes, a few teenagers even sporting guitars. The scene looked like a busy summer camp!

"Well, hello!" Stan heard a familiar voice call out through the crowd. "I'm so glad you could come!"

It was the grandmotherly woman from the grocery store.

"And this must be your wife and baby . . . come on in. Let me introduce myself," she said more to Christine than to Stan. "Your husband and I have already met."

"Well, not really," Stan said. He realized that he had never even given the woman his name. "I'm Stan. This is my wife, Christine, and our daughter, Natalie."

"My name is Mary," the woman said, smiling as she helped Christine with Natalie's jacket. "Welcome to our church."

"We're real sorry to impose on you," Stan said, "but we didn't have anywhere else to go. So I thought maybe we could take you up on your offer for tonight. Sorry to bother you."

"No bother at all!" Mary gushed. "We're so glad you are here. Make yourself at home. Don't be bashful. Let me show you around. This church is the greatest thing in the world!"

"Really?" Stan replied. "I've never heard a church described like that before."

"Well, maybe you've never been to a real church," the grandmotherly woman responded sprightly. Again, Stan noticed the twinkle in the woman's eyes, just as he had back in the grocery store.

Mary took Christine by the arm and led her and Stan toward the front of the sanctuary. "Those fellows are taking food back to the food bank," she said, pointing to three young men who looked to be in their early twenties. "Come on, I'll show you where it's at, so you'll know where to go if you need anything." Mary pointed out the kitchen area and the food bank storage area. "As you can see, we have a clothing cupboard, a food pantry, and a soup kitchen, and it's all available to you. If we have something that you need, all you have to do is ask and someone will help."

"Wow, look at all that food!" exclaimed Stan, visions of the empty store shelves still fresh in his mind.

"Yes, we have quite a lot," said Mary. "Our people have been laying in supplies for some time now, so we can take care of our own congregation and folks like you and your family who might need a little help. We love helping people as an expression of our love for Jesus.

"Right now, everyone who is staying inside the church is eating breakfast and dinner together in our fellowship hall, just off the gymnasium.

Lunch is on your own, but if you or the baby gets hungry, there's always plenty of food here in the food bank."

"Thank you so much," Christine said. "Our baby hasn't had much to eat all day."

"Well, we'll have to do something about that, now won't we?" Mary said as she picked up several jars of peach baby food and handed them to Christine.

Tears trickled from Christine's eyes as she hugged Mary with one arm and held on to Natalie with the other. "Oh, Mary! How can we ever thank you?"

"Don't thank me. Thank God. And His people. They are the ones bringing in all the food. But the church is more than just a place for food and shelter. We are especially interested in helping people who have been spiritually hungry to find real satisfaction."

The group walked back toward the main sanctuary as Mary continued. "In our church we're seeing all sorts of wonderful things happen," she said. "You know how difficult it is to get an appointment with a doctor these days."

Stan nodded. "That's the truth." Recently, doctors and hospitals had been having problems accessing their patients' medical records. Then there were the telephone outages, as well as the gas shortages. It was such a frustrating hassle to attempt getting to a physician that, unless it was an emergency situation, many people simply put off medical attention as long as possible.

"Well, in our church, God has been performing wonderful miracles of healing," the saintly woman continued.

"You don't say," Stan interjected skeptically, as thoughts of opportunistic, moneygrubbing, so-called "faith healers" flitted across his mind.

Mary didn't seem to notice Stan's cynicism, but instead kept right on extolling the virtues of the church. "Oh, yes, but it's not what you might think," the woman replied, unwittingly pulling the rug out from under Stan's skeptical attitude. "We don't have any big-name preachers coming to the church for special healing services—although I've heard of some people who have been healed at those kinds of services."

"No professional faith healers?" Stan asked.

The woman smiled. "No, not in our church. As a matter of fact, our pastor has warned us that nobody should attempt to take credit for what

God is doing. The healings have been taking place quite naturally, or should I say *supernaturally?"* Mary winked at Stan.

"It's just been ordinary people like you and me, praying for people who need a touch from God. Like those folks over there." Mary nodded toward a group of about ten or twelve people at the front of the main sanctuary, and Stan and Christine followed her gaze. It looked as though the people were praying together quietly.

"We believe that we are seeing a time of supernatural healing restored to the church," Mary explained. "It's simply been mothers and fathers praying for their children and grandchildren, neighbors praying for neighbors. We pray for each other so often, nobody notices who is praying for whom; we just see the results as God answers prayer."

"Do you mean that people actually feel better after somebody prays for them?" Stan probed.

"Oh, they don't just feel better. They *are* better! We've had folks who have been healed of cancer, heart disease, kidney failure; one fellow was even healed of AIDS. Take Melody, there," Mary said as she motioned toward an approaching young woman who Stan guessed to be in her late thirties. "Melody was diagnosed with an incurable case of colitis. The doctors said she'd just have to live with it. Well, as you can see, she is living quite well, but she no longer has the colitis, do you, Melody?" The young woman hugged Mary as she passed by and said, "No, I don't, Mary, and the doctors have been baffled."

"God is doing remarkable things," Mary continued, "and it seems that He is willing to do even more, as long as we don't try to rob the glory that belongs only to Him. The more difficult things have gotten in the world, the more we are seeing God work wonders, supernaturally." Mary guided her guests out of the sanctuary and toward a wide, long corridor, as she spoke.

"Hmm, I'll bet people are pushing and shoving, trying to be first in line to get healed, huh?" asked Stan.

"Not exactly. As a matter of fact, it seems that the people in our church have a renewed love and concern for each other. It didn't happen overnight. When all the natural disasters started—you don't need me to tell you how terrified everyone was over those news reports that an asteroid was soon to collide with earth—we were suddenly thrust together, and many of us were forced by our circumstances to live in close proximity to each other. At first, some people were constantly getting into arguments over who gets how much food, and who gets to stay at the church, and all sorts of other things. We just weren't really accustomed to functioning the way the body of Christ is described in the New Testament. I'm embarrassed to tell you this . . ."—the woman looked sheepishly at the floor— "but we had never done it before."

"Done what?" Christine asked.

"We had never actually lived as a Christian community. We attended church services, and most of us were quite content with that—until the time of real tribulation began."

"Are you saying that for all these years your congregation wasn't really a *church?*" Stan asked in amazement, surprised at the woman's candor.

"I'm afraid that's so," Mary replied. "But please don't be too hard on us. We honestly thought that we were doing God's work." She motioned toward the classrooms on each side of the corridor as they walked. "And many people were helped by the church. We weren't a bunch of pagans or anything like that. We just had never truly considered how a genuine New Testament church should function. We had never *had* to take care of one another before. Oh, sure, we always had our benevolent funds to help people whose homes had burned down or had been damaged in a storm. We helped lots of people who suffered with some debilitating disease that had hospitalized them or impaired their ability to take care of themselves. But most of us considered ourselves to be self-sufficient. We didn't need each other. We didn't need anybody . . . or so we thought.

"But then calamity after calamity started to happen. At first it was awful. Everybody was at one another's throats, arguing over all sorts of silly things, but little by little, the Lord began a marvelous refining process in our congregation. I'm not sure, but I think that's what the Bible means when it says that Jesus will return one day soon for a church without spot or wrinkle. I think He's getting the spots and wrinkles out of us by using all these tribulations we've been going through . . ." Mary paused in front of two large sets of double doors.

"And this is the gymnasium," she said. "This is where we will sleep tonight. It might get a little noisy when some of our folks start snoring," she said, smiling as she spoke, "but if you've ever spent the night in a storm shelter, you know that we can adjust to just about anything for a while. In the morning, we pick up the cots and mats, so the children have a place to play. It stays relatively warm in here, but you'll want to keep the baby's jacket on."

"You sure are learning to live in cramped quarters, aren't you?" Stan asked as he noted the large number of cots and mats on the floor.

"Cramped quarters? Yes, I suppose so," Mary replied. "One thing I know for sure, the members of our church have a new attitude toward each other. Everybody has gotten into the habit of putting the other person first. We've realized that we are all part of Christ's body, and when one person has a need, we all have a need. When one person is celebrating, we all celebrate. We enjoy sharing whatever resources we have with each other, and it is such fun!

"Not only that, it has been amazing to see how God provides for even the little things we need. Why, just the other day, little Billy Brown bent a rim on his bicycle. He actually cried, he was so upset. But then, Walter Robinson, a man in our church said, 'Son, I used to own a bike shop. Bring your bike over to my place, and let's see what we can find in the back room.' Wouldn't you know it? They found an old rim, and Walter was able to fix up Billy's bike like new.

"It works the same way in the bigger things, too. No matter what somebody in our body needs, somebody else is able to help out. It's as though God has already thought of that need and has made provision for it to be met within our own body."

"But don't you all get on each other's nerves?" Stan asked, thinking about how he tended to get claustrophobic in the small apartment in which Christine, Natalie, and he lived.

"Yes, we did at first. But it's amazing what love will cover. When you really love somebody, you hardly notice the little inconveniences, and what you can't ignore, you learn to forgive. And do you want to hear something really interesting?"

Stan suddenly realized that he was enjoying this conversation with the saintly woman. "Sure, I'd love to hear it," he answered.

"Well, before our church started living as a Christian community, a lot of our single people and especially some of our senior citizens were extremely lonely. You know how isolated recent events have caused many of us to become. A large number of people barely have had a social life at all. They can't get out much; they have little resources to spare, and no way of getting together with their friends, even if they could afford to do so.

"But now, since we have been living more closely as the family of God, nobody complains of loneliness anymore. We're always working together, helping each other, fixing one another's cars or houses, cooking for one another, or doing some little thing for each other; we are together all the time. And people love it! It's like we have a large, extended family that is watching out for us. People who felt that they no longer had a purpose in life are finding an incredible sense of meaning and significance."

"How can you afford to help so many people?" Stan asked. "Doesn't it cost an enormous amount of money to do all that?"

"I suppose it does," the woman replied. "But we all contribute whatever we can, and God seems to multiply and prosper our efforts. When the stock market crashed a while back, we had a number of people who lost large amounts of money. They had invested heavily in stocks and bonds and mutual funds—all those things that I don't understand much about. Well, our pastor had tried to warn people not to place their security in the financial systems of this world, but you know how possessive people are about their money. Many of the wealthiest members of our congregation lost nearly everything they had. But God is good, and He is taking care of those rich people who are now poor, just like He is taking care of us.

"In fact, even in these dire economic days, we are adding on to our church by building a family life center out back. It's not going to be a big, ostentatious building, but everyone is pitching in, and the people have a mind to work. The job is getting done!"

"It sounds as though you have your own little club going here," said Stan with a smile.

"Oh, not at all. In fact, our church is winning more people to Jesus than ever before. Every day new people show up at our door. Some come, of course, because they heard that we have food available and are willing to help. Others come because they have no place else to turn. But a lot of people want to be a part of a church that cares."

Stan and Christine instinctively looked at one another. "Yeah," Stan said, more to himself than to anyone else. "I guess that's why we're here, too."

Mary paused to introduce Christine and Stan to another young couple, Stephanie and Tom. After the couple went by, Mary commented, "Stephanie and Tom came to the church for the first time as spectators, but they were so impressed by what God is doing, they said, 'Wow! We always wanted to be a part of a church like this.' They stayed and got involved. Before long, they were excited about the Lord, and they started helping others find what they have found.

"Funny, we used to have evangelism classes, church growth programs, and all sorts of other programs in our attempts to get people to come to church. We once had helicopter rides for the kids after Sunday school, and one time we had a hot-air balloon ride for the person who could bring the most people to church on a particular Sunday. All those things were nice, but usually once the promotion was done, the impact on our church was barely noticeable. But now, we don't advertise or promote, and still the people keep coming."

"That's pretty impressive," Stan agreed.

"Oh, my! We're just scratching the surface of what God has for us!" Mary exuded excitement. "We have a sister church in Northern California where the members of the church are building a new sanctuary and cutting their own trees! Even the youth group is helping to work on the church, doing the wallpapering, and learning how to lay blocks. It is a wonderful experience for them. Another sister church in Las Vegas is now meeting in a place that used to be known as the Desert Hotel. Are you familiar with it?"

"The Desert Hotel? Heh, heh . . . err, ah, well, yeah, I am," Stan admitted reluctantly. He didn't want to tell Mary that he had spent thousands of dollars, gambling away his hard-earned money at the Desert Hotel's casino and indulging in other less-than-admirable behavior during his business trips to Vegas. Oh, yes, he knew the Desert Hotel.

"Well, do you remember in the Old Testament that when God delivered His people from the hand of the Egyptians, He said that they would go out with the riches of Egypt?"

Stan nodded. He had no clue what the woman was referring to, but he was not about to interrupt her.

"The Bible says that the wealth of the evil has been laid up for the just. That means that God has prepared the riches of the world for God's people. These days, now that money is so tight, there aren't as many people gambling in Las Vegas, except for those who are foolishly hoping to strike it rich so they can escape the turmoil that the world is in. But where are they going to go? The whole earth is being shaken. So the Desert Hotel donated its entire property to our sister church there. We are housing people, feeding people, and ministering to them right there in what used to be a casino! It's wonderful!"

For some reason, the woman's ebullience at the transformation of the Desert Hotel bothered Stan. "Aw, come on, Mary," he teased. "You must be on some kind of drugs, aren't you? Can you get me some of that stuff?"

Mary burst out laughing. "Dear me, I haven't even taken an aspirin in ages! But, yes, I will be glad to give you what I have. You come. Even after this crisis is over, come and be a part of our fellowship. You'll see what I mean. We're not closing up. These are exciting days, and you are more than welcome to join us."

"So what's the catch?" Stan's cynical side still remained unsatisfied. "After you get me in the church, you bilk me out of all my money, is that it?"

"My, my! God doesn't need your money, Stan. Do you think these calamities have taken the Lord by surprise? Don't be silly! Jesus told His disciples to watch for all these signs of the times, to get ready, and that is exactly what we have done. We're not discouraged. We are excited because we know that Jesus is coming back for us soon!"

"Like those Hale-Bopp people?"

"You are a cynic, aren't you?" Mary said with a smile.

"It's difficult not to be skeptical after being exposed to all the news-casts nowadays."

"Yes, I understand. Yet despite all the bad news, there's good news, too. Jesus said that when you see all these things happening, look up because our redemption is near. He told us that we should take a cue from these signs and get ready. So that's what we are doing. The church is getting ready for the hard times that the Bible says will precede the Lord's coming. That's why we've been prepared for these days for some time now, so we can help each other and help good folks like you."

"Are you sure we won't we be an imposition?" asked Christine.

"Why, heavens no!" Mary replied. "That's what the church is all about. You are welcome here."

"But with so many people hurting, aren't you afraid that your supplies will run out?" Stan asked.

"No, God keeps blessing our people. We learned a long time ago that we can't outgive God. The more we give to Him, the more He gives back to us in so many ways."

"Well, we might be here for a little while," Stan said sheepishly. "We ran out of gas in front of the church."

"You are welcome to stay here as long as you like," Mary said, as she tucked her arm around Christine's waist. "And don't worry about the gas. I'm sure one of the men here at the church can get you some in the morning. Right now, it's getting late, and that baby needs some sleep, and you probably do, too. Let's find some cots and a place where you can rest."

"I am pretty bushed," Stan said. "But Mary, tell me one more thing. Why are you being so kind to us? You don't owe us anything. We are total strangers to you."

"Not anymore," Mary replied with a smile. "Besides, what we give to you, we give in the name of the Lord Jesus as an expression of His love for you. He's filled our lives with love, peace, and joy, so we just want to allow some of that to overflow to you. Then as you receive His love, you can pass it on to others. Like I said, that's what the church is all about."

TROUBLES UP AHEAD!

THE STORY IN THE preceding chapters is, of course, fictitious . . . for now. In the near future, however, I believe that it may become an all-too-real scenario. Catastrophic calamities will soon strike the earth; economic systems are going to crumble; life as normal will be severely disrupted; and the world will be plunged into a time of tribulation such as we have never before experienced. It is not a question of *if* these things are going to happen; the Bible clearly predicts their occurring. The only questions are, When will these things occur? and Will we be ready for them?

Unfortunately, many people—even many sincere Christians—have been lulled into apathy concerning "end-time" events. The recent spate of apocalyptic books, movies, and the nonevent of Y2K have served only to dull our sensitivities to the real dangers of meteor showers, earthquakes, floods, famines, economic unrest, and widespread panic in the streets.

Someday there will be many Stans, Christines, and Natalies to care for; far more people than we might imagine will be looking to the church for physical as well as spiritual help. What if such a young family came to your church? Better yet, what if they came to your home? Would you be able (and willing) to help them?

And what about you? How do you plan to make it through the difficult days the Bible says are definitely coming? How connected are you to the body of Christ right now? The truth is, Christians need each other simply to get through the "ordinary" events of life, let alone the catastrophic or tragic times. God does not intend for His family members to live alone, in isolation physically or spiritually from one another.

To understand why it is so important that we rediscover the church in these days, we must understand the backdrop against which we are living. To do that, let's refresh our memories concerning some of the signs of the times that Jesus told us to watch for.

Jesus said that in the last days there will be false christs, wars and rumors of wars, famines, and earthquakes (Matt. 24:5–7). Certainly, we are seeing the rise of cult activity today. We can also track the increase in unusually devastating natural disasters in the daily news. Beyond that, Jesus said, "nation will rise against nation, and kingdom against kingdom" (Matt. 24:7 NKJV). Interestingly, the word He used for "nation" was *ethnos*, from which we get our word *ethnic*. In other words, Jesus predicted "ethnic cleansing" long before it became a descriptive term on our newscasts.

Jesus also informed us that there will be a flagrant increase in lawlessness, people will betray one another, and many people's love will grow cold (Matt. 24:10–12). Love for the Lord will wane, as well as love for each other.

Skeptics scoff, saying, "We've always had these natural disasters, and men and women have been at each other's throats since the beginning of time. What's new?"

Plenty. Jesus stated plainly that "when you see all these things, recognize that He is near, right at the door" (Matt. 24:33 NASB). Jesus implied that the awful things that are to come upon the earth will intensify, that they will converge at one point in human history, and they will be so bad that our very survival will be in question. He said, "For then there will be a great tribulation, such as has not occurred since the beginning of the world until now, nor ever shall. And unless those days had been cut short, no life would have been saved; but for the sake of the elect those days shall be cut short" (Matt. 24:21–22 NASB).

APOCALYPSE NOW!

The book of Revelation reveals more of the devastation that is soon to occur. Exiled to the isle of Patmos, the apostle John described the deceptive rise of the Antichrist (Rev. 6:2), the evil emissary of Satan himself. John also told of a coming time of terror (Rev. 6:4), which very well may include terrorist acts such as the detonation of nuclear bombs in our major cities, massive germ warfare attacks on civilians, or the terror of people slaying each other senselessly in schools, churches, and synagogues. Furthermore, John described a coming economic collapse and famine (Rev. 6:5–6).

Even more frightening, John informed us that more than one-fourth of the world's population will soon be destroyed by the sword—and here's where it gets really scary—and by hunger, "death," and the beasts of the earth (Rev. 6:7–8). By studying the meaning of John's words in the original Greek language in which they were written, I discovered that this word *death* means plagues, pestilences, or diseases. I believe that many of the new and enigmatic viruses such as AIDS, Ebola, "mad-cow" disease in England, the Hong Kong bird flu, and strange strains of deadly encephalitis, such as that carried by mosquitoes to birds to humans in New York in the fall of 1999, may be related to the predictions in the book of Revelation.

The United Nations has repeatedly reported that AIDS is killing more Africans than war. The U.N. Children's Agency estimates that thirteen million children will be orphaned over the next eighteen months, due to the AIDS epidemic in Africa alone! The AIDS epidemic is traced back to the monkey, a direct fulfillment of Revelation 6:8, death by disease and beasts of the earth.

WHAT COULD BE WORSE?

Beyond that, I am convinced that a monstrous asteroid will collide with the earth, causing massive destruction, flooding, and darkening of the sky for as much as a year. I base my conclusions on the Scripture, not simply on scientific evidence, although a plethora of such data now exists. (For a detailed description of the potential destruction to come as a result of meteors and asteroids, see my book *Prosperity and the Coming Apocalypse*.)

Unfortunately, few political leaders in our world are willing to talk about the possible annihilation of our planet. That shouldn't surprise us. A planet populated by people convinced that they are faced with possible extermination might be totally ungovernable. Besides, few politicians other than Winston Churchill ever campaigned successfully on platforms of preparing for the worst. We shouldn't expect much in the way of warning from our government officials.

What is baffling, however, is the silence of so many spiritual leaders on this issue. "Oh, yes, I've noticed those passages in the Bible before," one esteemed pastor told me, "but I can't see any sense in getting our congregation all worried about it."

Another ministry leader commented caustically, "So Jesus is coming soon, and bad things are going to happen before He does. What am I supposed to do about it?"

Do about it? How about informing the Christian community that we may very well be the generation that sees Jesus Christ return? How about preparing our people for some rocky years ahead?

I have been appalled at the complacency of so many people in our churches. Sadly, many people do not want to hear the truth. It is too horrible to ponder, so they'd rather escape into denial or some more comfortable doctrine that tickles the ears, soothes the mind . . . and embalms the spirit! Most people would much prefer to listen to messages promising that we will escape the troubles ahead, rather than even consider the possibility that we will have to go through them. Such blatant spiritual denial is nothing new.

VOICES FROM THE RUBBLE

Within forty years of the resurrection and ascension of Jesus Christ, the Roman general Titus laid siege to the city of Jerusalem. Month after month, the Jewish people remained trapped inside the city walls. Soon food became scarce. Water was in short supply, despite the Jews' ingenious method of storing water in cisterns buried beneath the city of Jerusalem. In addition, the Jews obtained water through an incredible engineering marvel known as "Hezekiah's tunnel" (which can still be seen today). The tunnel facilitated an underground water system, which transported water all the way from Megiddo (where the Bible predicts that the Battle of Armageddon will be fought) to Jerusalem. Although the Jews could survive inside the city walls, nothing changed the truth that the Roman army was encamped outside their gates, waiting to destroy them.

Morale deteriorated and internal stress increased horrendously. Still, the Jews refused to give up. False prophets glibly predicted the Jews' imminent victory over the Romans, despite signs to the contrary all around them. The acclaimed historian Josephus recorded the people's gullibility in believing the false prophets who insisted that everything was going to work out okay. Josephus wrote:

> A false prophet was the occasion of these people's destruction, who had made a public proclamation in the city that very day that God commanded them to get up upon the temple, and that there they should receive miraculous signs of their deliverance. Now there was then a great number of false prophets suborned by the tyrants to impose upon the people, who denounced this to them, that they should wait for deliverance from God; and this was in order to keep them from deserting, and that they might be buoyed up above fear and care by such hopes. Now a man that is in adversity does easily comply with such promises; for when such a seducer makes him believe that he shall be delivered from those miseries which oppress him, then it is that the patient is full of hopes of such deliverance.[1]

What insight on the part of Josephus! When people are looking for deliverance from their troubles, they will believe just about anything, and anybody . . . even an antichrist. I'm convinced that we are nearing that state of gullibility in our culture, that when the Antichrist appears on the scene, offering solutions to some of the worldwide chaos and suffering, even normally discerning, intelligent people will be duped into following him.

Josephus also reported that the Jewish people ignored the highly visible signs that were right before their eyes:

> Thus were the miserable people persuaded by these deceivers, and such as belied God himself; while they did not attend, nor give credit, to the signs that were so evident, and did so plainly foretell their future desolation; but, like men infatuated, without either eyes to see or minds to consider, did not regard the denunciations that God made to them. Thus there was a star resembling a sword, which stood over the city, and a comet, that continued a whole year. Thus also, before the Jews' rebellion, and before those commotions which preceded the war, when the people were come in great crowds to the feast of unleavened bread, on the eighth day of the month Xanthicus [Nisan] and at the ninth

hour of the night, so great a light shone round the altar and the holy house, that it appeared to be bright day-time; which light lasted for half an hour. This light seemed to be a good sign to the unskillful, but was so interpreted by the sacred scribes as to portend those events that followed immediately upon it.[2]

Notice, not even the yearlong sighting of a comet and the unusual star that hovered over the city could shake the people away from their confidence in the false doctrines they had been duped into believing.

Josephus further recorded more down-to-earth signs that were also ignored by God's people:

The eastern gate of the inner [court of the temple], which was of brass, and vastly heavy, and had been with difficulty shut by twenty men, and rested upon a basis armed with iron, and had bolts fastened very deep into the firm floor, which was there made of one entire stone, was seen to be opened of its own accord about the sixth hour of the night. Now, those that kept watch in the temple came thereupon running to the captain of the temple, and told him of it; who then came up thither, and not without great difficulty was able to shut the gate again. This also appeared to the vulgar to be a very happy prodigy, as if God did thereby open them the gate of happiness. But the men of learning understood it, that the security of their holy house was dissolved of its own accord, and that the gate was opened for the advantage of their enemies. So these publicly declared, that this signal foreshewed the desolation that was coming upon them.[3]

The people, according to their own preconceived notions, interpreted this unusual opening of the eastern gate. Some saw it as a sign that God was opening up a great future to them. Others, more accurately, saw the opened gate as a symbol that the end was near.

Indeed, by A.D. 70, the Romans' patience had been exhausted. The long siege had taken its toll on both the people trapped inside the city and the soldiers waiting for them to submit. According to Josephus, when finally the wall was breached, the Roman soldiers went wild. In an uncontrollable frenzy, they sacked the city, raping, killing, destroying, and pillaging. Despite the efforts of their officers to contain the violence and salvage some of the spoils for the empire, everything in the temple area was torn apart. Huge stones were pulled down, and walls were set ablaze so the soldiers could steal the gold and other precious treasures inside the Jewish temple area.

Interestingly, a few days prior to His crucifixion, Jesus and His disciples had discussed just such a destruction of the Jewish temple. As they sat together on the Mount of Olives, across the Kidron Valley, overlooking the city of Jerusalem, the disciples admired the resplendent temple area, which recently had been remodeled under the direction of Herod the Great, a project that had taken forty-six years to complete.

Jesus must have devastated the disciples when He told them, "Do you not see all these things? Assuredly, I say to you, not one stone shall be left here upon another, that shall not be thrown down" (Matt. 24:2 NKJV).

It was in response to this statement that the disciples begged Jesus, "Tell us, when will these things be? And what will be the sign of Your coming, and of the end of the age?" (Matt. 24:3 NKJV).

Jesus' reply must have shocked the disciples even more as He described "the signs of the times" that they (and we) should look for (Matt. 24:4–51). Most students of biblical prophecy believe that Jesus' comments about the destruction of the temple were fulfilled in A.D. 70, well within the lifetimes of most of the disciples. Many of the other details that Jesus and the disciples discussed, such as Jesus' second coming, have a future-tense fulfillment, which we are seeing come to pass before our eyes today, just before Jesus returns to earth again.

DAYS OF PREPARATION

God is giving us a chance to prepare for the difficult days ahead. Jesus said that before the big event, everything will go along pretty much as normal. He compared the last days to the time of Noah:

> But as the days of Noah were, so also will the coming of the Son of Man be. For as in the days before the flood, they were eating and drinking, marrying and giving in marriage, until the day that Noah entered the ark, and did not know until the flood came and took them all away, so also will the coming of the Son of Man be. (Matt. 24:37–39 NKJV)

In an interesting comment on Noah's actions, the writer to the Hebrews gave us the inside story:

> By faith Noah, being divinely warned of things not yet seen, moved with godly fear, prepared an ark for the saving of his household, by which he condemned the world and became heir of the righteousness which is according to faith. (Heb. 11:7 NKJV)

Notice, Noah prepared the ark as a result of his faith, but he also had a godly fear, part of which may have been an awesome reverence for God, and part of which may have been a fear of what was about to come upon the earth. In any case, while preparing the ark, Noah must have appeared quite foolish to the world around him. Bad enough that he was building a huge boat on dry land, in a place that had never even experienced rain as far as we know. Worse yet, imagine him gathering the animals, stocking the ark with food, water, candles, and other basic essentials for survival through a calamity, when he could not possibly have had a clue about what to expect. All he had was God's word to him, saying, "Noah, get ready." No doubt, Noah was the frequent object of derision and entertainment among his neighbors . . . until the first raindrop fell.

For us, these are days of preparation. God has told us in advance what He plans to do. Some Christians scoff at the idea of preparing. "Oh, brother, I'm not worried," they tell me. "I'm just going to trust God."

I'm going to trust God, too, and frankly, I feel that it takes even more faith to take Him at His word and prepare in anticipation for what He has said will come to pass. By faith, Noah prepared the ark. And God has made it clear that the vehicle for surviving the storms to come is not a big boat. The ark today is His church, the body of Christ, the true Christian community.

Part of our preparation involves stocking the shelves with food, water, and other supplies to help meet the basic survival needs of His people. We need to avail ourselves of practical survival hints that will be helpful, whether we are preparing for a flood, hurricane, tornado, or some other natural disaster. While nothing but the grace of God will make us immune to the Tribulation, these tips may come in handy and make life more bearable during those awful days, as well.

But much more important, in this book, you will find keys to your spiritual preparation, so that as the Tribulation begins, you will be ready to meet the challenges and hold on to your faith in Christ until you see Him face-to-face.

Until that day, the Christian community must function more effectively than ever before, rapidly becoming efficient at providing for each other's basic needs. Where will you go? How will you meet your basic needs for food and water, shelter, basic hygiene products, heat, and gasoline when supplies run short, or rationing begins, or worse still, if you are alive when the Antichrist declares that you will neither buy nor sell without the mark of the beast on your body?

More important than mere physical sustenance, how do you plan to survive spiritually? What sort of support network will you have? Who are you going to call on for help when things get tough?

In the days ahead, the only place you will find the help you need will be the community of believers, the church, the *refuge*. And the best place for you to help meet the needs of other hurting people will be in the church. We need to be preparing now; we need to be bearing one another's burdens now, we must be functioning now as the body of Christ, the community of believers, the church.

Where does such a refuge exist? Where can you find a Christian community committed to bearing one another's burdens, dedicated to helping each other find wholeness and healing?

I found just such a Christian community . . . in a most unexpected place.

NEW TESTAMENT
EXPERIMENT

DURING MY FINAL YEAR in prison, I was incarcerated in Jesup, Georgia, a small town about 250 miles from Atlanta. It was there—in prison—that I experienced the best Christian community I had ever known. Now, that is saying something, when one considers that we had more than eighty services every week during my last years as president of Heritage USA, a Christian retreat center that saw nearly six million people go through our gates in our last full year of operations. Beyond that, I had been involved in Christian church services, camp meetings, and other "church" activities for most of my life. I had experienced some mighty moves of God, and I had enjoyed fellowship with some wonderful people of God around the world. But it was not until I went to prison that I experienced a New Testament church, a community of believers, unlike anything I had ever been a part of in my life.

When I arrived at Jesup, I was surprised to find a large contingent of Christian inmates. They welcomed me as though I were a long-lost brother who had come home. They took me in, encouraged me, and nurtured me back to spiritual health.

The Christian men in Jesup prison loved one another; we cared for each other; we bore one another's burdens. When one guy had a problem, we all helped him with it; when one fellow was down and out, ready to give up on life after receiving a "Dear John" letter from his wife, fiancée, or girlfriend, the other guys were right there to encourage him. When a man was on the verge of saying, "I don't need this Jesus stuff anymore," the other guys were in his face, saying, "Come on, buddy. We're going to Bible study, and you're coming along. We need you."

Similarly, when someone had something to rejoice about, we all rejoiced together, as though something good had actually happened to us, too, which in a way, it had. The Christian guys in that prison interacted with each other *daily*. We didn't simply see one another occasionally, or sit in an isolated row during a chapel service. We spent time together on a regular basis. We ate and worked together; we studied the Bible and attended all sorts of chapel services and spiritually uplifting programs together. We shared communion together, we witnessed to other inmates together, and when a new group of inmates got off the bus at Jesup, a group of Christian men were right there at the front gate, waiting for them, with a batch of "goodies," including toiletries, shower shoes, and other practical items that the men had to leave behind at their last place of incarceration. We gave each new arriving inmate a Bible and invited him to chapel services.

"How could you guys do all that?" I have been asked. "It must have been because you had so much time on your hands."

Not necessarily. Sure, we were doing time, but the prison system knows that too much idle time can lead to problems within the prison, so inmates are kept on a fairly tight work schedule. But like life on the outside, the secret to squeezing everything into what free time we had was by making prayer, Bible study, and fellowship priorities in our lives.

Instead of wasting time in the television room, during my last year of incarceration, I watched less than four hours of television all year long! We had prayer meetings and Bible studies at 5:00 A.M. Prior to that I barely knew what 5:00 A.M. looked like—I didn't realize that five o'clock came twice a day! Of course, I'm being facetious, but I am not exaggerating about the power of God that was in that place. The presence of God was so powerful in that prison, I actually could not wait to get out of bed to go study the Bible and pray with my Christian brothers each morning. The Bible came alive to me during those early morning sessions!

Interestingly, evangelism became a natural result of being involved in the Christian community. As nonbelievers brushed shoulders with men who were experiencing the presence of God in the body of Christ, they became curious at first, then interested, then hungry for what they saw in the Christian men. Often ten to twenty men each week came to know

Jesus Christ in that prison. We had *revival*—not just services every night, but genuine, life-changing encounters with God. We had Bible studies in which new converts and established Christians could grow in the Word. We prayed with and for each other continually throughout each day. We brought more speakers, evangelists, singers, and teachers from the outside than most churches will ever have. As far as I know, every man who was part of our Jesup Bible study group is still serving God today!

One of the keys to our successful functioning as the body of Christ was our accessibility to each other, our availability. The layout of that particular prison lent itself to easy access, since the "cells" were open cubicles, with six-foot-high cement block walls partitioning off each set of inmates, but with no bars or heavy doors to keep the men separated. I felt as though I were sleeping in the window of a Macy's department store! Obviously, that arrangement diminished our personal privacy, but it also meant that if someone wanted to talk, we were available to each other, day or night. There was no place to hide, even if we had wanted to. In fact, when Larry Wright, one of our outstanding "in-house" Bible teachers, wanted to find a quiet, secluded spot to study, pray, and prepare to teach, the only place he could "get away" was in a mop closet! Even there, men found Larry and sought his counsel and spiritual insights.

As strange as it may sound, the Christian men in that prison during the time I was there were the family of God to me. I experienced the body of Christ in such a powerful way that I am not the same anymore. I have never claimed to be a great Christian, but I know that my spiritual life was at its optimum during the year or so I spent as part of the Christian community at the Jesup prison.

ONE REALLY IS THE LONELIEST NUMBER

On July 1, 1994, I stepped into the warm North Carolina sunshine as a free man for the first time in five years. No longer was I referred to as Inmate 07407-058, federal prisoner (although the prison stigma never really leaves an ex-con). I was free—free from people telling me when to wake up, when to go to sleep, where I could go, and what I could do. Most of all, I was free to start life over again.

I settled in a small, quaint farmhouse in a pastoral setting in Hendersonville, North Carolina, a friendly little town outside Asheville.

The house was hidden well off the highway, tucked in between a strip of pasture, complete with cows mooing on one side of me and a cemetery on the other side of me. It was perfect. Nobody to bother me.

I rarely ventured off the farm. I just wanted to stay out of the public eye, to spend time with my children and grandchildren, and to get reacclimated to life on the outside. I had spent five years living with hundreds of men in federal prisons, in an environment that provided precious little privacy. We were constantly exposed to the incessant (and frequently grotesque) noise and activity of prison life. No wonder by the time I reached the farm in North Carolina, I was ready for some solitude, peace, and quiet.

But then a surprising thing happened. As I slowly became accustomed to real "life on the outside," I discovered that I was extremely lonely. Jim Bakker lonely? The man who had preached to millions of people around the world—lonely? A fellow who once had to have security guards just to be able to relax in his own home due to the constant press of people—lonely?

It was true. No matter what I did, I could not shake the awful feelings of isolation that dogged me night and day.

I enjoyed the opportunities that solitude provided to spend time with God, to study His Word, to pray, sometimes just walking around the house talking aloud to Him, sometimes sitting in the yard, contemplating the beautiful, natural setting around me. But I was alone.

Oh, sure, people came and went. My children and grandchildren visited often. Other close friends dropped by. But it wasn't the same. After having been surrounded by people for most of my life, suddenly I felt disconnected. It was then I realized that it was not so much that I was disconnected from society—I had never fit in with the politically correct crowd anyway—but I sensed an awful void in my life because I was disconnected from the body of Christ, the people of God. I didn't need to be preaching or teaching or building, but I desperately needed to be in fellowship with other believers on more than an occasional basis. I needed people with whom I could pray regularly, with whom I could worship the Lord, to whom I could confide my fears, and with whom I could celebrate my spiritual victories. I realized that what I really needed was the church.

During my first year out of prison, I concentrated on writing my book *I Was Wrong* and taking baby steps toward establishing a new life. I didn't plan on beginning a new ministry, yet I had much to share when anyone asked me to speak. Wherever I went to preach, I admitted to my audience that one of the problems I continued to combat was an awful, gnawing sense of loneliness. Inevitably, my confession resonated with multitudes in every congregation, who seemed as if they were silently crying out, "Me, too, Jim! Me, too!"

To my deep chagrin, I discovered that despite the church's growing numbers, marvelous ministry programs, and excellent fund-raising techniques, the body of Christ was largely populated with lonely people! *How can this be?* I wondered. *We are the family of God! There has to be a better way,* I thought. *We have large, beautiful sanctuaries, but we are filling them with people who are just as lonely as I am living alone out on the farm. Surely, this is not how the Christian community is meant to function.*

A DREAM COME TRUE?

Then in late 1997 and early 1998, Pastor Tommy Barnett invited me to speak at the Los Angeles International Church, an inner-city ministry known as the Dream Center. Founded by Tommy and his son Matthew Barnett, who pastors the church, the Dream Center is located in what used to be the Queen of Angels Hospital, the massive 1,400-room medical facility, in which most of the L.A.-born baby boomers took their first breaths. Matthew and Tommy Barnett had opened the Dream Center on the premise of bringing hope back into people's lives through the power of the gospel, and indeed, that was happening. The former medical hospital was now a spiritual haven. The place where much of the L.A. population had been born was now a place where many people living in the Los Angeles inner city were being "born again"!

There, for the first time since I had experienced the body of Christ functioning in the prison at Jesup, I caught a glimpse of what the Christian community could be . . . and should be. At the Dream Center, I accompanied Pastor Matthew as he went into some of the toughest neighborhoods in L.A. to share the gospel with hurting people. I watched a lily-white young man without a hint of prejudice sit down amid the filth and squalor of the inner city and minister to various ethnic and racial groups. And I saw lives transformed. Again, I thought, *This is how the body of Christ can really work!*

Functioning under the loosely knit covering of the Dream Center, dozens and dozens of ministries flowed into Los Angeles. Ministries to the homeless, ministries to drug addicts, drunks, and prostitutes, as well as mobile ministries to children in the ghetto areas, all streamed into the city from their home base at the Dream Center.

But the good-hearted people who minister at the Dream Center are not content to see people converted and then continue to live in the same conditions. They provide follow-up ministries with an emphasis on discipleship to Christ, not simply a fire-escape commitment that might keep a person from hell, but a growing relationship with the Lord, one in which the Christian's desire is to live as closely to Him as possible.

The Dream Center opens its doors to anyone who needs a place to stay or some food to eat. Many of the people who have committed their lives to Christ through the center's various ministries literally move into the former hospital rooms and live at the center, all free of charge, the costs defrayed by the donations of God's people around the country. Those who live at the Dream Center are expected to work in some way at the facility, whether their job is to sweep the floors, work on the grounds, or to help renovate the old hospital. The overriding vision is that "we are working together for God's glory and to help other people." All are required to attend the worship services and Bible studies conducted at the church.

In addition to the hundreds of people of every age, race, and color who live at the Dream Center full-time, hundreds of other people visit the center weekly to help with the various ministries. The place is a virtual human beehive, buzzing with activity night and day.

When I first visited the Dream Center, I was duly impressed by the many smiling faces, all seemingly content, serving the Lord and working together to help minister to the underbelly of the city. As I preached my first sermon there, I told the audience how I had lost everything I owned and had spent five years in prison. Many in the congregation nodded their heads in understanding. Feeling a tremendous sense of freedom, I ventured to ask, "How many of you in this church tonight have been to prison?"

A large number of men and women in the audience put up their hands. I knew that I had found my new home. Ironically, for the first time since I had been released from prison, I suddenly felt accepted.

One of the young men who immediately embraced me following the service was Armando Saavedra, a tough-looking Hispanic fellow whom I guessed to be in his early twenties, with flashing eyes and a shaved head.

I later learned that Armando was a former gang member who had met the Lord in one of the most dangerous neighborhoods in L.A.

"Jim, I love ya, man!" Armando said, throwing an arm around me as we walked down the hall, as though we were two long-lost buddies who hadn't seen each other for years. "I've been in prison, too," Armando told me, "and I know what it's like. I'll see ya around." After Armando left, somebody at the Dream Center informed me of the rumor that Armando and his gang had murdered twenty people. Whether or not that was true, I accepted Armando as a brother in the Lord. I had been around all sorts of convicted criminals in prison, so although I certainly didn't condone Armando's past record, it didn't overwhelm me as it might have before I had gone to prison myself.

In February 1998, with nothing more than what I could fit into my Jeep, I traveled from North Carolina to Los Angeles and moved into a room at the Dream Center to be a part of what I considered to be a tremendous example of New Testament living. Shortly after that, my son, Jamie, moved into the room next to mine, and we shared the bathroom between the two rooms. Jamie had a heart to reach the kids known as "Generation X-ers," so he and several of his friends brought their ministry, "Revolution," to the Dream Center. Armando Saavedra lived next door; Armando became my friend, and I became his spiritual mentor.

Interestingly, I went to the Dream Center to minister to the inner-city people. In fact, the inner-city people ministered to me. One of the young men at the Dream Center whom God used in a mighty way to encourage me was Aaron Jayne. A sharply dressed fellow with a striking resemblance to 1960s singer and television personality Rick Nelson, Aaron was a former drug addict and alcoholic whose life had been radically transformed by Jesus Christ. Aaron was serving at the Dream Center as a youth pastor. For the first few weeks that I was there, Aaron took me on as his personal discipling project.

One of the meanings of the word *disciple* implies "to attach yourself to" somebody. That is what Aaron did with me. He attached himself to me and wouldn't let go. Everywhere I went, Aaron was there, encouraging me, helping me, doing whatever he could to make my initial days of transition at the Dream Center easier. He helped me get some food. He did everything from washing my clothes (or arranging to have them washed), to introducing me to everyone, to helping me to secure basic living items from the store. He was a pastor with a servant's heart. I was a stranger, and Aaron and the others at the Dream Center took me in.

He constantly affirmed me, "Man, you are good, Jim. You are one of the best preachers I have ever heard." Aaron's words reinforced my self-image, which at that time, as I was trying to put the denigrating images of prison behind me, was still in desperate need of bolstering. No doubt, if even one person at the Dream Center had rejected me or said, "Jim, you're a real jerk," or "How could you have been so stupid?" or "You're nothing but an ex-con," or in any way put me down, I would have fled the Dream Center as fast as I could.

But nobody rejected me.

Instead, the inner-city people wrapped me in unconditional love and acceptance. Although to many people, I was well on my way to recovery—I had, after all, written a stomach-wrenching book and had appeared on national television talking about my experiences—internally, I was still bruised and beaten down, damaged, and hurting. The people of the Dream Center picked me up, like a little baby, and cared for me.

Ironically, I was the preacher who had come to preach and teach, but the people of the inner city taught me much more about the body of Christ than I could ever have taught them. Everywhere I went around the Dream Center, the Hispanic children (who have a habit of using all of a person's names, such as Juan Carlos Maria Rivera!) called out, "Jim Bakker, we love you!" Grandmothers smiled and said the same, "Jim Bakker, we love you!" I had never felt so affirmed in all my life, not even when I was appearing daily on television before millions of people around the world.

I poured myself into teaching the Bible to Armando and anyone else who would listen. Many of the ghetto kids were eager to listen; in fact, they didn't want me to stop teaching them the Word. (I'll share more with you about those Bible studies later in the book.) Before long, however, I noticed that the new converts were not the only ones at the Dream Center who were hungering for more of the Word of God. The staff members wanted (and needed) more of the Word, too.

As I analyzed the need at the Dream Center, I recalled one of the mistakes I had made at Heritage USA, where I had at one time headed a staff of over three thousand paid workers and innumerable volunteers. In the early days of our ministry, we took time for staff Bible studies and prayer services. But when our ministry grew larger, we became so busy working for God, we had little time left to study His Word together. Besides, our accountants estimated that it was costing us more than $200,000 in lost work time when we pulled our people off the grounds for an afternoon staff Bible study. The bucks won out over the Bible, and that is a tragic mistake for any ministry.

So when I recognized the hunger for the Scriptures among the staff members at the Dream Center, I knew that I had to do something. I began a midday Bible study for the Dream Center staff members as well as people from the inner city. Before long, more than two hundred people attended our daily, lunchtime Bible study. With the help of Connie Elling, a Dream Center volunteer, and a few helpers, we provided free, sandwich-style lunches for anyone who wanted to attend, and each afternoon, while they ate their lunch, I taught them from the Bible. It was a time of tremendous spiritual enrichment in my life. I felt fulfilled in my desire to teach the Word, I felt that I was contributing to the overall ministry of the Dream Center, and most of all, I knew that I was serving the Lord by serving others. In addition, I had numerous young people who regarded me as a personal mentor in their spiritual lives. I love the people there and would be perfectly content to live and work in the ghetto until the day I die.

GATHERING TOGETHER

Besides teaching the staff Bible study, I poured myself into ministering to the inner-city people, and before long, I recognized that there were so many people to counsel, as well as other ministry needs, that I needed help. Slowly, I assembled a small staff around me. After I had been in L.A. for several months, Shirley Fulbright, my assistant with whom I had worked in ministry for more than twenty years, transferred from our Charlotte office to help with our ministry in Los Angeles. To do so, Shirley left her comfortable home and moved into one room at the Dream Center. We had little money and virtually no office equipment, but Pastor Matthew provided us with a phone and office space at the Dream Center, and we furnished it with cast-off, refurbished desks and old, rebuilt computers.

I met Leanne and Howard Bailey, a couple in their mid-forties, at Christ for the Nations, a Christian training center where I spoke at the graduation ceremonies in the spring of 1998. Leanne and Howard had both prepared for the ministry and were seeking the Lord's direction in their lives concerning what they should do after graduation. When I told them about our work at the Dream Center, their eyes lit up. Leanne had a background in catering services, but her heart's desire was to develop intercessory prayer ministries. Howard's background was in business and computers. More important, I recognized in both of the Baileys a quality that is becoming increasingly rare nowadays: a servant's heart. Leanne and Howard said, "Anything we can do to help, we're available." Although I couldn't pay them a dime, by the summer of '98, the Baileys were living by faith and working with us at the Dream Center.

Harvey Martin, a construction company owner, was watching television in Kelowna, British Colombia, one night, when he flipped the channel and saw me being interviewed by Charles Grodin on his late-night talk show. Harvey was searching for fresh direction in his life, so he listened intently as I told my story.

"I felt that if I could just talk to that man for five minutes," Harvey later said, "he might be able to help me." A few months later, Harvey committed his life to Christ.

In April, Harvey heard about the Dream Center and the need for someone who was licensed to install fire prevention sprinklers. "Well, I have a license," Harvey said. Two weeks later, at his own expense, Harvey made a trip to Los Angeles to help install the fire sprinkler system at the facility. When Harvey walked through the Dream Center's door, I was the first man he met. We talked briefly, and I was on my way to another speaking engagement, but to Harvey, it was a sign. Harvey returned to Kelowna in May, and by July, he was back at the Dream Center helping me to work on the room where I had been conducting my Bible studies. Harvey's construction and carpentry skills were a tremendous boon to our work.

Despite the sweltering summer heat, and the auto and bus exhaust fumes that permeated our Bible study meeting place in the former hospital laundry room, which was located under the tar-covered parking lot with no air-conditioning, our lunch-hour Bible study group continued to grow. Some days we actually had to tell people, "I'm sorry, there's no more space in this room. You'll have to come back tomorrow." I didn't mind the adverse conditions. My staff and I were content; I was discipling the older students at the Dream Center Academy, and we felt that we were making a difference. We would have been glad to stay there forever, but God had different plans for us.

SURPRISED BY LOVE

In mid-July, I met Lori Graham, an attractive, vivacious woman who had come from Phoenix First Assembly, at the encouragement of pastor Tommy Barnett's wife, Marja, to speak at a special women's meeting at the Dream Center. Lori had been active in ministering in the inner city as well as to women's groups, especially women who had experienced the traumas and guilt associated with abusive relationships and abortion. Like me, she had been married previously but had been single and celibate for the past ten years. We were two broken people whom God brought together to form a whole person. Lori and I fell in love and married in September. (You can read the complete story of our courtship in Lori's forthcoming book.)

After our fairy-tale wedding in the backyard of the home of our friends Joyce and John Caruso, who had also become active in our ministry, Lori and I headed to London. While there I spoke at historic Westminster Chapel, pastored by R.T. Kendall, whose book *God Meant It for Good* had been so instrumental in my spiritual growth while in prison. From London, Lori and I set out on a whirlwind schedule of speaking engagements in Australia, and then across America. Some honeymoon!

WHEN GOD SHUTS THE DOORS, HE OPENS A WINDOW

Back at the Dream Center, Lori moved into my one-room accommodations. When my son, Jamie, moved back to Atlanta to revive an inner-city ministry there, Lori and I inherited his room. We felt as though we were basking in luxury—two rooms and a bath!

My afternoon Bible studies had been put on hold prior to our wedding. I felt bad, almost as if I were abandoning my spiritual babies, but from the time Lori and I announced our engagement, my schedule was crammed full. We were gone from the Dream Center more than we were home. At the same time, I felt that a new aspect of our ministry was about to be born.

Ever since I had been released from prison, a desire burned in my heart to open a "restoration center," a place where broken, bruised, or burned-out, fatigued pastors and ministry workers could come to find spiritual help and healing. Part of Pastor Tommy's, Pastor Matthew's, and my vision for the Dream Center was to renovate the ninth floor of the old hospital and turn it into a place of healing and restoration for ministry workers and others who had suffered great losses in their lives. Having experienced what I had at Heritage USA, both positively and negatively, I felt that I could empathize with the ministers' struggles. I believed that God was also leading me to establish a restoration ministry in conjunction with, but separate from, the Dream Center. Consequently, everywhere I traveled, I searched for opportunities to develop such a ministry to ministers.

I didn't find a place to establish a new restoration ministry in L.A. and, although the renovation of the Dream Center's ninth floor was important, it was currently on hold. I began to feel in my spirit that my present time of ministry at the Dream Center was drawing to a close. I didn't say anything to anyone; I just kept the matter to myself.

Despite my increasing sense of unrest, I continued my plans to help renovate the Dream Center and to create further ministry opportunities for the converts in the inner city. One of my dreams was to develop a new television ministry from the center. Pastor Tommy and Pastor Matthew were already doing a television program that originated at the Dream Center and aired on Trinity Broadcasting Network. I felt that I could help train young people at the Dream Center in television production skills, which would help them learn a profession while they were helping the ministry.

At the same time, I sensed a rekindling of a desire to return to a television ministry myself. I had no interest in ever being in a position similar to what I held at PTL, where I lived with the intense, constant pressure of having to raise nearly four million dollars every week to stay on the air and to pay the other ministry bills. Yet I could not deny the fact that from the earliest days of Christian television, I have felt called by God to be involved with that medium.

Excited about the possibilities, I wrote up a proposal and presented it to Pastor Tommy and Pastor Matthew. Few ministers in the world are more encouraging and motivating than the Barnetts. But when they out-lined their own plans for the Dream Center's future, I could clearly see that my call to Christian television was not consistent with their plans. To have my dreams dashed so abruptly caused me to wonder even more if my time at the Dream Center was indeed coming to a close. Even Tommy's and my plan to build a restoration center for pastors on the ninth floor of the Dream Center had to be delayed until the fire exit, fire walls, and sprinklers could be brought up to codes. Completion of that process, we realized, was still several years away. Regardless of what I tried to do there, it seemed that God was shutting the doors for me at the Dream Center.

One morning, my wife, Lori, woke up and shocked me with her state-ment. "Jim, I feel that we are going to move . . . to Charlotte."

Had Lori hit me in the face with a shovel, I would not have been more surprised.

Charlotte! Why Charlotte? I thought.

Lori had told me previously that she had no desire whatsoever to go to Charlotte. She did not want to live in the shadows of my past. For Lori to say that she felt we were moving to Charlotte would be like the presi-dent of Ford Motor Company waking up one morning and saying, "I'm going to drive a Chevrolet!"

As for me, Charlotte was the last place on earth I wanted to be. Although I had many wonderful friends and many great memories from my years of living and ministering in that city, it was also the scene of some of the most painful memories in my life. To me, Charlotte was the city of my humiliation. Why would I want to go back there?

Although I knew that God was gathering a group of Christians in Charlotte who had a desire to do something great for God, only one thing could possibly motivate me to move back to Charlotte. It would take a very clear word from the Lord.

That year, I spoke at the New Year's Eve services in Charlotte, spon-sored by Morningstar Ministries, which was led by Rick Joyner. I had known of Rick since I was incarcerated—when I first read his books. While I was in prison, Heritage USA was bankrupted, closed, and many of its assets had been sold off. The new owners opened it to be used as a conference center. Although I had no more legal authority at Heritage, Rick still regarded me as the spiritual leader of the ministry that had thrived there. He was so respectful of my position as the former head of

Heritage USA that he contacted me in federal prison and said that he refused to hold a conference on the property without asking my permission. I was awed that he would have such respect for God, and for me, an inmate in federal prison! In the years following my release from prison, Rick and I became close friends. He is now a member of the board of directors that I work under at New Covenant Fellowship, along with Pastor Tommy Barnett, of Phoenix; Pastor Tommy Reid, from Buffalo; Dr. R.T. Kendall, of Westminster Chapel in London; and Julian Carroll, former governor of Kentucky.

During some of our casual conversations at the New Year's Eve conference, Rick spoke prophetically to me: "Jim, I believe that your time of ministry in Los Angeles is drawing to a close." Rick wasn't saying that I should pack up and move out the next day. He was simply informing me of what he felt the Lord had laid on his heart to share with me. Little did he know that God had already begun speaking to me along that same line.

But where was I to go? What was I to do? And what of the people who had gathered with me to work at the Dream Center? I had a lot of questions and very few answers, so I kept quiet and kept my heart and mind open to the Lord's direction. Besides, I had learned the hard way not to make hasty decisions. The last major decision I had made in haste and under duress had cost me my ministry at Heritage USA.

Early in 1999, a pastor whom I respected immensely called with an unusual message. After a brief conversation, he said, "I don't exactly know how to say this, but I feel strongly led of the Lord to tell you something."

"Why, sure, Pastor. Go right ahead. Let me hear it."

"Well, I feel that your ministry in Los Angeles is drawing to a close."

This pastor lived nowhere near Rick Joyner, yet they both had declared the same message to me. I thanked him and admitted that I was not sure what the Lord had in store for me, but that I was willing to go wherever He wanted me to go and do whatever He told me to do.

In April, Lori and I went back to Charlotte for another Morningstar conference. One day, out of the blue, Rick Joyner approached us and said, "I believe that you are to move to Charlotte. You can live at our cabin." Lori and I looked at each other in amazement. Besides a confirmation of the word that Lori had felt strongly about, we both realized the significance of Rick's words. The cabin he mentioned was surrounded by more than five hundred acres of lush wooded property, but it was not a hunting cabin. It was a huge house, built by an Amway magnate, Dexter Yager. The "cabin" was large enough to house our office equipment and our entire ministry team!

5

CAN NEW TESTAMENT COMMUNITY REALLY WORK?

FOR MONTHS BEFORE RICK Joyner's offer, I had been talking about and teaching about the body of Christ. My teaching had provoked many interesting and stimulating discussions among our staff and Bible study members concerning the Christian community. Now Rick was presenting to us an ideal opportunity to test the biblical concepts.

But does it really work? I wondered. *Is it actually possible for people to live together in a sharing, caring community this side of heaven? Or are the scriptural accounts merely an ideal to shoot for, a nice idea, but one that nobody really expects to achieve?*

The more I thought about it, the more convinced I became that the New Testament church is the standard. Yet I am also a realist. In the early church some compassionate people sold their possessions and generously shared their profits or goods with others who were needy. At the same time, other people in the church were selfish, lazy, grab-all-you-can-get-for-free users. We have no reason to believe that these two extremes (and people everywhere in between) have disappeared from our church ranks. Moreover, the church is still populated by sinners who have been saved by grace, many of whom have brought their carnal, worldly ways along with them when they joined the church. The great "temple of the Lord" is still very much under construction!

Yet something deep within me said that God would not have given us so much information on how we are to treat one another if He did not intend us to live in a close-knit community. We really would not need much of the New Testament's practical instructions about how we are to interact if we were simply to gather together for an hour or so each week. Almost anyone can be civil toward each other under those circumstances. It is when we live in close proximity to each other, interacting on a daily basis, often in stressful or pressure-packed conditions, that we need spiritually based principles to keep us from killing one another.

With as realistic an approach as possible, Lori and I decided that it was worth a try. We would establish the restoration center in Charlotte, based on principles of New Testament Christianity.

MOVING AGAIN?

Rick's offer was incredibly generous, but the more I thought about it, the more I wondered how I'd even have enough money to pay the utility expenses at such a large house. We gathered our team together, and I presented Rick's offer to each person on our staff.

"We can't pay you," I told them, "but you can live with Lori and me for free, and we'll all trust God together to meet our needs." At that point, we weren't even sure how we were going to scrape up enough money to pay for our cross-country move, let alone how we were going to feed, clothe, and provide for other basic needs. "We will live in the house together, work together, and be a New Testament community, not just in theory, but in real life!"

By now, Harvey and Shirley had announced their engagement to be married. "How about it, Harvey? Are you in?" Lori asked Harvey.

Harvey looked at Shirley and smiled. "You bet we're in." Harvey sold off his business in Canada and the majority of his possessions, taking a severe penalty on the currency exchange rate. For a new believer, it was an incredible step of faith.

To a person, we were united as a body, and we agreed to move to Charlotte. We all started packing what meager belongings we had in our rooms at the Dream Center.

Seven of us decided to make the move: Armando, a single, twenty-four-year-old young man; Leanne and Howard, a couple who had been married more than fifteen years; Shirley and Harvey, who were soon to be married; and Lori and me, who were newlyweds. We certainly spanned the spectrum in the area of personal relationships! But could we all live together as one happy family? That was another question.

We figured that if we didn't take any furniture, we could pack our clothes and boxed possessions tightly enough to fit into one rental truck. Anything that did not fit into boxes would have to be left behind in storage.

The week of the move, Shirley's daughter, Cathy Brock, who was employed by Dexter Yager's son, Jeff, came to the Los Angeles area for a large Amway convention in Long Beach. Her employer had shipped a tractor-trailer load of materials from Charlotte to the convention in L.A. The truck was scheduled to return to Charlotte immediately following the convention—the exact day we had planned to leave Los Angeles. When Cathy learned about our plan to move all our belongings, she generously suggested, "Maybe you could fit some things in the back of our truck if there is any room left over."

Most gratefully, we accepted Cathy's offer. All we had to do was to get our belongings to Long Beach from Los Angeles. We diligently packed our rental truck with the boxes we planned to load onto the Amway truck and took off for Long Beach. We were excited, yet a little discouraged at having to leave behind many of our belongings that wouldn't fit on the truck. When we arrived in Long Beach, however, we were pleasantly surprised.

Whether it was the hand of God or merely an enthusiastic bunch of Amway representatives, I'll never know. What I do know is that the conventioneers had bought up every box of product Cathy's employer had shipped from Charlotte, leaving that entire tractor-trailer empty for the return trip. The truck drivers agreed to take *all* of our possessions to Charlotte—we just had to go back and bring them from Los Angeles, about an hour and a half away. We hastily unloaded the rental truck and raced back to L.A., where we enlisted the help of some friends and frantically loaded our battered furniture and other items that had been in storage onto the rental truck. Then we raced back to Long Beach where the Amway truck was waiting for us. We must have looked like "The Beverly Hillbillies," but all seven of us got all our possessions loaded onto the trucks.

With our possessions gone, there was nothing left for us to do but to say good-bye to our friends at the Dream Center. We left on good terms and planned to continue working together with the wonderful people in the heart of Los Angeles.

We all set out by car on our way to Charlotte by way of Atlanta, where my son, Jamie, and Amanda Moses were scheduled to marry on June 5. Lori and I traveled toward Dallas for a speaking engagement. On the way, we decided to divert from the direct route long enough to stop by the Grand Canyon. As we crossed the Arizona–New Mexico border, we saw the most wonderful sight. A bright, double rainbow stretched across the sky. I had been teaching in our Bible study how the rainbow was a sign of God's promises and of new beginnings. As we drove from the Grand Canyon, the rainbow remained in the sky, almost like a radiant gateway to a fresh start. Although we didn't know it at the time, we later learned that Shirley and Harvey had also taken time to stop by the Grand Canyon, and they, too, saw and photographed the double rainbow in the sky. We all felt that the rainbow was a confirmation of our step of faith to move back East.

THE REAL THING

Following Jamie and Amanda's beautiful wedding in Atlanta, we all piled into our vehicles again and set out for Charlotte. But we had one more stop along the way. On Sunday, June 6, I was scheduled to speak in Georgia for the dedication ceremonies at a new church, pastored by Robert Rutherford. I didn't really know Robert, so I had no idea what to expect, but as soon as we drove up to the church, I knew this stop was God-ordained.

Robert and his congregation were *doing* what we had been talking about in theory—living out New Testament community in an entire local congregation. The church building was sleek and new, with metal exterior walls and a beautifully appointed interior, pleasant and appealing yet extremely functional. The members of the body had helped raise the building, with everyone pitching in and helping, even the children. As Pastor Robert showed us around, he pointed out some of the wallpaper work that had been done by the young people in the congregation. Tears filled his eyes as he pointed to a crooked seam in the wallpaper. "Our kids did that," he said, choking back the tears. "Sorry," he apologized, wiping his eyes. "Every time I see that place where the paper doesn't quite fit together, I have a hard time keeping back the tears. I am so proud of our youth for the way they worked together to help build the church.

Sure, we have some imperfections, a few places where things don't look as good as if they had been done by professionals, but I wouldn't trade those imperfections for all the paid workers in the world."

We were so intrigued with this church's pioneer spirit, we decided to stay over to see the whole picture. The next day, Pastor Rutherford showed us how the congregation was growing its own food, sinking its own wells, and generating its own power in anticipation of the days when food, water, and electricity may be in short supply. Food and clothing banks at the church were well stocked. Many members of the church have built homes either on or nearby the church property. Volunteers from the congregation built most of the homes, working together to provide housing for their people. "We call ourselves 'Amish with an attitude,'" quipped Pastor Robert.

For some time, the church had operated its own sawmill. Church members had cut and hewn most of the trees used in the log cabins that dotted the property. To help newlywed couples who had helped others in the body build their homes, the church provided a beautiful, brand-new log cabin, built by the congregation. Following the New Testament principle of "Those who do not work, do not eat," only those couples who helped others build their homes were eligible for the wedding gift of a free log home.

Undergirding everything the church did was a spirit of cooperation and service, as unto the Lord. They gathered together regularly to study the Word of God, to pray together, and to fellowship together. A major emphasis was placed on ministry to the youth. Most of the families homeschool their children, and the children's work ethic blew us all away. Rather than looking for what somebody could do for them, the children all wanted to help. "What can I do to help?" was a question we heard again and again. The youth of the congregation ran a thrift store downtown, as well as a coffeehouse ministry in town.

As we toured the property and met the people of Pastor Rutherford's congregation, we marveled at how they were effectively living in Christian community and how much they loved each other. It dawned on us that by showing us this example of true Christian community, combined with our experience of living and working together in close quarters at the Dream Center with few luxuries beyond our basic needs, God had been preparing us for the lifestyle we were about to enter. He showed us that not only was it possible to live in Christian community, it was preferable!

MORNING HOUSE

"It looks like the Ponderosa!" Howard exclaimed when we first got out of our vehicles and everyone looked in awe at the huge "log cabin" Rick Joyner had made available to us. Tucked in the forest, well off the main highway, the house had eight bedrooms, a large kitchen and dining area, a "garage" that had been turned into a two-hundred-seat conference room by the previous owners, plenty of office space, and more! Compared to our one-room existence at the Dream Center, this place was a mansion! And we were going to live here for free! We all just shook our heads in awe at God's marvelous provision.

Lori, Shirley, and I assigned the rooms, and we all worked together to bring in our belongings. After unloading the last box, I called everyone together around the large table in the kitchen.

"I've never done this before, not even at Heritage USA," I began slowly and quietly, "but I am going to do it here. I want everyone in this house to understand that I am the boss. I am the head of this house. If we are going to live together as one big family, there needs to be one person where the buck stops, and I am that person. I don't intend to be a dictator or a slave driver, but if this community is going to work, somebody has to be in charge. I love each one of you, and I will make every decision as fairly as I can, and I will always do what I believe the Lord wants me to do, even if it is not my own preference. But I will be the last word."

I paused for a moment to let my words sink in. The group of people around me looked at me as though I were Winston Churchill, telling them that I had nothing to offer but blood, sweat, and tears. I continued, "We must keep short accounts with God and with one another. We cannot allow disagreements or offenses to fester and turn into bigger problems. If you need to confront someone, do it in love or not at all. We must treat one another with love. We'll live by the golden rule: Do unto others as you would have them do unto you. Be kind to one another. And remember the old saying, 'If you can't say something nice about someone . . .'"

The group finished the saying in a chorus, ". . . say nothing at all!"

We called the home "New Covenant House" (we later changed it to Morning House) because we were beginning afresh with a new promise to God and to each other, to love the Lord and to love one another. We plunged into the work of setting up the house and establishing a place where broken ministers could come to find healing. At the same time, much of our initial ministry efforts revolved around me, since I continued to travel, speak, write, and minister around the country. Within a month of getting the house together, we had our first of many seminars for people to come and begin the healing process. Lori renewed her ministry to women, especially women who have had abortions and who need to find healing from the guilt, shame, and pain from the past.

THE PROBLEMS AND THE OPPORTUNITIES

Living together in Christian community provides plenty of problems that must be addressed and opportunities to do what Jesus would do. The most obvious problem is the lack of privacy. As I write these words, we now have eight people living at Morning House, with a constant flow of invited visitors who fill the guest rooms. In addition to our "full-time live-ins," my daughter, Tammy Sue, works in the ministry full-time; Shirley Phillips and Joyce LaBaron, both widows, also help with the ministry on an almost daily basis; and several other men and women help with everything from data entry into our computers to the housecleaning each week. Although the house is large, it is usually crowded with people.

Basic privacy issues such as closed doors are always respected. Well, almost always. Not long after we arrived, we were conducting an early morning seminar, when two guests decided to wander through the house. They opened a closed bedroom door and ran smack into former Green Bay Packers defensive lineman Reggie White and his wife, Sarah, who were staying with us that weekend and were just getting out of bed. I'm not sure who was more shocked!

Ordinarily, however, we attempt to give each other as much privacy as possible. Not everyone wants to get up at 6:00 A.M., and not everyone wants to stay up until midnight every night, so we try to respect each other's individuality. Since we have people of all ages living in close quarters, differences in taste regarding music, lifestyle, dress, and other individual preferences must be respected, while the individual must also submit to the majority wishes or the defined spiritual standards of others living in the group. Basic manners and consideration for each other are absolutely essential if we are going to live in harmony with each other.

Certainly, all the other issues that any family must address are relevant to us, too. For instance, since I am the "father" of the house, who is in charge when I am gone? What about money issues? When money comes into the ministry, how is it spent? Food and clothing budgets must also be decided. Most of the people at Morning House are volunteers, but somebody has to go out and bring home some income to pay for basic living expenses. As the head of the ministry, that responsibility usually falls to me, but it would not necessarily have to be exclusive to me. Anyone who wanted to work outside the ministry and contribute to the overall budget could do so. Currently, our ministry workload simply doesn't allow time for most of us to maintain outside jobs.

How are the resources and work assignments distributed? In the book of Acts, the disciples had to appoint deacons to distribute food to those who needed it, while the apostles gave themselves to studying the Word and to prayer. In our case, that means that my primary responsibility is to be in the Word, preparing messages, and studying so I can teach the Word to the others; Lori's responsibility is similar to mine. Meanwhile, Harvey's responsibility is to take care of the physical plant, maintaining the house, and making sure that everything is working properly. Armando works with Harvey on the property, as well as going around the world to preach. Shirley and Howard operate our offices, and Leanne heads up our intercessory prayer ministry and handles most of the grocery shopping and food preparation. It is not a matter of one of us being more important than the other. It is simply a matter of each of us having different gifts that we are using for the cause of Christ. Regardless of our positions, we all pitch in together to do whatever needs to be done to help further the ministry—whether that is researching Bible subjects or cleaning the toilets.

Certainly, someone must do the mundane chores. The garbage needs taking out. The grass needs cutting. Carpets must be vacuumed. Meals need to be prepared. Grocery shopping must be done. And commodes need to be cleaned. Most of living together in the Christian community is not glamorous or super "spiritual." It is work. Pure, simple work. It means that some of us are going to have to get used to living in cramped quarters, sharing our resources with others, and constantly keeping in mind common sense and consideration for others. Doing the "little things" means a lot, such as wiping out the bathtub after using it. Cleaning off the mirror when you spatter soap spots on it. Picking up your messes. Putting away clothes or anything else that would interfere with the common good of the community.

As my friend Bill Wilson of Metro Ministries in New York says, "If you see something that needs done, you don't make a big deal about it. You just do it."

Nevertheless, we are still human. And our human pride can easily raise its head and create divisions in the body of Christ. Jealousy, bitterness, resentments, insecurities, and power grabs can all be heightened by living in close proximity to each other. The only way to keep minor irritations from developing into major problems is that each of us must die to ourselves on a daily basis. When Paul said, "I die daily," he must have had the Christian community in mind.

As in any family, communication is key. Although the personality traits, temperaments, and psychological profiles of the people living at Morning House span the spectrum from spontaneous "sanguines" like Lori to introverted, bashful "melancholies" like me, each of us must make a conscious effort to keep the lines of communication open, even if sometimes it is difficult or goes against our individual grain. We do not have the luxury of being related to each other by blood, but we are related by the blood of Jesus.

For us, the absolute key to maintaining fellowship and keeping communication lines open has been our after-dinner devotional time. Similar to many modern families, often the only time we see each other is at the end of the day, at supper. So each evening, after our meal, we have a Bible study and discussion time, usually led by me when I am home. Not only has this time been central in our understanding of Scripture, but it has also been a time of dealing with gripes and concerns, and it has been a time in which our relationships can be healed. It is the Word of God that pierces and purifies our hearts and does what no amount of human rules and regulations can do. Without any manipulation by me or anyone else, the Holy Spirit will frequently speak to us through our Bible study time. Often the Scripture for the day (chosen "arbitrarily") will pertain to a particular subject or a problem being faced by one or more of our group. Many times, the answer has come as we have sought the Lord together. Sometimes we've had as many as thirty-five people joining us for dinner and for this special time of ministry.

Have we done everything perfectly? No way! Do we mess up, make mistakes, or occasionally lose our tempers with each other? Absolutely. Indeed, I have often felt more pressure, frustration, and sheer anger living in close community with eight dear people on a shoestring budget than I ever did when I was leading a multimillion-dollar ministry and employing three thousand people. It's like putting your life under a magnifying glass; everything looks bigger, whether for better or worse.

Yet I am convinced that what we are doing at Morning House is soon going to be the "norm" in Christianity. No, we all won't move in together, nor should we. It's tough enough to live with eight people, let alone eighty or eight thousand! But in the days ahead, I believe that the only way the Christian community can really function is by living out our faith in close-knit groups of people who can help each other and care for one another.

Yes, we will still have large church buildings in our towns and cities, but it will be impossible to have everyone's needs met at their local church house, when they are hoping to find a place to live, eat, sleep, or survive in practical ways. We must do this in microcosms. If you have a house that can accommodate two more people, that is your community opportunity. If you have an apartment into which you can take in one more person, that may be your opportunity for Christian service. Yes, we need to assemble together at the church meetinghouse regularly, but the real ministry must take place on a much more personal level, in your house, yard, or apartment.

Please understand, I am not advocating communism. Communism takes away rights, while genuine New Testament living empowers people to live together in love, supernaturally, and to tap into God's supernatural provision. I don't even like to use the term *communal*, because it is so easily misconstrued. Yet, in a way, authentic New Testament living involves a communal attitude, people living and working together. The difference is that in communism, the sacrifices are made for the state, but in the Christian community, people are living and working together to help one another and to glorify Jesus Christ.

The concepts you will discover in the pages ahead are based on New Testament Christianity, applied to twenty-first-century living. The lessons learned and practical applications of those truths are drawn from my experiences in the various Christian communities in which I have been privileged to live. Does New Testament community work? Yes, it does. Is it easy? Not on your life. Is it worth it? It's worth it now, and it will be worth it a million years from now.

6

THE CHURCH
IS NO
DISNEYLAND

WHAT IS THE CHURCH, anyhow? Is it that group of pious, self-righteous, or superficial Christians who meet at certain places every so often, with everyone pretending that they have it all together, that nobody has a problem in the world? I don't think so.

We tend to think of the church as a building or an organization. Nowadays, it's common to hear people say things such as, "I'm going to church" and to hear pastors or church leaders talking about "building a great church." In most cases, such comments refer to a place, a building, some structure where God's people meet every so often to do their religious exercises.

Interestingly, none of the New Testament writers referred to the church as a building to which people went to conduct religious services. In the truest biblical sense, Christians really don't go to church; rather, they *are* the church. The church is not a building; the church is the *body*, the people—people who were lost and on their way to hell, but who reached out in faith to Jesus Christ, who saved us. He adopted us and allowed us to become part of His family, despite our imperfections.

In fact, the impression is never given in the Bible that the church is a gathering of perfect people, Christians who have it all together spiritually. Quite the contrary! The church is a fellowship of forgiven sinners, people who may have failed miserably and sinned horribly, but who have trusted Jesus Christ as Savior, asked God for forgiveness. And He has washed them and made their hearts whiter than fresh, clean snow.

Forgiven? Yes! Saved? Yes! Perfect? Absolutely not! Many of the people in the church are still struggling to overcome habits from their pasts. Others are struggling with "new" sins that dog them. The church is not a pristine picture of piety and purity. Instead, it is a rogues' gallery, comprised of former liars, cheats, thieves, murderers, pornographers, drunks, and prostitutes—people who should have been condemned to eternal destruction, if it were not for the cleansing blood of Jesus Christ and the grace of God.

Nor is the church a Disneyland where all is well all of the time. It is not a place where all our hopes, dreams, and fantasies come true, where "never is heard a discouraging word . . ."

Somehow, we have gotten the impression that the church is some idyllic group of people who are immune from real-life problems, who never have a need, who always get along, and who go around all day long singing "Hallelujah." We have been duped into believing that the body of Christ constantly flows together in one harmonious river, euphorically bubbling along toward heaven.

The truth is that we are much more like the bumper cars attraction at an amusement park. We all start off in the same direction, but before long, we bang into one another, sometimes scraping and grating against each other. Sometimes we hit each other from behind and sometimes head-on collisions occur, creating all sorts of awful screeches, crashes, and other unmentionable sounds. More frequently than we care to admit, we get stuck, spinning our wheels, thwarting progress, or simply going in circles.

Is this really the church, the body of Christ, the people for whom Jesus gave His life and through whom He intends to finish His work? Yes, believe it or not, it is. And we need to learn how to live together in love, not that we will eliminate all bumps and bruises, but that we might be the "place" where people can find healing for their hurts when they occur.

In fact, I believe that like gemstones that have been thrust together to be polished, part of our refining will take place as we grate against each other and allow God to smooth out the rough places in each of us.

WHAT IS THE CHURCH?

But just what is the church, and what in the world is it supposed to do?

The Greek word that is translated "church" in the New Testament is *ekklesia* (pronounced: ek-lay-see-ya), which means "a group of people called out to assemble together."

Throughout the New Testament, *ekklesia* has a twofold meaning. First, it is used to describe the church universal, the whole body of Christians everywhere, from New Testament times until now, and, if you can imagine it, all the Christians who are yet to be born into the kingdom of God. In other words, the church comprises the saints— which means "true believers" in Scripture—who have gone before us, the believers who are alive presently, and the believers yet to be born. Second, the word *ekklesia* also describes a local community of believers, a local church.

The Universal Church

It is important to understand that the universal church includes all people who have trusted Jesus Christ as their Lord, regardless of their race, skin color, nationality, social status, or denominational affiliation. There is no such thing as a "black" church or a "white" church, a "Chinese" church, or a "Canadian" church; we are all one family. This explains why Christians who visit foreign countries and meet fellow believers frequently discover that although they may not share the same language, liturgy, or cultural values, their common faith in the Lord Jesus binds them together in an incredible love. They are "one in the Spirit." Ironically, it does not explain why some Christians can get along better with believers in Bogotá than they can with fellow Christians across the street. Please understand that if you have trusted Jesus as your Savior and have acknowledged Him as Lord of your life, you are a member of the universal church, the body of Christ.

The Local Congregation

The second and more frequent use of the word *ekklesia* in the New Testament refers to a local congregation of Christian believers. These believers are part of the universal church, and they are living out their Christian commitments together in a community, doing their best to follow the principles taught by Jesus Christ—serving the Lord and each other in a local situation. The local community of believers may be a large group that meets regularly in a church, or it may be a small group that meets in somebody's home, field, or boxcar. The size of the group or the appearance of the building in which the body meets is irrelevant.

Jesus promised that wherever two or three people are gathered in His name, He would be in their midst.

Now, here's where all this talk about the church can sometimes get confusing. It is important to understand that participation in a local Christian community is not necessarily synonymous with membership in God's church. Getting your name on the church roll, singing in a choir, serving on a committee, playing on a church softball team, putting money in an offering plate, or even teaching a class or preaching a sermon or appearing on Christian television does not necessarily mean that you are a member of God's church.

An old saying puts it this way: "Going into a church building does not make you a Christian any more than going into a garage makes you a car, or going into a barn makes you a cow." The late singer Keith Green often quipped, "Going to church doesn't make you a Christian any more than going to McDonald's makes you a hamburger!"

To be a part of Christ's church, you must know Him, and you must believe some basic things about God, about the Bible, about the person of Jesus Christ, and about your own need to trust Him as your Lord. Granted, individual churches may add their own doctrinal distinctions when it comes to membership "requirements" in their particular denomination or group. You may or may not choose to adhere to those doctrines, but the essential elements of the Christian faith are nonnegotiable.

What are those basic Christian beliefs? Perhaps one of the best statements of faith, distilled from the Bible and grouped in a compact package, can be found in the ancient collection of statements known as the Apostles' Creed.

No one knows who actually wrote the Apostles' Creed (the apostles themselves probably did not write it), but some form of the creed dates back to the earliest days of the church. While the creed is not a divinely inspired document as the Bible is, to this day the Apostles' Creed is an accurate, succinct statement of what Christians believe. Many sincere Christians believe much more than the basic doctrinal statements the creed presents, but no genuine Christian who has even a rudimentary understanding of the Bible should believe less. The Apostles' Creed says:

I believe in God the Father Almighty, maker of heaven and earth:
And in Jesus Christ His only Son, our Lord; who was conceived by
the Holy Spirit born of the Virgin Mary, suffered under Pontius

Pilate, was crucified, dead, and buried; He descended into Hades; the third day He rose again from the dead; He ascended into heaven, and sitteth at the right hand of God, the Father Almighty; from there He shall come to judge the living and the dead. I believe in the Holy Spirit, the holy Christian church, the communion of saints, the forgiveness of sins, the resurrection of the body, and the life everlasting. Amen.

There, in a nutshell, is the common denominator of what most Christians believe. Certainly, in most public church services, there will be people who do not truly believe even the basics of the Christian faith, as reflected by the above creed. Those people may be in the church building, but they are not a part of Christ's body. Similarly, in nearly every church service there are people who have never been "born again." In fact, I'm convinced that a large number of people in our Christian congregations nowadays have never been born again! Our job is to do all that we can to win them to Christ by our loving example, not to ostracize unbelievers and force them out.

Sometimes even our best efforts will be unfruitful. When that happens, we must remember that Jesus taught that wheat will grow up alongside tares, the chaff, and we ought not to be overly concerned about tearing up the tares or casting out the chaff. Jesus instructed us to let the wheat and tares grow up together (Matt. 13:28–29). In the last day, the angels of heaven will separate the good from the bad, the just from the unjust. That is not our responsibility. Our job is to invite as many people as possible to become part of God's family and then to nurture them as we would members of our own physical families. Jesus told us to make disciples, not simply converts.

How do you become a member of the community of believers? There is only one way: you are added to God's church by grace through faith in Jesus Christ the moment you are born again. You are not added to the universal church merely by joining a local church. Getting your name in the Lamb's Book of Life does not happen after you get your name on an official church membership registry.

Nor do you become part of the body of Christ when you suddenly get inspired to involve yourself in the church. As author Max Anders poignantly stated, "We do not become the body when we agree to work together in harmony. We are automatically the body, regardless of whether or not we decide to work together in harmony. The question is only whether we will be a healthy body or an unhealthy one."[1]

If we are truly Christians, we are already members of the community of believers; if we belong to Christ, we are His members. The purpose of belonging to a local community of believers is not to "get you saved"; it is because you are saved. It is because you have already decided to put your faith in Christ and to follow Him. The best (and perhaps only) way you can live out your salvation is by joining with, belonging to, and functioning in a local group of people with like faith and living out that faith together.

Rabbi Harold Kushner, author of *Why Bad Things Happen to Good People*, reminded us that we are searching for significance, that human beings are social creatures, and that we are affected by the people around us. In an interview with Peter Lowe, Rabbi Kushner said:

> Do you want to feel good about yourself? Be part of a community of people who are dedicated to doing good. It's not easy to be the only person in your crowd that pays his taxes honestly. It's not easy to be the only person in your group who refrains from malicious gossip. Find yourself a sub-community, a sub-set of people who believe what you believe . . . Bounce off each other; reinforce each other; encourage each other. This is what churches and synagogues do. You don't go to church to become a good person. You become a good person, you go to church; you surround yourself with other good people. You have your values and your commitments reinforced. You don't have this sense that "I'm out of step with the community; everybody else is trying to get their own thing, to fill their own pockets, and I'm the only lonely saint out here." Just the opposite. You find that you are part of God's army and it becomes a lot easier to do it when the people around you are doing it.[2]

Rabbi Kushner is right. Positive peer pressure can be a powerful force for good in our lives. And the most loving, kind, compassionate group a person can ever join ought to be the church of Jesus Christ.

Now, here's an interesting paradox: Membership in a local congregation does not necessarily mean inclusion in God's church. However, inclusion in God's universal church means that if we are to mature spiritually, we must become an active part of a local congregation that espouses and attempts to live out the ideals of Jesus. It's not enough to say, "I'm part of God's universal church, so therefore I don't need to be connected to a local community of believers." Or, "I'm a part of the universal church, so that supersedes my responsibility to be involved in helping my brothers and sisters in my town. I'm above all that. I'm too busy looking at the broad, worldwide picture to concern myself with what is happening in the local Christian community."

Nothing could be farther from the truth. Yes, God wants us to be concerned about the world. Jesus gave us a mandate, the Great Commission, to take the gospel to the ends of the earth (Matt. 28:19–20). But our primary duty is not to "win the world to Jesus." Our top priority is to fall in love with Jesus and to live out our relationship with Him wherever He puts us. As we do that, we will indeed "win the world" to Christ.

Motivated by the Great Commission, for many years I was convinced that the way to win the world to Christ was through Christian television. I am still convinced that television is an effective tool to communicate the gospel, but I now realize that God always places His children in families, which is why throughout the New Testament we find an emphasis on the local church.

Let me show you what I mean. In the introduction to his first letter to the Corinthians, Paul wrote, "To the church of God which is at Corinth, to those who are sanctified in Christ Jesus, called to be saints, with all who in every place call on the name of Jesus Christ our Lord, both theirs and ours" (1 Cor. 1:2 NKJV).

Notice the reference to the local congregation—the church of God at Corinth. Then Paul spoke of the local congregation as a part of the universal church, the church in every place that calls on the name of the Lord. Throughout Paul's letters, the apostle referred to specific, local communities of believers.

Similarly, the apostle John, writing from the isle of Patmos, in chapters 2 and 3 of what we now know as the book of Revelation, addressed the church of Smyrna, the church of Sardis, the church of Pergamos, Thyatira, Philadelphia, Laodicea, and Ephesus—in other words, he wrote to the local community of believers in each town. All of these churches were part of the universal church being manifested in local communities.

It's an inadequate comparison, but imagine being a member of a national political party. Although you are linked together with the national organization, you meet regularly with a grassroots group on a local level to "work out" your political beliefs, to encourage one another, and to go out into the community to spread the word about your party and to serve your fellow citizens.

The difference, of course, is that the church of Almighty God is a living, breathing, supernatural organism, not simply a human organization. The church is God's work, inhabited, instructed, and empowered by the Holy Spirit. It is not controlled, energized, or motivated by human personality, power, or charisma. If the church is to be built, it will be the Lord who builds it, not mere human effort, charm, or manipulation.

WHOSE IDEA WAS THIS?

Interestingly, it was Jesus who first mentioned the church, when He looked at Simon Peter, in the company of the other disciples, and said, "You are Peter, and on this rock I will build My church, and the gates of Hades shall not prevail against it" (Matt. 16:18 NKJV). The Roman Catholic Church has traditionally taken the position that Jesus was pronouncing Peter as the first pope, the "rock" on which the rest of the church would be built. Most Protestant denominations believe that Peter's confession of Jesus as the Messiah, the Christ, the One they had been looking for, is the "rock" foundation on which His church is built.

In other words, Jesus was saying, "Upon the revelation of who I am, I will build My church and the gates of hell will not be able to hold it back, to keep it from impacting the world." Any way you interpret the statement of Jesus, one thing is clear: You can't accept Him without accepting the importance of His church.

The fact that Jesus said, "I *will* build My church" (future tense), rather than "I *am* building My church" (present tense), leads many Bible teachers to assume that the church didn't "officially" exist until the day of Pentecost. On that day, three thousand people were added to the 120 believers who had experienced the supernatural outpouring of the Holy Spirit, forming the nucleus of the first Christian church. In subsequent days, the Bible tells us that the Lord added to the church those who were being saved (Acts 2:47).

In his wonderful book *What You Need to Know About the Church*, Max Anders pointed out that the New Testament writers employed several word-pictures to describe the church. The church is pictured as a body, as the bride of Christ, and as a building—a peculiar people, a chosen race, and a spiritual house.[3]

The apostle Paul most frequently compared the community of believers to a body, giving the church anthropomorphic characteristics such as hands, feet, a mouth, and other parts. Clearly, Paul intended to imply that the community of believers is figuratively the hands, feet, and voice of Jesus in our world.

While every Christian is part of the body, it is important to remember that Jesus Christ is the head of the church. "And He is the head of the body, the church," we read in Colossians 1:18 (NKJV). And we are to be His body in this present world. In 1 Corinthians 12:13, Paul reminded us, "For by one Spirit we were all baptized into one body" (NKJV). In Ephesians 1:22–23, Paul wrote, "And He [God] put all things under His [Christ's] feet, and gave Him to be head over all things to the church, which is His body, the fullness of Him who fills all in all" (NKJV).

The purpose of the body is to fulfill the desires and commands of the head. Since Christ is the Head, and we are His body, what should the church be doing? Whatever fulfills the desires and commands of Christ. The Bible makes it abundantly clear that the body of Christ should represent Christ, to show the world what Jesus is like—or you could say, we are to *re-present* Christ—in such a way that the world can once again see the love, character, power, and personality of Jesus Christ . . . in us!

In his book *The Road to Reality*, author K.P. Yohannan probed,

If we're rightly connected to the head in this way, it would be hard to imagine making any decision without first submitting it to Christ for His approval. What would that do to the way we spend our time? What does Christ say about the TV and the films we view, the music we listen to, or the catalogs and magazines we read?

What about our activities—church, clubs, leisure time, friendships, hobbies, prayer, service, sports and study?

What about our relationships with boyfriends, girlfriends, mentors and role models? Whom do we idolize and pattern our lives after?

What about our purchases, both large and small? Is our shopping basket under His control? Does He direct the checks we write? What about the "big buys"—our car, home and insurance?

What about our intake of food and drink? Is Christ or our appetites in control?

And of course, there are those major decisions in life—full-time missionary service, career and job plans, education and the choice of a mate.

For the Christian, none of these things is any longer a personal decision. It is not what others say, what self says, or what circumstances dictate. The only valid question is always, What does Christ say to me about this decision?

But most of us find ourselves making even the big decisions without prayer and waiting for guidance from the Holy Spirit.

Obviously, the gap between this kind of biblical Christianity and the shallow spirituality of our day is a significant one. How different is this kind of self-sacrificing faith from the pleasure-seeking, self-serving, wimpy religion so often preached and practiced in our churches![4]

Yohannan is right! All too often, there is little difference between the contemporary Christian community and the world at large. Rather than showing the world what Jesus is like, many Christians have become so much like the world that it's hard to find the "Jesus" in them. We talk like the world, act like the world, pursue the same worldly goals, and participate in the same worldly recreations. We squander our time, resources, and energy in pursuit of pleasure. We have lowered our standards so far that our values have become blurred and distorted. For instance, nowadays, we consider a movie to be "clean" if it only takes our Lord's name in vain or uses the "F" word three or four times! Shouldn't the body of Christ have the same "mind" as Christ?

The popular slogan "What would Jesus do?", recently revived from Charles Sheldon's classic book, *In His Steps*, is an extremely appropriate question for us as individual parts of the body and for the body as a whole. The church, the body of believers, should be doing what Jesus would do if He were here in a physical sense.

Clearly, if the local church is an important part of God's plan for His people, it ought to be high on our priority lists, as well. We need brothers and sisters to link arms to arms, hearts to hearts, and to live out our Christian experience together, so that we might become the image of Christ on earth. It is not enough to sit home alone reading the Bible, listening to Christian sermons and music, or watching Christian television programs. We need to be a vital, functioning part of the local church, as well as the invisible church universal. Otherwise, we will shrivel up and die spiritually.

The Lord Is Magnified in His Church

Throughout the Psalms, David often implied that the Lord is magnified in the midst of His congregation. What does it mean to magnify something? Does it mean that you make it bigger? Not necessarily.

Imagine yourself at a ballet performance (or a football game, if you prefer), and your seats are high up in the nosebleed section. To help you enjoy the event, you take along a pair of binoculars. As you focus your binoculars on the action, suddenly, it seems that ballet dancer or football player is just about sitting in your lap! What happened? The performer didn't get any larger; you simply saw him or her more clearly.

Similarly, when we gather together to worship the Lord with other believers, the Lord is magnified. That magnification doesn't make God bigger than He is. It simply allows us to see Him more clearly. Don't miss that: *Something about gathering together as a community of believers causes us to see the Lord in a way that we do not see Him in our personal worship of Him.*

Certainly, I love spending time alone with God, and in no way am I minimizing that. Quite the contrary. Each of us needs to establish and maintain a personal time with the Lord, in which we study His Word, have intimate conversations with Him, focus our attention on Him, and receive personal attention from Him. But David implied that my personal devotional life is no substitute for gathering together corporately with the community of believers. Solitude and isolation are certainly disciplines advocated in Scripture, but they do not exempt me from my need to be a part of the congregation of God, for when I get together with God's people, He is magnified. That is one of the reasons why believers are commanded (not simply encouraged) to gather together regularly with other believers (Heb. 10:24–25).

What's the Church to Do?

While every group of Christians that gathers together is part of the universal church, not every group of believers is a bona fide church. For instance, a large group of believers may gather for an evangelistic crusade, or a Promise Keepers rally, or a Women of Faith conference, and those Christians who attend those functions are part of the universal body of Christ. The gathering itself, however, does not necessarily constitute a church. On the other hand, a small group of believers may meet in someone's home to study the Bible, and they may indeed be a church. What makes the difference?

Following the patterns set by New Testament churches, to be considered a church nowadays, the local community of believers, no matter how large or small, rich or poor, must be composed of a group of Christians who commit themselves to doing at least two key things together.

They Commit to Meet Together Regularly

A number of years ago, I heard a song on the radio with lyrics that went something like, "Me and Jesus—we got our own thing goin'." Not only is that bad grammar, it's also bad theology. Nowhere in the New Testament do we find "Lone Ranger"–style Christianity. God does not intend for us to live our Christian lives alone, isolated from other believers. Saint Augustine, one of the early church fathers, realized the error perpetuated by anyone who wishes to have a relationship with God but does not want to be involved with His church. Augustine said, "He cannot have God for his father who does not have the church for his mother."

Following the mighty outpouring of the Holy Spirit on the day of Pentecost, the early Christians gathered together frequently. This is recorded in the book of Acts (NKJV): "And they continued steadfastly" (2:42); "all who believed were together, and had all things in common"

(2:44); "So continuing daily with one accord . . ." (2:46); "the Lord added to the church daily" (2:47); "the churches were strengthened in the faith, and increased in number daily" (16:5); and they "searched the Scriptures daily" (17:11). The early Christian community was not a group that met for an hour once a week, on Sunday mornings. Nor did they limit themselves to an annual conference or monthly meetings. They interacted daily.

While living and working at the Dream Center in the inner city of Los Angeles, I got into the habit of describing our ministry as "twenty-four/seven," because the ministry to hurting people was constant. It continued twenty-four hours a day, seven days a week. It didn't stop when the clock struck five; nor did it stop at midnight or take a break on Saturdays. Helping hurting people was a daily venture. And that is normal New Testament Christianity. It is the way the body of Christ should be!

The early believers ate many of their meals together; they went to the temple together to witness for Christ and to worship the Lord. No doubt some of them lived in the same areas of the city; or possibly they may even have shared the same houses. They studied the Scriptures together, and they discussed the application of those principles in their lives. They celebrated communion together, and they prayed together. They served one another and watched out for one another.

How can we be a New Testament community today? Practically speaking, most modern-day Christians will not be able to physically move into the church building and sleep on the floor, nor should we have to. Our churches are not designed to handle such communal living. Nor can we all buy homes in the same neighborhood or move to a large plantation in the country. It is simply not feasible for all of us to be together all of the time.

Beyond that, we all have responsibilities in life—we have made commitments to our families, to schools, to civic organizations or clubs. Being part of the body of Christ does not negate those commitments.

But if we are going to take seriously being part of the Christian community, it must have a priority place in our lives. Consequently, we need to carefully examine our schedules to see if we are missing the *best* for the sake of the *good*. We need to be interacting with God's people on a regular basis. Daily interaction, of course, is the ideal standard to aim at, but if you can't get together with fellow Christians every day, make whatever adjustments you must to maintain as close a contact as possible. Perhaps you can share a lunch together, work on a Habitat for Humanity house together, or attend a sporting event together. We don't always have to be at the house of worship to be interacting with the Christian community. Something uplifting occurs in our spirits as we gather together with God's people, even if the reason for which we have gathered is not overtly "spiritual." Just being with "family" is worth any sacrifices we must make.

They Commit to One Another

Wherever the Lord leads you to become a part of the local church, you must commit yourself to that group of people. You need to decide that you are going to meet regularly with that group and that you will follow Spirit-set and Spirit-led leadership. That does not mean that you follow mindlessly or naively, as many cult members have done in recent years. Images of Jim Jones, David Koresh, and the Hale-Bopp comet cults are fresh in our memories, and they ought to be red flags, warning us against blindly following any spiritual leader who contradicts or distorts the Scripture. The apostle Paul told his converts, "Follow me as I follow Christ" (see 1 Cor. 11:1). The implication is obvious. Paul hinted, "If at any point I am not following Christ, you are under no obligation to follow me."

Similarly, no local congregation, and certainly no human pastor, should be followed if they are leading contrary to biblical principles. Only the Lord Jesus Himself deserves our unequivocal trust and irrevocable commitment. If a church or a spiritual leader begins to go astray and is unrepentant, or if false doctrine is being taught or false christs arise in your midst (and many will in the last days!), you have a duty to God, your family, and yourself to extricate yourself from that fellowship.

Certainly we should not part company with our church over insignificant issues; we should never leave a church lightly or cavalierly, any more than we would break up our family over something trite or silly. Years ago, I preached a message titled, "Nitpickin' over Corn-Pickin'," based on the account of the Pharisees nitpicking at Jesus because His disciples picked a few ears of corn to eat on the Sabbath. We tend to forget that the Pharisees were often correct in their doctrines; they knew the rules and kept them meticulously, with an outward righteousness that was unrivaled in Jesus' day. But they still killed Jesus and tried to snuff out His gospel.

Of course, this is one of the reasons why I stress so strongly that in the last days Christians must study the Word of God. Otherwise, we will be vulnerable to aberrant interpretations of the Bible, to false teaching and all sorts of other destructive ideas, and we will not even be able to discern the error that has crept into our community. (I'll deal at length with this subject in a later chapter.)

But if the Christian community is not a Disneyland, neither is it a country club, where you simply pay your dues and drop by whenever you feel "led" to partake of its services. Nor is the church a "recovery" group (though many in the church are recovering from some of life's toughest trials), a dating service, an encounter group, or a social service. The church is the family of God.

Some people say, "Oh, I just can't seem to find a church home, someplace where I fit in, where I feel comfortable," so they drift around from congregation to congregation. They have no roots, and not coincidentally, they assume no responsibilities. They are spiritual leeches, sucking lifeblood from others, while giving nothing in return. That is not the picture of the Christian community we find in the New Testament.

Granted, your match with a community of believers might not be where you are currently attending church services. Fine. Find where God intends for you to be joined to the body and get busy there. Stop nit-pickin' over corn-pickin', quit looking for excuses, and stop trying to avoid the responsibility that comes along with commitment to your brothers and sisters in Christ.

Other people say, "I see some things in that church that I don't really like." I hate to be the one to burst your bubble, but the perfect church does not exist. And if you happen to find one that you think is perfect, don't join it, because you'll ruin it! Seriously, none of us are perfect.

The church is not a fellowship of perfected saints; the church is a fellowship of broken people who have found forgiveness through the blood of Jesus Christ and the grace of an everlasting God to help us face another day. Sure, you will find problems in the church—any local congregation has problems, just as any hospital attempting to help sick people has its share of difficult cases. But as someone has aptly said, "The church is like Noah's ark. The stench on the inside would be unbearable if it were not for the storm on the outside." You need to get in the boat and live this Christian life together, helping one another and caring for each other.

Wherever the Lord plants you, make it a practice to worship together with that portion of the "family." Openly declare your allegiance to that part of the Christian community, letting it be known that "I am a part of this group. I am going to become a part of this church, I am going to work with you, I am going to serve the Lord with you; I will be taught by you, and I am going to help teach your children. You are my spiritual family." If your family is hungry, you feed them; if they need financial help, you make your resources available to them; if they are in the hospital or in prison, you visit them. Jesus said that as we do to the very least of these, we do so unto Him (Matt 25:40).

This type of commitment to a local church, though, is rapidly becoming a thing of the past, especially in the modern era of megachurches.

Megamonsters?

Most major cities in America now have several churches in which multiplied thousands of people gather to worship God each week. That's the good news. The bad news is that it is all too easy to hide in a congregation of three, ten, or fifteen thousand people. Furthermore, it is easy to become a spectator, to attend "church" as you would a theatrical production or sporting event—to simply attend services, pay your tithes, watch the "show," and then leave, without ever becoming connected to the community of believers. You can attend services for months or possibly years and never get to know another person in that church. Sometimes, you don't even have to say hello to anyone.

While this sort of "worship experience" might be attractive to many people, it is not an environment conducive to New Testament-style Christianity. Perhaps that is why in most major American cities nowadays, there can be found a transient, "floating" congregation that drifts around the city from church to church. They go to a Baptist church for a while, then they try out a Methodist congregation before hopping over to a nondenominational, charismatic fellowship or two, then they loop around through a "Faith" church, then on to First Nazarene, then to some idyllic-sounding congregation such as "The Gathering Place" or the "Flowers and Butterflies" fellowship, before floating back to their original congregation.

The floaters are under the illusion that they are getting the best of all the churches. They might spend a few weeks here or there until they tire of that style of worship or that particular preacher, but they are only scratching the surface of what the church is truly about. The church is about living out our faith together; it is about loving each other, caring for one another, bearing one another's burdens.

The megachurch can be a wonderful rallying center, but the real-life, practical caring for and sharing with one another must take place in smaller groups within the Christian community. This shouldn't surprise us. On the day of Pentecost, three thousand people were added to the church, but they did not immediately go out and build a huge, arena-style building in which to meet. They continued to meet in homes throughout the community, small segments of the larger group, fellowshipping together and ministering to each other. This sort of community life not only works, but it also takes the strain off our pastors and other spiritual leaders.

In his book *The Purpose Driven Church*, Rick Warren tells a story drawn from his experience as a pastor in Saddleback, California. He went to the hospital to visit someone from the church, but the nurse on duty said, "I'm sorry, sir. You can't go in."

Rick replied, "Ma'am, I am his pastor."

The nurse answered, "I'm sorry, nine of his pastors have already come today."[5]

You don't find that kind of concern, compassion, and love simply by dropping in and looking at a congregation for a few weeks, and then moving on down to the next church on your tour card and milking them for all they are worth. Indeed, you may not discover what the church is all about until you have a need, until some calamity strikes your life—a spouse dies unexpectedly, your son gets picked up for possession of an illegal substance, your daughter gets pregnant out of wedlock, your business goes bankrupt, or your spouse walks out, saying, "I don't love you anymore." It is in those times that the church gathers around, wraps its arms around you, and says, "You were there when we went through it. We are going to walk with you and your family through this thing."

You won't get that sort of commitment from a traveling evangelistic ministry or a healing crusade; nor will you get that sort of loving care from a television ministry. Those ministries may be helpful, but they cannot replace the local church in your spiritual life. Nor were they ever meant to. I used to encourage my television audience to become established in a local church. I cautioned, "When you are sick or in the hospital or just need a hug, that television can't hug you. That's why you need to be involved in your local church."

I am convinced that if you truly want to live effectively for God, you must find a group of people with whom you can meet regularly and to whom you can commit yourself and say, "These are my people; this is my immediate spiritual family, and this is where I am going to work."

Certainly, we thank God for our "second cousins" in the family of God; we thank God for our "great-aunts and -uncles" in the family of God. But the people with whom I am going to live out my days doing the work of God are not my extended family. I must have an "immediate family," a group of spiritual brothers and sisters, mothers and fathers, with whom I can meet regularly and to whom I can commit my life to work alongside them for God's glory. That is how the church has survived in the past, and I am convinced that the community of believers will be the means of our survival in the next few years as the world moves into dark days and nightmarish nights.

The Scripture says that we are to "love one another" (1 John 3:11 NKJV). Love covers a multitude of sins. It sees the best in each other; it cheers for and encourages the other person to be what God wants that person to be.

God wants the various parts of His body to build each other up, and we simply cannot do that floating around from church to church, not knowing anybody beyond the realm of fickle superficiality. Nor can you find that sort of caring community by traipsing after the "latest and greatest" evangelist, singer, or television ministry; or worse yet, not being connected to any church at all. You have to get into people's lives to do the things that the New Testament instructs us to do—and you have to allow other believers to be able to get into your life.

We are to minister to each other not from the recesses of our lives, but from the overflow of what God is doing in and through each one of us. God has poured His gifts into our lives; He is developing the fruit of His Spirit in each of us. Consequently, when we get around each other closely enough, some of God's blessings are sure to splash onto someone else. But that can't happen unless you are living in close proximity to the Christian community.

The Christian community is a household, a family, a home; it is not simply a group of people who are living individual, disjointed lives, never coming out of their rooms. It is a home where a group of people gathers around the supper table, where people love and care for each other, not just once in a while when they feel especially spiritual, but on a regular, if not daily, basis.

How would you like to be a part of a Christian community that actually does those things? We can be, but we must "submit to one another in the fear of God" (see Eph. 5:21 in various translations), which means we must willingly lay aside our own desires for the good of others out of reverence and respect for and awe of our Lord. Is there risk involved in this sort of relationship? Count on it. Untold numbers of people have been used, abused, or otherwise wounded psychologically, emotionally, or spiritually because somebody else took advantage of their willingness to submit. The only person to whom we should submit our human will is the person of the Holy Spirit, the Spirit of Jesus. But as we submit to Him, we can then trust His guidance in submitting ourselves to mere human beings.

On the other hand, some Christians are on the other end of the spectrum, unwilling to submit themselves to anyone or any group. They are full of pride, and their egos recoil at the very idea of settling into any one church and submitting themselves to anyone else's spiritual authority. They wouldn't think of saying, "See that fellow up there? That's my pastor, and these are my spiritual brothers and sisters to whom I am submitted."

If you want to be irreverent in your relationship to Christ, don't ever submit yourself to a local congregation; don't ever place yourself in accountability to brothers and sisters in Christ. Live your life as a Christian island, and you can say all day long that you and Jesus have your own thing going. But I would have some doubts about your relationship with Jesus, because after all, how can you claim to have such a close relationship to Him when you so flippantly ignore His church?

The church is God's sovereign work on earth. It is the one institution to which He has attached His name. It is the modern-day equivalent of the ark in Noah's day: a place of safety in the time of storm, a place where men and women can be saved. It is the one refuge we have in this world. Some might say, "God is my refuge," and that is correct, but clearly, the church is of paramount importance to God; it ought to be so to us.

7

First-Century Community in the New Millennium

In his book with a most intriguing title, *Early Christians of the Twenty-first Century*, Chad Walsh wrote:

> I suspect that Satan has pretty much called off his attempt to convert people to agnosticism [or atheism]. After all, if a person travels far enough away from Christianity, he or she is always in danger of seeing it in perspective, and deciding that it is true. It's much safer from Satan's standpoint to merely vaccinate a person with a mild case of Christianity, so as to protect him from the real thing.[1]

Chad Walsh's observation raises some interesting questions: Are we embalmed by the truth, or excited by it? Have we been vaccinated with a mild case of Christianity, or do we have the real thing?

The church of Jesus Christ at the beginning of a new millennium is suffering from an identity crisis. We don't know *who* we are, *what* we are, or *what* we should be doing in these days when our newscasts are punctuated with one earthshaking event after another. Many Christians today are similar to an amnesia victim waking up and saying, "Who am I? Where am I? What's going on? And why in the world am I here?"

Many wonder aloud in these last days, "Just what should the community of believers be doing? How do we decide our priorities? Should we be stockpiling food, spending all our energy on evangelism, feeding the hungry, clothing the naked, providing shelter to the homeless?

Should we be sending out more missionaries or building larger sanctuaries? Should we be involved in hot-button political issues with moral underpinnings—issues such as abortion, pornography, political corruption, or euthanasia? Should we be involved with politics at all, since we know that the kingdom of God is eternal and the kingdoms of this world are passing away?" All of these issues may deserve attention, but are they really the priorities on which we need to be focusing as we count down toward eternity?

When we read the accounts of the early church in the book of Acts, however, we are struck immediately by two things: (1) how focused the early church was in its purpose and activities, which we will discuss in this chapter; and (2) how far the contemporary Christian community has gotten away from the real thing—how caught up we've gotten in peripheral issues, spending enormous amounts of time, money, and energy on things that are not of primary importance. They may be good things, interesting things, spiritually invigorating services or activities, but we give inordinate attention to matters that are really not important for the generation of Christians that may well be alive at the second coming of Christ.

The early church didn't allow that to happen. They were committed to the Lord, and they were committed to each other. Their unconditional love proved to be more powerful than the mighty Roman Empire.

Why does this strange disparity exist between the early church and today's church? We're related to the same Person, aren't we? We love the same Lord Jesus, don't we? We have available to us the same supernatural power of the Holy Spirit that Peter, James, John, Andrew, and the other disciples did. We're called to the same purpose. In an academic sense, at least, we have much more biblical knowledge than any of the early Christians. Why, then, are we not impacting our world to a greater degree?

I'm convinced that the Christian community is confused about, and easily distracted from, our true purpose. Since we don't really know what God wants us to be doing, or what our priorities ought to be, we focus our attention on the "squeaky wheel"—whoever or whatever cries out the loudest, most often, or most obnoxiously. This is something that the first-century believers refused to allow for long. The early church didn't become foggy concerning their purpose.

They understood, although somewhat vaguely, that Jesus easily could have taken them to heaven along with Him, but He had chosen instead to have them remain on earth as His witnesses. Have you ever considered that? How easy it would have been for the early Christians to say, "Jesus went to heaven; we want to go, too!" But they didn't. Certainly they believed in heaven and looked forward to being reunited with Christ for eternity, but they knew that they had a purpose to fulfill here on earth first, before they graduated to heaven. They did not simply sit around and debate the details of Christ's promised return. They likely were not debating when, where, or why the latest persecutions might pummel the body. They had a mission to accomplish, a Great Commission to fulfill! In the midst of end-time events, we must rediscover that same sense of passion and purpose.

In light of our strategic position in human history, we need to ask afresh, What practices, procedures, and principles ought to rank atop our priority lists? What kind of leadership will it take for the Christian community to make an impact upon our society? How are we to live in these tumultuous times, and how can we best reach our family and neighbors with the gospel?

The model can be found in Acts 2:42–47, where we discover the essential elements in a New Testament church, including availability, instruction, worship, and fellowship.

> And they continued steadfastly in the apostles' doctrine and fellow-ship, in the breaking of bread, and in prayers. Then fear came upon every soul, and many wonders and signs were done through the apos-tles. Now all who believed were together, and had all things in com-mon, and sold their possessions and goods, and divided them among all, as anyone had need. So continuing daily with one accord in the temple, and breaking bread from house to house, they ate their food with gladness and simplicity of heart, praising God and having favor with all the people. And the Lord added to the church daily those who were being saved. (NKJV)

Any Christian community that claims to be based on the New Testament example must include these activities.

1. AVAILABILITY

Clearly, there was an attitude of openness among the first-century com-munity of believers. Notice that they went from house to house, breaking bread together (2:46), which some scholars interpret to mean that they celebrated communion together in their homes, while others say that the people simply had their meals together. Quite possibly, they did both. One thing is certain: they were together often in each other's homes.

In the days ahead, if God gives you a house, it will not simply be a place of refuge for you and your family. It will be a means of providing opportunities of spiritual blessing to the body of Christ. We dare not get upset when somebody tracks mud onto the carpet, or someone accidentally spills something on one of our prized pieces of furniture. If you have a house, and you open it to the body, people will come— and inevitably some things will get marked, marred, or broken. But it is a small price to pay for making your home available for use in the kingdom of God.

At the Dream Center, we were available to each other around the clock. We didn't consider it an inconvenience when somebody knocked on the door early in the morning or late at night in need of spiritual help. Similarly, at Morning House, if there is a spiritual need, or sometimes simply a practical necessity such as getting out our monthly newsletter, we go "off the clock" and work until the job is done. It is impossible to put "ministry" opportunities on an eight-to-five schedule. We must be available to each other, and sometimes that may involve sacrifice, inconvenience, or going the extra mile.

2. INSTRUCTION

Notice that the early believers were devoted to the apostles' doctrine (2:42). Some translations say that they "continued steadfastly in the apostles' doctrine." No matter how it is translated, it is clear that teaching, or you could say, education, was a perpetual priority among the early believers. The Christian community that does not educate its people will not last for long. And I'm not simply referring to the "3 R's: Readin', 'Ritin', and 'Rithmetic." First and foremost, we must educate our people in the Word of God.

Sadly, many modern-day believers suffer from a terrible dearth of biblical knowledge. They simply do not know the Word. They sit in service after service, and they look as though they are listening. They nod their heads every once in a while—sometimes the right way, sometimes the wrong way—but they are not growing in their knowledge of the Word. They are not learning!

Many others seem to be unaffected by the messages they do hear and understand. They come to church, mentally ingest a lot of interesting information, but they never seem to absorb anything into their lifestyles or attitudes. No wonder, then, that they do not have a biblical worldview.

But in the days ahead, it will not be enough simply to be able to quote the Bible. No doubt, the Antichrist and the false prophet of Revelation will readily quote Scriptures as well. We will need a twofold emphasis: (1) we will need to know the Word better than ever before, drawing regularly upon our reservoir of biblical knowledge; and (2) we will need a biblical worldview, in which we examine everything through "biblical glasses"—correlating all of life with a biblical outlook. We will need to know the biblical perspective on science, history, philosophy, psychology, literature, and other fields. But it will be impossible to know what is biblically accurate if we do not have a good understanding of the Bible itself.

The church that does not educate its members in the Bible becomes a social club! It might as well be the Kiwanis, or the Ladies' Aid Society, or the Rotary Club—all of which are wonderful organizations, but they are not the church of Jesus Christ. Biblical education is not an option for a Christian; it is an essential. Yet the tragic truth is that we have people in our churches who have been "good church members" for years, but, as that study revealed, they still can't answer some of the basic, elementary questions about their faith.

This spiritual complacency must be changed before it is too late. In the days ahead, when everything that can be shaken will be shaken, these casual church attenders are going to be terribly vulnerable to false doctrines, temptations to backslide, and being duped by the devil's deceptions. There is no such thing as maintaining a spiritual status quo. If you are not going forward with God, you will soon slip backward. If you are not learning and growing as a Christian, you will soon be sliding into error. If you continue to slide in the wrong direction, the results could be disastrous.

Ironically, some people in the church think they know so much about the Bible that they have no further need to be taught. I heard of one woman who had the audacity to say, "I will *teach*, but I will not be taught!" Such arrogance! Such sin! We all need a better working understanding of God's Word. Moreover, we need the "spiritual washing" that comes from the Word.

Besides, true instruction and understanding of God's Word involve much more than the mere accumulation of facts, or the ability to recite by rote certain verses or creeds. We need the Word working in our hearts, renewing our minds, refining us, transforming us on a daily basis, and causing us to become more like Jesus and more attuned to His Spirit's voice. Frankly, the more I learn about God and about His Word, the more I realize how little I know and how much I have yet to learn.

If you are serious about growing as a Christian, here is a simple suggestion that has helped me: start taking a pen and paper to church. Take notes on your Sunday school class, the Sunday sermons, the Bible studies you attend, or other opportunities you have to increase your knowledge and understanding of the Word. Jot down insights that the Holy Spirit gives to you as the Word takes root in your heart and mind. Periodically review your notes, and you will be pleasantly surprised at what you have learned.

I have dozens of notebooks crammed with insights from conferences I have attended or Bible studies in which I have participated. Sure, some of the pages contain mundane information, but many others are priceless. One insight into God's Word is worth all the effort.

Why do good, effective teachers encourage their students to take notes in school? It helps the students to remember the material they have studied. If it is important to know who the other general was in the Battle of Waterloo, how much more should we be concerned about learning and remembering the Word of God!

My wife, Lori, came to know Christ after living a wild life that I frequently refer to as a life of "sex, drugs, and rock 'n' roll." But when Lori trusted Christ, she made a radical commitment to the Lord. She became a student of the Scriptures, not merely a reader. She wanted to learn all that would help her live closer to Jesus. Early in her transformed life, she began taking copious notes on her pastor's sermons, her Bible study materials, and other sources of biblical information. Lori also has scores of notebooks filled with scriptural truths. To this day, she takes notes on every sermon she hears (even mine!).

Once when I mentioned Lori's passionate desire to take notes on the Word, a woman later protested, "A notebook wouldn't match my dress!"

Who cares? Do you attend church to put on a show, or do you go to church hoping to learn and grow spiritually? If you are not progressing in your lifelong biblical education, I suggest that you begin to take advantage of the opportunities to grow before it is too late and such opportunities are no longer available. For instance, you could get involved in a community Bible study. Sure, it may take some effort on your part to turn off the television, step out of your comfort zone, and go to where the community of believers are studying God's Word. But it is incredibly helpful, not to mention stimulating and challenging, to study the Scriptures corporately, with other believers, and not simply by yourself. You should never neglect personal Bible study, but you will also benefit greatly from receiving biblical instruction from gifted teachers and pastors whom God has placed in positions of spiritual leadership for that precise purpose. Besides, we need each other for balance. Especially in these days, we need to test our interpretations of Scripture, to make sure that we are on target, that no alloy or error has been unwittingly included in our understanding of God's Word. We must take time to be instructed in the Word, even if it means getting rid of some other "good" things in our lives, or if it means revising our priorities.

Prayer a Priority

So often, the attitude of many Christians today is: "When all else fails, pray." Or how many times have you heard this: "Well, brother, just pray about it." *Just* pray? How about *starting* with prayer? How about believing that if anything good is going to happen in the church, it must begin with prayer! To the first-century Christian community, prayer was their first choice, not their last resort (Acts 2:42). They prayed about almost everything: spiritual direction, food, finances, the freedom of imprisoned preachers, and supernatural healing. Throughout the Scriptures, we are encouraged to pray, even commanded to pray, yet prayer continues to be one of the last resources we turn to when problems, decisions, or opportunities arise.

I was greatly encouraged when one of the prophetic words that I was privileged to hear at a recent conference concerned the prayers of the body of Christ. The prophet shared a message that clearly proclaimed that God planned to restore divine healing in the last days. Not contrived or manipulated "healings"; not psychosomatic healings (although mental and emotional healings will no doubt be included); not sweeping, broad generalizations regarding healing ("I believe somebody in the audience is being healed of a throat problem"); not the sort of "pay-per-prayer" manipulation of people's sincere faith that has been so prevalent among healing ministries. But God is going to restore genuine, supernatural healing on a widespread basis.

The prophet shared a vision he had received from the Lord, in which hundreds and hundreds of people were praying for each other and multitudes were being healed of their ailments and afflictions.

Interestingly, the prophet reported that, in the vision, the people who were praying appeared to be "faceless." He interpreted this to mean that the healings would not take place through "high-profile," well-known ministers, but through common, everyday folks. Furthermore, the message implied that God will continue to do miraculous healings so long as we do not care who gets the glory. And when we really stop to think about it, all the glory for any genuine healing belongs to our Lord God, not to the vessel through which He chooses to bring about the miracle.

3. WORSHIP

Another essential element in a New Testament community is worship. Worship is a missing key ingredient in most churches today. Oh, yes, most local congregations have a designated time—usually on Sunday mornings—that we call "the worship service." But it doesn't make any difference what label you put on the bottle if the bottle is empty!

Nowadays, many Christian groups speak much about praise and worship—and it is refreshing to see that many congregations are developing fresh methods and habits of praising the Lord. But when it comes to *worshiping* Him, we get lost; we have very fuzzy ideas of what worship is, or what kind of worship is pleasing in God's sight.

Here's an extremely simple definition of worship: "Worship is your personal response to a divine revelation."

Ask yourself: Am I responding to what God has said through His Word? Am I responding to what the Spirit is saying through various messengers today?

"To worship means that we offer ourselves completely to God."[2] Nowadays, I fear that much of what we call worship is merely hype and hoopla. Our worship leaders work hard to stir us into a spiritual frenzy by having us sing choruses, clap our hands, and engage in various spiritual gyrations for a half hour to forty-five minutes. Ostensibly, the purpose is "to prepare our hearts," which in many cases should be translated as "to get us pumped up" to hear the Word of God. In most cases, their intentions are good, although in a few cases, I've felt that pastors were almost held hostage by the worship leaders, who refused to surrender their place in the limelight until they had performed all that they had planned to do, despite the fact that the poor congregation was dying on its feet! But if, as Max Anders says, and I concur, worship means that we offer ourselves to God, our attitude should be more like that of Abraham, who was willing to sacrifice his own son, Isaac, on Mount Moriah, in obedience to God.

You may recall that somebody died on Mount Moriah that day, but it was not Isaac. It was Abraham who died to his own hopes, dreams, plans, and even his family legacy as he laid his son—his *only* son, the son he loved, the miracle son that God had given him—on the altar (Gen. 22:2, 9).

An often overlooked, but extremely interesting insight into Abraham's attitude can be found in the account of the journey itself. After a three-day trek into the hill country, the group stopped. Abraham saw the mountain and knew what it implied. But prior to Abraham and Isaac's ascending the mountain, Abraham told the two young men who accompanied him and his son, "Stay here with the donkey, and I and the lad will go yonder; and we will worship and return to you" (Gen. 22:5 NASB).

Is that faith, or what? But notice that Abraham, knowing what God had called him to do, regarded his willingness to give up his most priceless treasure, his son, as an act of worship!

In the Scriptures, the word most often translated as *worship* means "to prostrate oneself, to fall down on one's face." When we prostrate ourselves before someone, we are recognizing that person's authority and affirming his superiority, a gesture of our absolute submission to that person's will. As much as we may agree with this definition of worship, to actually do it is another matter.

Max Anders commented:

In the land of the free and the home of the brave, in the land where all men are equal, in the land of rugged individualism, we can hardly imagine prostrating ourselves like that. But if we did, we would be saying, by our body language, "You are greater than we are, and we recognize that. We humble ourselves before You, place ourselves at Your mercy and disposal, and agree to do anything You tell us to do."[3]

Many of us have the idea that it is the church's responsibility to put on a good show that we enjoy, that moves us emotionally, and that we feel comfortable with. We see the ministers, the special music, the choir and instrumentalists as the actors on a stage, with ourselves as the audience. If the show is good, we reward the actors with our approval, presence, and our financial support. If the show isn't so good, we may reduce our response.[4]

Chuck Colson hit the nail on the head: "True worship . . . is radically countercultural, being directed not toward self but toward God. Richard Neuhaus puts it in sobering terms: 'The celebration we call worship has less to do with the satisfaction or the pursuit of happiness than with the abandonment of the pursuit of happiness.'"[5] Colson continued, "True prayer and worship also run counter to the prevailing ethos in the church, which equates God's blessings with growth and material success."[6]

The concerted point that these writers make is one that has been lost in recent years in many Christian communities, namely, that true worship is not for our benefit; its purpose is to please God. He is the audience; we are not. We worship Him because He is worthy, not so we can elicit some response from Him, or from the congregation.

We sing the words *I worship You.* But do we do it?

Some people think praise and worship are the same. Granted, praise and worship may overlap and involve some of the same elements, but they are not really the same. Think of it this way: worship is like inhaling, breathing in, and praise is like exhaling, breathing out praise.

Worship may take many forms, sometimes loud and boisterous, sometimes quiet and simple, but in a nutshell, worship is that attitude of reverential awe that we have in the presence of God. Interestingly, in the description given in Acts 2:43, worship follows biblical instruction. It does not precede it. Consequently, I've often wondered whether we have our services backward. In most services I have attended, we worship the Lord through music, prayers, offerings, communion, or other expressions, and then we listen to someone expound the Scriptures.

Maybe we should reverse that order. Perhaps we ought to have prayer, then Sunday school, perhaps a time of praise, then the sermon or teaching, and then worship, because worship automatically flows out of biblical instruction and knowledge. You could say that worship of the Lord is a direct result of genuine biblical learning. The more you realize how awesome God is, the more you want to fall on your face and worship Him. Granted, some people have worshiped the Lord in ignorance, but it is difficult to worship in "Spirit and in truth" a God you do not know or One about whom you know very little.

In any given "worship service," a significant percentage of the people in attendance don't know God. Others don't know Him very well. They don't know what He has said, how He feels about certain things, or what He has done in human history. But if they remain in the presence of the worshiping community for long, they are bound to be affected.

That's another reason why these days are so exciting: God is speaking and He is not stuttering! Believers are hearing His voice clearly, and when God speaks to us, our response ought to be one of worship.

The moment that God speaks, you ought to worship—adore Him, exalt Him, express to Him your absolute awe that the Holy God of all creation would speak to you. Whether He speaks through the written Word, the spoken word, or the manifestation of His gifts in our presence, our response should be one of worship, drinking in His Majesty, and expressing our love and our adoration of Him. When we do not worship the Lord, we cease to be New Testament Christians at that point. No wonder our spiritual lives are so dry; no wonder we endure such anemic spiritual health; no wonder we have to use all sorts of motivational methods to "hype" ourselves into God's presence, and then have to pretend that God is pleased with our miserable, fleshly efforts. We have not learned how to adequately express our worship of a supernatural God!

We Need a Power Surge!

I travel a lot, and I meet many Christians who are frustrated in their spiritual lives. Sincere believers often ask me, "How can I get motivated in my spiritual life? I just don't feel like doing anything anymore."

They complain, "How can I get it together? I'm so bored and dry in my spiritual life. What can I do?"

Sometimes I feel like answering, "Why don't you try stepping into about forty million volts of electricity?" Because if you back into such an awesome power source, you are not going to turn around and say, "Excuse me, did you say something?"

No! You will respond! You will move! You will be motivated!

Similarly, when you come in contact with the supernatural, holy, living Lord Jesus, it is virtually impossible for you to remain unmotivated. If you are not motivated in your walk with God, it is either because you have stepped away from His presence, allowed something or someone to interfere with His presence in your life, or you have never really been in His presence in the first place. If you are living in the presence of a holy God, you cannot possibly remain complacent!

When you hear the Word of God or experience God's presence some other way, yet remain untouched, something is drastically wrong with you! I'm not saying that when you hear a *particular type* of sermon or song, or when you experience some sort of ecstatic spiritual phenomenon, you will be overwhelmed by the presence of God. But on the other hand, if God speaks and you remain unaffected, recognize the fact that you have backslidden and need to be revived, refreshed, revitalized, or restored.

Worship and Work Go Together

In church after church, I hear the same story: "We need more workers." In most churches, a few people are willing to work, and the majority are willing to let them work. It's gotten to be almost a given that 20 percent of the people do 80 percent of the work in most churches. Even in modern megachurches, most of our workers are overloaded.

Certainly, most ministries could use more warm bodies, but I am convinced that the solution to the problem is not just recruiting more workers. We don't merely need more workers; we need more worshipers! We don't simply need more willing hands; we need more willing hearts.

I have never seen a true worshiper of Jesus Christ who did not want to go to work for Jesus. When you have been in His presence, and you acknowledge Him for who He is and what He has done for you, something inside most of us wants to give something back, to express our deep gratitude to the One who has saved us, who has done so much for us.

One principle I learned the hard way at Heritage USA was that it was easier to recruit workers than it was to develop worshipers. With some motivational preaching and some inspirational programming, my staff and I were able to recruit nearly three thousand dedicated, wonderful workers. Yet in the process of building a great facility, ostensibly for God's glory and for the benefit of His people, we somehow allowed our worship of Him to slip down the priority list.

Please learn a lesson from my experience: If you are working without worshiping, you are probably working in the energy of the flesh, and I have to tell you, it is extremely dangerous to do so. When we go to work for the Lord in the power of our own flesh—our own human energy—we are not solving a problem; we are creating a problem! Perhaps that's why there are so many problems in the body of Christ today—because we are attempting to build so much in our own efforts. On the other hand, as we learn to worship the Lord in everything we do, we will do even mundane tasks well, because we are working for His glory rather than our own.

A Natural Expression

Taking action to meet the needs within the body of Christ is a natural outgrowth of worship. Notice how this expression takes place in the lives of the people who are instructed in the Word, and who are sincerely worshiping the Lord. In Acts 2:44, we discover that "all who believed were together, and had all things in common" (NKJV). The Word and worship working within the hearts and lives of the believers caused them to move and meet the needs of the body. That is the inevitable response when people have been instructed in the ways of the Lord and have been worshiping Him. They want to help meet the needs of the body in practical as well as spiritual ways.

Notice that the early believers were not satisfied to respond with some sort of unrelated spiritualizing of problems: "Oh, yes, brother. You have a definite need. You are out of food. You have no place to live. You have no way to get to work; come to think of it, you have no job. Your life is in danger . . . Well, we will pray for you!"

No, the early believers moved to meet not only the spiritual but also the physical and financial needs of the body! Those members of the original Christian community took seriously their Lord's words: "As you did it to one of the least of these My brethren, you did it to Me" (Matt. 25:40 NKJV).

According to James 2:15–17, a passage written by Jesus' brother in the face of difficult days in the first-century church, it is a mockery of Christ to say to the hungry man, "Be blessed—be filled—I'll pray for you," when you have it in your power to help him! James said, "That kind of faith without works is dead!" (see James 2:26).

In the book of Acts, these people who were instructed in the Word and were worshiping the Lord wanted to know, "What are the needs of the body? How can I help?"

Similarly, if we are really serious about Christianity, we must ask, "What can I do to help meet the needs of the body?" The Lord may or may not lead you to sell your possessions and give the proceeds to some ministry to distribute to those who have a need. It seems that in the early church, this drastic step was voluntary, not compulsory. Nevertheless, it is rare when God shows us a need and doesn't ask us to do something to help meet it!

Yet at the same time, we need to understand that our mission includes more than merely meeting the needs within the body. Indeed, that is where we must start, but we are called to meet the needs outside the body, as well. Our mission is to penetrate the society for Christ, to transform society by the power of Jesus Christ.

4. FELLOWSHIP

Another key element in the Christian community is fellowship.

No doubt, the early Christians celebrated communion together, reminding each other of the death, resurrection, and return of the Lord Jesus. In a later chapter, we will look more closely at that intimate, family affair. But notice, too, that the early Christian community also ate together frequently: "Breaking bread from house to house, they ate their food with gladness and simplicity of heart" (Acts 2:46 NKJV).

Something wonderful happens when people are able to sit down to a meal together. Although we tease quite a lot in Christian circles about our potluck dinners—group meals to which everyone brings something to add to the selections—fellowship around food is a time-honored tradition in the Christian community. When we eat together, the barriers and walls often come down. People are nicer to each other—usually. They talk while they eat and enjoy each other's company.

Some of my fondest memories of church life during my youth involve eating together with the body of believers. I can still recall Mrs. Johnson's chicken and noodles, and my mom's chocolate cake, as well as the macaroni and cheese. Mom's "Bakker Beans" were legendary among believers in our community. Our entire life revolved around the church. We had frequent church fellowship dinners and Sunday school picnics, where people not only ate together, but they also sat around afterward and talked with one another, laughed together, and usually ended up praying together before heading to their homes as the sun dipped below the horizon.

I have often said that if I ever build another church, I am going to include a cafeteria or a dining hall. Not so the church can make money off the sale of food, but so God's people don't have to run off so quickly after a service. They can have Sunday lunch or dinner right at the church and continue fellowshipping with one another.

But fellowship involves more than food. Have you ever wondered how the early church could possibly have fellowshipped without coffee and doughnuts, cakes and pies?

The answer is simple: They had something better, something even stronger than sugar to pull them together (no, not sugar-free, fat-free cake and ice cream). They had *persecution!* Yes, they endured real, body-battering, life-threatening persecution for their faith in Jesus and their testimony of His resurrection power. And the persecution—rather than destroying their faith—made them stronger. An old saying claims, "That which does not kill me makes me stronger." No doubt, that is true. I believe that in the days ahead (and I am not referring to some time in the far-off, distant future), Christians are going to experience intense persecutions from the nonbelieving world. In many parts of the world, believers already endure harsh persecutions. According to statistics gathered by Prison Fellowship, more than two hundred Christians are martyred for their faith each year! Atrocities against Christians can be expected to increase and intensify as we draw nearer to our Lord's return, but do not despair.

The irony is that the more the world persecuted the early church, the more the church flourished! It is much the same today. Not long ago, I heard of a church that had grown behind the Iron Curtain in one of the communist countries dominated by the former Soviet Union. The Christians were being persecuted, and they were having all kinds of severe problems. But their biggest problems were not the threats against their lives, although they experienced such challenges almost daily. The toughest problem that church faced was that they could not have enough services. Too many people wanted to come! They had to start two services, then three, four, and five services every Sunday. Finally, the elders got together with the senior pastor and said, "Pastor, we have a serious problem."

"What's that?" asked the pastor.

The elders said, "We have some people who are going to more than one service!"

The next Sunday, the church leaders confronted the congregation and said, "Look—one service—and one service only. You can only attend one service each Sunday. If we see you in more than one service, we are going to ask you to leave, because you are taking somebody else's seat who also wants a chance to join in the worship!"

That solution worked for a while, but the church kept growing, so the pastor and elders came up with another idea. They said, "Okay, in this church, if you come this Sunday, you must stay home next Sunday, so somebody else can come. Got it? One Sunday on, one Sunday off!" Ironically, that's the way many believers attend our churches in America— only for different reasons!

What caused that church behind the Iron Curtain to keep growing? It was their intimate fellowship with the Lord and with each other. And what caused their fellowship to be so close? Persecution from the world.

Let's suppose that we were currently experiencing that sort of persecution here in our country. Suppose that a real danger existed: the moment you stepped out the door of the sanctuary or the home where you were meeting for a Bible study, you could be shot on the spot for your identification with Jesus Christ. Imagine what kind of fellowship we would have in the Christian community.

If you looked to your left or to your right during a time of praise and worship, and you knew that next week, one of you would be dead because of your uncompromising testimony of Jesus Christ, what do you think that would do to your fellowship? Would that help put your priorities in proper perspective, or what?

In most churches, fellowship has degenerated to shaking hands after church services or occasionally sitting around the table and talking for a while. Oh, yes, every once in a while we break out of our holy huddles long enough to go out on an evangelical mission, where we might venture into enemy territory. But if we get shot at a bit, we run right back into our holy huddles and hide. Then we get up at the next church gathering and say, "Beloved, I was persecuted for righteousness' sake!" Most of us have no idea what real persecution is like, and maybe that is why our fellowship is often so fickle and superficial.

Fellowship in the New Testament community was no nice, warm, mushy feeling. They were *galvanized* together! Every time they gathered as the body of Christ, they left each other with the stark realization that they might never see each other again! And I believe we ought to live with that same sense of fellowship today—one from which we can say, "Brother and Sister, if I never see you again on earth, I'll see you in heaven!"

That's not negative thinking. That's a positive reality!

The purpose of Christian fellowship is to encourage and inspire the saints of Jesus Christ to function as His representatives in society. We gather together regularly to be taught the Word, worship the Lord, have fellowship with each other, and then we go into the world representing Jesus Christ.

Kefa Sempangi's book, *A Distant Grief,* is probably one of the most powerful books written in my generation. In it, Sempangi tells the story of how the church of Jesus Christ was persecuted and terrorized under the reign of Idi Amin in Uganda. During Amin's despotic rule, thousands of Christians were raped, robbed, tortured, and killed in an attempt to replace Christianity with Islam. One of the most poignant insights Sempangi shared came not from surviving Amin's tortures, but from what happened to him when he finally got out of Uganda and came to the United States to study for the ministry at Westminster Seminary in Philadelphia. Even after all he had been through, Kefa said that he began to take God's grace for granted.

In Uganda, they had never talked about tomorrow. It was, "Give us this day our daily bread." But when he came to the luxury, comfort, and security of the United States, Kefa not only began to take the next day for granted—but the next week, and the next year, unlike in Uganda where he knew his next breath might be his last.

Kefa Sempangi admitted that while in Uganda, "I read the Bible for hope and life. We read to hear God's promises, to hear His commands, and to obey them. There was no time for argument and no time for religious disputes, discrepancies, and doubts."

But in Philadelphia, he began to read the Scriptures to "analyze the texts and to speculate on the meaning." He said he came to enjoy our abstract theological discussions, and before long, his fellowship revolved around ideas about God, rather than the daily work of God in his life.

Kefa's prayer life changed, too. In Uganda, he had prayed with a tremendous sense of urgency. He said that he refused to leave his knees until he had been in the presence of the resurrected Christ. In Philadelphia, the sense of urgency evaporated. More and more he found himself coming to God with vague requests for gifts that he did not expect to receive. One night, Kefa Sempangi said his prayers in a ritual fashion. And he was about to get up off his knees when the Holy Spirit said to him, "Kefa, whom are you praying for? What is it that you wanted? I used to hear the names of children in your prayers. I used to hear you crying out for friends and relatives by name. Now you pray for 'the orphans.' Now you pray for 'the church.' Now you pray for those 'poor refugees.' Which refugees, Kefa? Which orphans, Kefa? Which believers are you talking about? Who are the people and what is it that you want for them?"

Sempangi—a godly man who had trusted God through intense tortures and persecutions, but who had grown comfortable in his Christianity—fell onto his knees before God and began begging God for forgiveness. Forgiveness for his unbelief. Forgiveness for his lukewarmness. He said, "I knew it was not just a bad memory that had caused names to vanish from my mind. God Himself had become a distant figure. He had become a subject of debate—an abstraction. I no longer was praying to Him as a living, loving Father, but as an impersonal being, who didn't mind my inattention and my unbelief."

Sempangi repented and later said, "From that night on, my prayers became specific." He believed again in a real God, and the Word of God burned in his heart and mind. He was able to truly worship the Lord once again—in Spirit and in truth. He was able to express his Christian commitment in tangible ways, not simply in pious platitudes.

And once again, he entered into real fellowship with God and with his fellow believers.[7]

This is what it means to be a Christian, to be part of the body of Christ, to be a New Testament church in the twenty-first century.

CHURCH IS A VERB

"LET'S DO LUNCH SOMETIME" is a commonly heard statement nowadays. A few years ago, we didn't *do* lunch; we ate lunch, went to lunch, had lunch, or even lunched at the park. But we didn't do lunch. Equally confusing sometimes is the term *church*. Is *church* a noun or a verb? I heard a story of a dad and his son who were working together on the elementary-school-age boy's English homework, highlighting the nouns and verbs in a series of sentences. They were doing fine until they came to the word *church*.

"That's a verb, Dad," the little boy said.

"No, son. A church is a place or a group of people, so that would make it a noun."

"I know, Dad," the son answered, "but think of it this way: church is something we do. It is something we're to be, and *to be* is a verb. So *church* is a verb!"

I'm not sure that an English teacher would buy the boy's logic, but I like the way the kid thinks! Church is something we do; it's who we are. We frequently hear similar statements, such as, "We went to church" or "We had church" and sometimes such statements tend to blur the truth that simply being a noun—the community of believers, the body of Christ—is not enough. We must actively *be* the church, doing the work of Christ. *Church* is a verb.

WHAT'S IN IT FOR ME?

Some questions concerning our involvement with the Christian community arise quite naturally: Why do I need the body of Christ? If I am saved by faith in Jesus Christ, and my sins are forgiven because of the blood He shed on Calvary's cross, why should I be bothered with other people in the church? Why can't I just live out my faith in the Lord along with my immediate family? With all the hassles and problems in the church, what good is it to me?

That age-old question—"What am I going to get out of this?"—apparently popped into Peter's mind as he watched and listened to Jesus define the cost of discipleship to a fellow we refer to as the "rich young ruler." When the young man came to Jesus asking what it might cost to enter the kingdom of God, Jesus hit him right in his wallet and, clearly, his heart. Jesus told the wealthy fellow to sell all that he had and give it to the poor, and then come follow Him. When the young ruler expressed his unwillingness to do what Jesus demanded, he went away sorrowfully, but nonetheless lost.

As Simon Peter and the other disciples observed this drama unfold, they may have wanted to cry out, "Jesus! You're blowing it. This guy has big bucks. He has power and influence. This young fellow could do a lot for us, and You are making it too hard for him to follow You—cut him a break. We could use a guy like this on our team."

But Jesus did not make it any easier for the rich young ruler to follow Him than He had for the other disciples (or us, for that matter). He watched silently as the wealthy young fellow walked away, rich materially, yet impoverished spiritually.

Always the rambunctious one, Simon Peter saw a perfect opportunity to score some brownie points with Jesus. Peter popped up and said, "Lord, that rich young ruler didn't make the commitment to You that you were asking for, but *we* have!"

I can see Jesus turning to look Peter in the eyes, and suddenly Peter's bombastic confidence dwindled, but he'd already gone that far so he continued on. "And, well, er . . . ah, Lord, the guys and I were just wondering, I mean, we were just wanting to check with You on this matter. We don't mean to offend You or anything, but, ah, You know, we have left everything to follow You, and we were sort of wondering, er, ah, what exactly do You have in mind for us?"

"What's in it for me?" Peter was really asking. "I've done what You asked me to do, and I believe that You will reward those who trust and obey You, but how? When? What sort of reward can I expect? Where is it? I've been serving You this long and haven't seen much from my efforts. When can I expect things to get better in my life?"

Jesus saw clearly the issue in question. It's a question most of us have asked at one time or another in our spiritual journey: "What can I really expect to get out of my faith in Christ?"

Matthew recorded Jesus' answer:

> And Jesus said to them, "Truly I say to you, that you who have followed Me, in the regeneration when the Son of Man will sit on His glorious throne, you also shall sit upon twelve thrones, judging the twelve tribes of Israel. And everyone who has left houses or brothers or sisters or father or mother or children or farms for My name's sake, shall receive many times as much, and shall inherit eternal life." (19:28–29 NASB)

Mark more specifically recorded Jesus as saying that His followers who have given up so much will receive "a hundred times as much now *in the present age*" (10:30 NASB, emphasis mine). Luke included even those who have been bereft of their marriage partners, for the sake of the kingdom of God, and emphasized that they, too, would receive "many times as much *at this time* and in the age to come, eternal life" (18:29–30 NASB, emphasis mine).

How does God repay a hundredfold in this life for a lost father, mother, wife or husband, children, brother or sister? The best way I can imagine Him doing so is by fulfilling the words of the psalmist, that He will take the solitary—the single person, the rejected person, the abandoned, the orphan, and the one left alone—and He will set them in a new family, the family of God (Ps. 68:6).

This was not simply spiritual schmaltz. Many of the early Christians lost everything they ever held dearly, all because of their commitment to Christ. Some lost their land and their homes. Others lost their jobs. Many men and women lost their spouses. For instance, in New Testament times, when a Jewish woman trusted Jesus but her husband did not, it was not unusual for that man to divorce his wife and disavow that she was even alive. As far as he was concerned, she no longer existed. Consequently, her decision to trust Jesus cost her everything, including her home, her security, her children, and, oftentimes, even a safe place to live or a respectable means of making a living. The words of Jesus—"Think not that I have come to bring peace, but I have come to set a sword between father and son, mother and daughter"—were quite real to those who were ostracized by their own loved ones.

To these people and to those in modern times who have sacrificed even their most precious relationships for the cause of Christ, Jesus might say, "It is not My intent to divide friends and families, but it is often the case that when a person makes a decision to follow Me, it costs them some of their closest relationships in this life. But," says Jesus, "I will restore; I will repay you a hundredfold."

Jesus was not prompting His followers to become materialists or polygamists. He wasn't saying, "You can expect to own one hundred houses in this life." Nor was He saying, "It's all right for you to marry one hundred men, or one hundred women." On the contrary, I don't think He was talking about possessions or marriage at all! I believe that Jesus was describing how His followers would find their every need met—and met abundantly—through His family's resources. My friend Dr. Mario E. Rivera, author of *Emotional Freedom* and numerous other books, and the developer of a Christian counseling program known as "Theo-therapy," told me, "A fully functioning, Christ-centered church is the best group therapy in the world. A truly functioning body will meet the total needs of the members."

For example, I believe that Jesus would be pleased if we who claim to know Him would take that single mother and welcome her into a body called the church; in that church will be men and women who will help her, and they will be "fathers" and "mothers" and "sisters" and "brothers" to her. When she needs her car worked on and she doesn't have the money to pay a mechanic to do it, that is where the church steps up, and men (or women) who can help volunteer to get or keep that car on the road. When she needs work done on her electrical outlets, some electricians in the church will say, "We want to help, because God has put us in a community, and He has told us that we belong to one another."

Similarly, when a brother in the church loses his wife, there will be men and women who will surround him with the support and help he needs to carry on with his life. Perhaps if he is a young father, some of the members in the fellowship can help baby-sit. If he is elderly, maybe inviting the fellow over for dinner once in a while will help him deal with the loss of his wife. Whatever the case, it is not God's plan that the man should grieve alone. He is part of us.

When we see children who have been orphaned or otherwise torn apart from their families because of their commitment to Christ, the Christian community must rally around and say, "We will help care for these children," whether that means feeding and clothing them or actually opening our homes for the children to live with us. Even though they may not be related to us genetically, they are related to us spiritually. We are family. We belong to one another.

Granted, we may have different roles and functions, but we are all members of the family. In Romans 12:4–5, Paul said exactly that: "Just as there are many parts to our bodies, so it is with Christ's body. We are all parts of it, and it takes every one of us to make it complete, for we each have different work to do. So we belong to each other, and each needs all the others" (TLB). Notice, we not only need each other, we belong to each other.

With the enormous growth of megachurches in or near most large American cities, we have all too frequently lost sight of the truth that we belong to one another. Not only are we disconnected from the other churches in town, but oftentimes, the people sitting in the seats in our huge churches also are disconnected from each other! If you are not willing to belong to the people sitting around you in your local body of believers, you have yet to understand or take seriously the commitments that you have made to Jesus Christ. God has called us to belong to each other as the members of His church. You belong to me. I belong to you. Each of us belongs to one another.

How committed are you to God, to His church, to the people sitting around you in your local congregation? If everyone treated the church the way you do, would the church be a caring, comforting, safe place, or would it be an indifferent, unconcerned, dangerous environment? If everyone was investing in the Christian community what you are investing, would it be a place where spiritual maturity is promoted, spiritual safety is procured, and spiritually motivated care is provided?

If everyone treated the church and functioned in the body with the same commitment level that you do, would it be prospering?

Some may say, "Well, I've given up on the church." Have you? God hasn't.

What are the advantages to us as individuals in belonging to one another, when we become involved in a local community of believers? Certainly, when Jesus returns to earth for His church, or if we should die before that day, we can be confident that He will take us to heaven to live with Him eternally. But what about in this life? Not just in heaven by and by, but as fellow members of God's church in the nasty here and now, what benefit do we procure from belonging to one another in God's church? What's in it for you and me?

AN ENVIRONMENT THAT FOSTERS SPIRITUAL GROWTH

One of the main benefits I have found in belonging to the community of believers is the opportunity for spiritual growth and maturity that living out our Christian lives together affords. Maybe you are much stronger than I am, but I need to be around people who are talking about Jesus. I need to be involved with people who are studying His Word and trying to apply Christlike principles to every aspect of their lives. Simply put, it is much easier to grow spiritually when you are being nurtured in an environment that is conducive to growth, where people are attempting to build each other up in the Lord, rather than tearing each other apart.

That doesn't mean that we Christians should move out to the wilderness and live by ourselves in cloisters, to remain separated from and "uncontaminated" by the world. Quite the contrary, Jesus commands us to be salt and light in the world (Matt. 5:13–14), to take the gospel to the world (Matt. 28:19).

Nevertheless, there is great value in coming apart from the world for a time and gathering together with fellow believers to be encouraged, taught, and strengthened in the things of the Lord. For some the time they can spend in close proximity to other members of the body may be limited. It may be only a matter of hours, while others are able to spend days at a time together, and some will actually be able to live in a community in which the prevailing culture is thoroughly Christian.

Nowadays, we take this privilege for granted, claiming that it is our right or choice whether or not to be in the presence of other Christians. Many believers around the world today, and certainly, down through church history, would relish the opportunities for spiritual growth that we take for granted: to spend time informally with other believers, to study the Word of God together, and to learn from godly leaders. Writing in the years just prior to Hitler's takeover, the German pastor and theologian Dietrich Bonhoeffer noted:

> An unspeakable gift of God for the lonely individual is easily disregarded and trodden under foot by those who have the gift every day. It is easily forgotten that the fellowship of Christian brethren is a gift of grace, a gift of the Kingdom of God that any day may be taken from us, that the time that still separates us from utter loneliness may be brief indeed. Therefore, let him who until now has had the privilege of living a common Christian life with other Christians praise God's grace from the bottom of his heart. Let him thank God on his knees and declare: It is grace, nothing but grace, that we are allowed to live in community with Christian brethren.[1]

Bonhoeffer's words were prophetic. Within a few years, Hitler controlled Germany, and Bonhoeffer was imprisoned for his refusal to compromise with the Nazi's "German-Christian" concept of watered-down, politically expedient "Christianity." On April 9, 1945, shortly before Allied troops liberated the prison camp where he was incarcerated, Bonhoeffer was executed by direct order of Heinrich Himmler.

I believe that we are facing a similar threat today, that animosity toward authentic Christianity is growing rapidly and soon we will enter a period of persecution unlike anything the body of Christ has experienced since the powerful fist of the Roman Empire attempted to pummel the early Christians into submission. Moreover, I'm convinced that one of the reasons we have such a low level of spiritual power in the body of Christ today is because we have discounted the importance of belonging to the local church. We are content to "belong to the great big family of God," while ignoring opportunities for spiritual growth and maturity—and yes, opportunities for Christian service—that happen quite naturally when we are tied into an active, local body of believers.

Taking it a step further, I contend that we will never reach the place of spiritual maturity to which God has called us—a willingness to lay our lives on the line rather than compromise our relationship with Christ—without interacting closely with the brothers and sisters in a local congregation. God has placed us in a family, and He expects us to function there, not just for others' benefit, but for our own well-being also.

BROTHER WHO?

In Ephesians 2:19, Paul wrote, "Now, therefore, you are no longer strangers and foreigners, but fellow citizens with the saints and members of the household of God" (NKJV).

Notice, the local church is not to be a group of strangers, whether we are part of a megachurch or a small assembly with just a few dozen believers. If the people with whom you worship God on a regular basis are strangers to you, something is wrong. You need to take a hard look at your commitment to that part of the body and the body's commitment to you. If you are not currently involved, you need to get involved or find yourself a segment of the body where you can become an active participant.

Certainly, if you are part of a large congregation, you may not know everybody who attends. If that is the case, then you need to become part of a smaller group—a Bible study group, a Sunday school class, or a home "cell" group—a more intimate part of the entire body that meets regularly for fellowship and to study, learn, and discuss how the Word of God works in our lives.

Another way of accomplishing the goal of connecting with a smaller group is to become involved in a ministry within the church. For example, Phoenix First Assembly of God Church, with its thousands of members, pastored by Tommy Barnett, must certainly be considered a megachurch. Yet the emphasis at Phoenix First is not so much on cell groups, but on every believer being involved in some sort of ministry. Consequently, the church has a virtual parade of more than two hundred ministries, including everything from the usual music ministries to drama and media ministries, ministries to the deaf, and ministries to children, singles, and senior citizens. Beyond that, the church also encourages the more "unusual" ministries, directed toward those with specific interests or needs. For instance, they have ministries to "Harley"-style bikers; to alternative punk rockers; to inner-city kids; to the Hispanic community; to hospitals; to athletes, coaches, and their family members; to former strippers; to AIDS victims; and perhaps one of the most unusual ministries I've ever heard of—one in which my wife, Lori, became involved as a single woman and is still involved today—a ministry to women who have experienced abortion.

Regardless of a person's interest and spiritual gifts, Phoenix First has a ministry area in which that person can become involved. These ministries, then, become almost like small churches within the megachurch, with the members working together on a regular basis, taking on the responsibilities of discipleship and accountability, and enjoying the benefits of the entire body of Christ.

My wife, Lori, credits one of these groups, Master's Commission, an intensive discipleship program at Phoenix First, as the key to her spiritual survival during the early years of her Christian life. Led by Lloyd Zeigler, a pastor at the church, Master's Commission requires its trainees to devote one full year of their lives to daily prayer, Bible study, and ministry. During this time, the participants are restricted from working outside jobs—in fact, they must pay more than five thousand dollars to be involved in the program—and single men and women in the program are forbidden to date.

Yet the "hands-on" discipleship training is life-changing. It includes evangelism, street outreaches, and college campus ministries, as well. More than 40 percent of the people who complete the Master's Commission program go into a "full-time" ministry, while another 30 percent continue on in "part-time" ministries. Perhaps more important, during the yearlong program, the members of Master's Commission serve as a church within the church to each other, praying with each other, helping one another, serving each other, and ministering together.

Similarly, at the Dream Center, at any given time, we had more than one thousand Christians living together. It was impossible for me to know every person there as a close friend. Instead, our ministry, New Covenant Fellowship, worked within the larger Dream Center ministry, and as a microcosm of the larger group, we functioned as the body of Christ, bearing each other's burdens, encouraging one another, and working together for the cause of Christ. Regardless of your circumstances, it is possible to find some group with whom you can actively live out your commitment to Christ. And you need to do just that. You cannot afford to remain an isolated stranger; you must be attached to the body.

PRIME PROPERTY

Paul went on to say that not only are we fellow citizens with the saints and members of the household of God, but we have "been built on the foundation of the apostles and prophets, Jesus Christ Himself being the chief cornerstone, in whom the whole building, being fitted together, grows into a holy temple in the Lord, in whom you also are being built together for a dwelling place of God in the Spirit" (Eph. 2:20–22 NKJV). The King James Version says that we have been "fitly framed together"; the *New Living Translation* paraphrases the text to read, "carefully joined."

Think about that for a moment. God not only has saved us, but He also has carefully joined us with His body. Being carefully joined to the body means that I can no longer willingly remain a stranger to other members of the body with whom I have regular contact. I cannot ignore the fact that whatever affects them affects me, and whatever touches my life touches theirs, as well.

Notice that the Scripture describes Jesus as the chief cornerstone, the One on whom everyone else rests and "in whom the whole building, being joined together, grows into a holy temple in the Lord." Do you see what is supposed to happen as we are joined together in the Christian community? We are to grow into a holy temple in the Lord.

Now some people feel that they are already so "holy" that they can't connect with "lesser" Christians. Yet if you want to be a dwelling place for God, you must recognize that you are going to have to brush shoulders regularly with God's people in community. You cannot isolate yourself from other people in whom God is chipping off the rough edges and still expect to be fitly framed together as part of His holy temple. Besides, God is probably knocking off a few rough edges in your life as well, shaping you so you will fit perfectly in His "holy temple."

So take off your halo. You might as well admit that: you need the rest of us imperfect people. And guess what? We need you! We need you to commit yourself to us, bringing your imperfections, mixing them with ours. Together, we must allow the Master Craftsman's hands to shape us into the holy habitation He wants us to be—a holy temple in which God dwells.

STIR IT UP!

The writer to the Hebrews also emphasized this truth as well: "Let us consider one another in order to stir up love and good works, not forsaking the assembling of ourselves together, as is the manner of some, but exhorting one another, and so much the more as you see the Day approaching" (Heb. 10:24–25 NKJV).

Not only do you and I belong to each other, we need to stir each other up to love and good works. I need my spiritual brothers and sisters to stir me up, not to agitate or aggravate me, but to provoke me to good works. Most of us go through our spiritual lives seeing only what we want to see, hearing only what we want to hear. We need other people to help us focus our attention on those things of eternal value, to speak into our lives, sometimes words of encouragement and sometimes words of rebuke.

Not long ago, I was one of the speakers at a large prophecy conference. Prior to presenting our messages to the congregation, the speakers gathered for a time of prayer and to present our messages to be tried and tested before each other, to make sure no one was off target or going off on some tangent. I shared the message that I felt God wanted me to speak, and the other ministers in the room concurred that what I planned to share with the congregation was an accurate and much-needed word.

When I got up to speak, however, I couldn't quite get the message together. I rambled all over the place, I stared at my notes, I quoted Scripture after Scripture, but nothing connected, not with the audience, not with the other speakers, not even with me. Instead of bringing a message filled with living water, I meandered back and forth, muddying the stream more with each curve in the flow.

After the session that day, the ministers gathered together again to evaluate what had been spoken. It was a precious time of prayer and encouragement. But that's not all.

The other ministers firmly rebuked me for not sharing the message God had given me. "You blew it, Jim," one man said kindly but emphatically. "You missed the message. God gave you the message, but you didn't present it. You never got the point across." The other ministers agreed that I had not been effective that day. They didn't make me feel like a heel, but they were not about to sit by idly, pretending that I had been a blessing when I had not been.

Did I enjoy that corrective rebuke? Absolutely not. Did I need it, learn from it, and grow from it? Count on it.

All of us need others who can look objectively at what we are saying or doing in the body of Christ, people who love us enough to tell us the truth, even if the truth hurts for a season. At the same time, we need people who can encourage us to do what God has called us to do, without kowtowing, flattering, or telling us simply what we want to hear. Honest encouragement must become a keystone in the last-days church of Jesus Christ.

Please understand, this sort of encouragement is not some ambiguous, ethereal connection with the universal church. God wants us to be stirring each other up in a local community of believers with whom we interact daily, week by week. He wants us to encourage and to be encouraged by spiritual brothers and sisters with whom we live out our Christian experience.

Notice again in Hebrews 10:25 how seriously God takes this matter. Scripture says that we are to stir one another up to good works, "not forsaking the assembling of ourselves together, as is the manner of some, but exhorting one another, and so much the more as you see the Day approaching." To the folks who think they don't need the church, the writer to the Hebrews makes it clear that we should make our gathering together a higher priority in these days. In other words, as we see the Day of the Lord approaching, the signs of Christ's coming all around us, we desperately need each other if we are to mature as believers.

In the days ahead, many will need the church for food; some will need the body for shelter, transportation, child care, and basic human services. All of us will need each other for spiritual encouragement to keep going, to keep trusting and believing. In these "getting ready days," we must take seriously the scriptural mandate that we encourage one another. If ever we needed the church, we need it now!

THE GIFT WE ALL CAN USE

I COULD TELL BY the expression on the young woman's face that something was wrong. I had just finished speaking at her church, after which many members of the congregation had responded to an invitation to commit themselves to the Lord and to each other in a fresh way. Now, as most of the remaining people ambled toward the exits, this young woman had returned to the sanctuary.

"I'm sorry to trouble you, Jim," she began politely, "but I feel that I can't go home until I ask you a question."

"Sure, go right ahead," I responded.

"Well, I heard you speaking tonight about how we all need each other in the body of Christ, how we are to bear one another's burdens, and how God has given each of us gifts and talents that He wants to use within the body."

"Yes, that's right." I nodded in agreement.

"But I don't have any spiritual gifts. Or if I do, I haven't discovered them yet. I want to contribute something of value to the body, but I can't sing, I'm not comfortable trying to teach the children, I don't play an instrument, I'm not the domestic type, so I don't cook for the missionaries when they come to visit our church. Frankly, I can't remember a time I have ever done anything of eternal significance for God. It's not that I don't love Him, or that I don't want to serve Him. I just don't have a clue what I am supposed to do."

That young woman's dilemma is much more common than most of

us might think. Millions of genuine believers, committed members of the Christian community, are frustrated and discouraged in their walk with God because they have not found a place of usefulness in the kingdom.

We talked further about her likes and dislikes and how God could use her personality traits for His glory. I suggested that she contact a Christian counselor who could administer a test that might help her discover her strengths and weaknesses, as well as her spiritual gifts. Most of all, I encouraged her to see that God had created her and poured into her the basic personality traits that He wanted her to have. Certainly, circumstances and her environment have had an influence on the person she has become, but the spiritual essence of her being was given to her by God. She needed only to recognize who she was in Christ and allow Him to use her life.

WE ALL HAVE GIFTS

Scripture is quite clear that all members of the body of Christ have a measure of faith (Rom. 12:3), a manifestation of the Holy Spirit (1 Cor. 12:7), and whatever spiritual gifts that the Holy Spirit imparts (1 Cor. 12:8–11) as He sees fit. All of these spiritual blessings are given by God for the building up of the entire body. In several places in the New Testament, the apostle Paul gave specific instructions concerning how these gifts from God should be used within the community of believers. He reminded the Christians at Rome:

> For just as we have many members in one body and all the members do not have the same function, so we, who are many, are one body in Christ, and individually members one of another. And since we have gifts that differ according to the grace given to us, let each exercise them accordingly: if prophecy, according to the proportion of his faith; if service, in his serving; or he who teaches, in his teaching; or he who exhorts, in his exhortation; he who gives, with liberality; he who leads, with diligence; he who shows mercy, with cheerfulness. (Rom. 12:4–8 NASB)

The list that Paul provided in this passage is often referred to as a list of "ministry gifts," which is a gift that God has given to you to enable you to help meet the needs of other people in the name of the Lord. God has given to every genuine believer in Jesus at least one ministry gift—and He often gives several ministry gifts to faithful men and women, and boys and girls who will use His gifts for His glory. Of all the gifts listed in this passage, perhaps the most underrated is the gift of exhortation (v. 8).

THE GIFT OF EXHORTATION

In the Bible, the gift of exhortation carries a fivefold meaning. Exhorters give (1) advice, (2) counsel, (3) comfort, (4) consolation, and (5) encouragement.

By far, the most descriptive term for the gift of exhortation is the word *encouragement*, which implies "a lifting, a buoyancy." Consider this: One out of two of us may have a special gift from God to be an encourager, a lifter of other people.

Exhorters usually function in a way similar to a mountain spring or a bubbling brook. Often they have been purified by the rocks they have encountered in their own journey, and now they are content to flow along in the stream of the Spirit, just looking for an opportunity to be a means of refreshment to someone else.

They normally operate at face value. Don't misunderstand. I'm not saying that those with the gift of encouragement are superficial people, just that they usually work best on the surface of matters. They know a little bit about a lot of things, so they can use their gift in a wide variety of circumstances.

Teachers and preachers, on the other hand, are usually "deep-well" people. They are not necessarily deep, and they are not necessarily well, but they function in the body best when they can plumb the depths of a matter, or when they are forced to dig into the Scriptures and come up with an answer or a solution to a problem. Preachers and teachers always seem to be saying, "Let's dig into the Word" or "Let's get down to it!"

You can tell the difference between an exhorter and a teacher by the way they approach the Bible. Exhorters read the Bible. I mean, they are always reading the Bible. They read, and read, and read the Bible, page after page, chapter after chapter, book after book!

Not surprisingly, you will often hear exhorters saying something such as, "I was just reading in the Bible the other day . . . and God showed me . . . !"

Teachers and preachers don't read the Bible; they *study* the Scriptures. They want to know what the Word means. Sometimes, it seems as though they never turn the page. They can stay glued to one spot, on one page of the Scriptures, for hours! Sometimes they'll study one chapter for days or weeks. Then they will get up to preach to you for what seems like months about one word in the Bible.

Exhorters don't do that. Not that they don't enjoy studying the Word—they do, indeed. But their approach is rather to pick up bits and pieces. They are always picking up a little bit about a lot of scriptural truth.

I am not implying that teachers, preachers, and evangelists cannot be encouragers; they can be, and many are, but it is not their natural gifting in many cases. Pastors are often blessed with a combination of gifts, which often include teaching and encouraging. But most scholars are not great encouragers, and most encouragers are not great scholars.

Ironically, exhortation is probably the most widely distributed, underused gift in the Church of Jesus Christ today. All sorts of people have this gift: short people, tall people, rich people, poor people, skinny people, Wal-Mart greeters, nurses, shopkeepers, factory workers, and pizza delivery boys. You don't have to be a Bible scholar to exercise this gift. You don't have to be a great speaker or a fabulous singer. All you need is a willing heart, an attitude that wants to be a blessing to others and to the Lord.

We don't all have the same spiritual gifts. Some people have gifts of discernment, some the gift of administration, others have gifts of healing, some have gifts of prophecy and other spiritual gifts. Moreover, God has placed within the body "some as apostles, and some as prophets, and some as evangelists, and some as pastors and teachers, for the equipping of the saints for the work of service, to the building up of the body of Christ" (Eph. 4:11–12 NASB). These are the men and women who have been ordained by God to lead His church. They are often the ones with great dreams and visions for what the people of God can be and do. And with all due respect to the leaders in the body, we can only handle a certain number of those types, or we'll all get tunnel vision. (I'll say more about visionaries in the body later in this book.) But all the various gifts and offices are important in God's plan to build up His church and to take His message of salvation to the world.

Yet as you ponder the list of gifts, perhaps you tend to become disappointed. You may be wondering, *What ministry gifts do I have? I can't preach, I don't feel comfortable teaching; I have never prophesied, nor have I ever been used of the Lord in a healing ministry. What could I do for God?*

Could it possibly be that you have a gift of exhortation?

Personality Counts

I didn't even know that this type of encouraging person existed until I met and married my wife, Lori. My temperament is what many psychologists refer to as a "melancholy," less spontaneous, and more of a "thinker," "dreamer" type of person. I can brood for hours over some problem or project. I am structured, organized (sort of), systematized, prioritized, and several other "-ized" words, as well! I love to pore over the Scriptures for hours, looking up New Testament words in the Greek and digging into the Old Testament Hebrew words.

My wife, Lori, is more like one of the exhorters, a spontaneous, sanguine, bubbly type of person. As soon as we were married, I set about my "spiritual duty" of helping her become a preacher's wife. At first, because of her love for the Lord and her love for me, Lori actually tried to cooperate with my renovation plans. But I soon discovered that God had made her the way she is, and I was wasting my time and hers trying to change her.

Then an awful revelation hit me: *Maybe God wants her to be that way!* After all, I had to admit that the Lord had done a much better job of creating Lori than I had in my attempts at re-creating her. Right there, I learned an important lesson—one that seems so ludicrously simple that we often miss it: God does not want all of us to be the same. He does not want all of us to be deep-well people. In fact, He is delighted that many members of the body of Christ are actually surface, bubbling-brook sort of people—and He created them to be that way. In the wisdom of God, He knew that we would need a large number of encouragers in the body of Christ in these last days.

If we can think of spiritual help in terms of medical assistance, there is a ministry to people that is more like first aid, and there is a ministry similar to surgery. Pastors, preachers, evangelists, and prophets are probably better at performing the surgical operations necessary in the body of Christ. Confronting and dealing with deep, dark, ugly sin in the body—that is best left to the wisdom of the spiritual leaders. But when it comes to first aid, nobody does it better than an encourager. With their hearts filled with kindness, love, and compassion, exhorters are usually excellent at providing spiritual first aid, bandaging up some bumps and bruises, washing out a shallow wound, or applying some healing salve to a cut that could easily become infected and cause much more serious problems.

Handle with Care

Two common errors exist concerning the gift of exhortation.

1. *The gift of exhortation is not "shaping up the saints."* Many Christians think that the word *exhort* means "to rebuke" or "to yell at," so they think the ministry of exhortation is one of clobbering and clouting the carnal, beating up on the believers, or depressing the disciples. They think the exhorter's role in the body is to tell relatively good people how bad they are!

But that is not the gift of exhortation. Exhorters are people who lift up and inspire other members of the Christian community, urging them on. They buoy up those who are discouraged, depressed, and frustrated in their faith. How badly we need some encouragers in the body today! And I believe we are going to need encouragers even more in the days to come as we head into difficult times.

2. *Those who discover they have this gift are immediately tempted to think that they are experts.* You know how it goes: somebody who is laboring under these two mistakes comes to the body and immediately attempts to shape up the saints. They approach a young couple, new in their faith. "Now we appreciate your coming to this church," says the misguided exhorter. "You've done well since you've given up those drugs, and have actually gotten married rather than living together in sin. But according to the Word, you've got some problems, and I want to help you deal with them."

"And, ma'am, we know you mean so well—you just don't do so well."

"And, we appreciate the way you can play the piano, but you've got some problems puffing on those cancer sticks. Don't you think it's time you stop killing yourself with those things?"

Obviously, that is not a proper use of the gift of exhortation. The ministry of exhortation is not pouring dirt on people who are already down in the pits. It is lifting up people who are down. It is encouraging them, inspiring them to face another day.

Some Christians seem to feel that they have the ministry of putdowns—putting other believers in their places through the use of snide remarks, sarcasm, or spiritual sledgehammer blows. I guess they feel a little taller if they can put somebody else down. But if you read the Bible, you'll quickly discover that there is no such gifting. God's gifts are given to edify the body, to build up, not to tear down.

Scripture says, "There is one who speaks rashly like the thrusts of a sword, / But the tongue of the wise brings healing" (Prov. 12:18 NASB). That wise tongue often is the ministry of exhortation.

A CONVERSATIONAL GIFT

The ministry of exhortation is a conversational gift. By that I mean, exhortation does not necessarily come in the form of a formal speech, planned teaching, or lecture. It is most often just casual, friendly conversation with another person and encouraging him or her to trust in the Lord. It is not the rumble of thunder from Sinai, but it is the flowing grace of the warm, friendly Jordan River. You will be amazed at how God will use this gift in your everyday situations, as you make a conscious effort to use your gift of encouragement.

You don't have to contrive situations or attempt to squeeze Jesus into every conversation. Just look for natural opportunities, and be willing to convey a message of hope and encouragement when the time comes. Nor do you have to speak in "Christianese." Have you ever noticed that when some people start talking about spiritual matters, the tone of their voice changes? They must assume that they have to speak in low, "godly" tones.

Speak naturally as you encourage. You don't have to sound like Charlton Heston when you speak words of spiritual truth. To be effective, exhorters just have to be genuine. Share what Jesus has done for you and what you know He has done for others.

Small Doses Are Better

Another interesting aspect of exhortation is that the gift is usually expressed in tiny "capsules," rather than in long, drawn-out sermons. Usually, an exhorter can get the job done in sixty seconds—really! That's all it takes to be an encourager.

Sure, there may be times when a longer conversation is necessary to convey your caring compassion and to offer whatever wisdom you can.

But in most cases, a word of exhortation is not a sermon or a lecture, it is just a power-packed spiritual capsule. These "capsules" originate in heaven, where God packs them with some much-needed wisdom, a word of knowledge, some common sense, or a word of Scripture that is especially appropriate for the need of the moment. The Holy Spirit delivers these nuggets of truth to you, dropping these little capsules into your heart and mind. He then instructs you when and where to drop them into somebody else's life, where they literally explode with supernatural power. Sometimes they explode with power to encourage, to lift up, or power to bring a word of wisdom, knowledge, or instruction to another person.

Often, these spiritual capsules penetrate to the heart, where they dissolve into the lives of people and become the medicine the Lord Jesus uses to totally transform somebody's life. For instance, after I did an interview with Barbara Walters, I signed my books for her staff members. I sincerely prayed before I wrote a few sentences in each book. When they received the books, I got numerous messages that the words I had written did indeed penetrate their hearts.

Now, here's some more good news about this gift: You don't have to be a preacher or an elder or a Bible scholar to deliver these words of encouragement. Your only responsibility is to make sure that the capsule came from God and that you deliver it with love.

Keep in mind that the devil loves to counterfeit the Lord's capsules. We've all heard of instances in which some evil person has laced a perfectly good medicine with cyanide or some other deadly chemical. What should be a means of healing then becomes a destructive poison. And it doesn't take much poison in a capsule to bring about deadly results.

Is That All There Is to It?

Maybe you are saying, "Jim, is that all there is to it? Why, just about anybody in the body of Christ could be an exhorter! Does this gift of exhortation really work that way?" Yes! People in the body are hurting. Is there a need for this gift of encouragement? More than we know.

Day after day, week after week, month after month, year after year, there is a need and an opportunity for you to express the gift of encouragement. You may say, "Oh! I wouldn't know how to talk to somebody about their problems!"

Who said you have to talk about their problems? When my wife, Lori, initiates a conversation, she simply starts where the person is—talking about the person's interests rather than his or her problems. Maybe all you need to do is to deliver the capsule the Lord has given to you. Let it be power-packed in heaven, dropped into your heart by God, and then deliver it when and where He tells you to drop it.

Many times when the gift of exhortation is working properly, you may not even be aware you said anything of great significance. Often I get letters in which somebody writes, "You know, what you said really helped me," yet I have no idea what it was that I said! It must have been just a little capsule, spoken at the right time.

Understand, these capsules don't need to be expanded into sermons, Bible studies, or seminars; they are just little capsules of truth that God puts in your heart and mind to share at just the right time, under the anointing and the direction of the Holy Spirit.

When somebody says, "Hey! What you shared with me really blessed me. You need to come teach our Sunday school class about that," don't get nervous; just smile and say, "Brother [or Sister], the Holy Spirit has given me a gift of exhortation, not exegesis!" And go merrily on your way.

Many Christians think that it is the pastor's job to encourage everyone. But most preachers take twenty-five to thirty minutes to make their point—some slow ones like me take even longer than that. Besides, not everybody has thirty minutes to listen to us, so that's why God has given so many people in the body of Christ these little capsules.

You can drop them all over your home, in your workplace, at school, day in, day out, night in, night out! And what God does will be explosive in and through your life!

Encouragers Must Be Good Listeners

If your gift of exhortation is going to function properly, you must learn how to close your mouth and open your ears. Exhorters listen; teachers and preachers are not usually good listeners. They like to do all the talking; in fact, they love to hear themselves talk! But a good exhorter knows how to listen with his or her head and his or her heart.

Have you noticed that there are very few listeners, nowadays? I've often shocked some of my "preacher-type" friends when I have suggested that what this world needs are more Christian bartenders. I'm usually only half joking when I say it. Yet most people do not go to bars to get drunk. Many don't even go there for the drinks. They go to the bars because they are lonely and looking for someone to talk to. Often that someone tends to be the bartender, a nonjudgmental listener, someone to whom the customer can pour out his or her heart without fear of condemnation.

That's what the exhorter needs to do within the body of Christ: be a nonjudgmental listener who will allow a hurting person to pour out his or her heart without turning the conversation into an opportunity to heap more abuse on the person who needs help.

As an exhorter, your job is not to preach a sermon or to recite the history of Christianity; you just have to open your ears and listen, and then drop the tiny capsule that God gives you, when He instructs you to do so.

I, NOT YOU

The ministry of the exhorter usually takes place in the first person. It is not, "Hey, *you!* Here's what *you* need to do." On the contrary, exhortation can often be indirect, offering suggestions rather than orders. Often it sounds something like this: "If *I* were you, here's what *I'd* do . . ." Or you might say, "Some of my friends tried this, and *I* can see how this has really helped them." Or "This is what helped *me.* Would that help you?" Or "*I* was just reading my Bible the other day, and *I* could hardly believe what happened . . ."

Exhortation is not yelling at someone else, or trying to convict them of sin, righteousness, or judgment under your own power. (Remember, that is the Holy Spirit's job, not ours.) Instead, the exhorter is merely saying, in a conversational way, "Here is what Jesus did for me. Maybe He would do the same for you, if you'd let Him."

Encouragement and Hope

The gift of exhortation always brings hope—not false hope, but hope based on the promises of God. The world is longing for such a message. If you talk to most people nowadays, the conversation won't go on for long before someone brings up some problems—all sorts of problems! The morale of most people is down in the basement digging holes! Why are they like that?

I don't know; maybe they have been watching the news on television. Or maybe they are beginning to realize that this world has run its course, that hope is in short supply, that the cataclysmic signs that Jesus predicted nearly two thousand years ago are happening right before our eyes.

Whatever the reason, engage most people in conversation and before long, they start bringing up all sorts of problems and negative garbage!

And what do we usually do? We agree!

"Oh, it's bad out there."

"Yeah, it's never been this hot before . . ."

Then in winter, we say, "It's too cold! It's never been this cold before!"

"Can you believe those guys in the White House?"

"Yeah, and what about our state legislature? Why did they need a raise?"

"Taxes? Don't even get me started!"

"Isn't this AIDS thing getting scary?"

"Yeah, how about that acid rain?"

"Oh, yes, I heard that the ozone layer is about shot, too, so the harmful rays of the sun are going to scorch us bald any day now."

"Yeah, well, that's probably true. If the glaciers don't melt and flood New York first, that is."

And on and on and on!

And most people—ninety-nine out of a hundred—will agree!

But the person who has the gift of exhortation will react differently. The encourager is not one to stick his or her head in the sand, pretending that everything is getting better. We know that is not the case. We understand that the body of Christ is going to experience some intense difficulties before Jesus Christ returns. But Jesus Himself said, when you see all these signs of the times, "Lift up your heads, your redemption draweth nigh."

Consequently, because the exhorter is aware of the troublesome times that are coming upon the earth, he or she brings a word of hope! The exhorter encourages people who are living in darkness to look to the Light of the World, Jesus Christ.

The exhorter brings a scriptural promise to bear on the situation. Or perhaps he or she has a definite word from the Lord that is applicable. Maybe the exhorter has a bit of instruction or positive guidance or wisdom from heaven.

The world desperately needs to hear some words of encouragement. Most everybody has the tendency to just spiral down to the bottom of the pits. But we Christians are exhorters! God has called us to lift people up!

Not only has He enlisted us to encourage people, but He also has empowered us to do so.

If you want to live and think and talk in a Dumpster, go ahead, but as the body of Christ, we need to encourage people every way we can!

And before you know it, the word will get around. People will start talking.

"Have you ever talked to that guy down there?"

"He is always so up, so positive, so encouraging! It's just good to be around a guy like that!"

"Have you ever met that secretary at the third desk over there? She's got more hope than anyone I've ever seen!"

"You know, honey, we've never had neighbors like the people that just moved next door. They are so happy; they seem to love each other and talk nicely to each other—even at breakfast."

As the body of Christ begins to encourage each other and the world around us, the word will spread like wildfire: Those people have a hope.

WHERE TO START

Some Christians say, "Oh, I wouldn't know how to offer hope to anyone; I wouldn't know what to say."

Okay, don't say anything!

"Say what?"

Don't say anything.

The first thing you do is just get into step with them. Just fall in beside the people you hope to encourage. That is exactly what the Holy Spirit does. He is the Paraclete, "the Comforter, the One called alongside" to help us. He is the Helper. And He will help you as you take the first step toward making an impact on your world. So just fall into step with the people you want to encourage, come up beside them, and offer to help them any way you can.

"Okay!" you say. "I get in step with them . . . then what do I do?"

"You listen!"

"But what if I don't have anything to say?"

"Then you listen some more!"

"Yeah, well, how long do I listen?"

"Until you have something to say."

"That's all?"

"Yep, just don't spiral down."

"Well, when should I say something?"

"When God gives you something to say."

"Okay, how will I know?"

"You listen."

"Then what?"

"Experiment."

"What if I blow it?"

We have all blown it at one time or another. But, as you become more comfortable with your gift of exhortation, the Lord Jesus will begin to use you in ways you never dreamed possible to have an impact upon your friends, family, coworkers, fellow students—even some folks you don't like and who don't like you!

You will be absolutely amazed at what the Holy Spirit will do in and through your life!

"Oh?" you ask. "What if I get into something I can't handle?"

No problem. Just point the way to someone who can help in that situation.

Have you ever been to Los Angeles or Chicago or Washington, D.C.? If so, then no doubt, you have probably been lost at one time or another on the freeways and highways around those cities. What did you do? If you are male, you probably circled the city for hours, refusing to admit that you were lost. If you are female, you probably insisted upon stopping and asking somebody for directions.

Did that person take you where you wanted to go? Probably not. Most likely, he or she merely pointed the way. That's what you can do as an exhorter. You don't have to be omnipotent or omniscient. When you get stumped, just point to someone else who might have a handle on that problem.

Maybe you meet somebody who has cancer and you'd like to encourage that person, but you don't know anything about what they are going through. Certainly, you can empathize with them, but you can also take it one step further. You can say, "You know, we have some people in our church who have survived cancer, and they would be glad to pray for you. I'll be glad to introduce you."

As an encourager, often your main role will be to make referrals. You don't have to have all the answers; you just need to stay alert to opportunities to lift somebody's spirits. All you need is a heart attitude to help and an availability to God to allow Him to work through you.

One night, while I was living at the Dream Center, I heard a knock at my door somewhere around midnight. There was Jorge, a young man barely in his teens. Accompanying him were several of the Dream Center kids who had led Jorge and his daddy to the Lord through the Dream Center's "Adopt-a-Block" program, in which four or five Christians work on a particular block, not only witnessing about Jesus, but doing physical work such as cleaning up the streets, helping to paint the houses, and other chores that help improve the living environment in the inner city.

Jorge's mom had returned to Central America, and Jorge had just learned that his daddy was dying of AIDS. The doctors gave him virtually no chance of recovery. When Jorge got the news that his dad would soon be dead, he was devastated. A believer for no more than a few weeks, the boy asked, "Where is God? How could a God who loves me take my daddy from me?"

The kids from the Dream Center tried their best to comfort Jorge, but he was inconsolable and ready to give up on God and on life. Finally, in desperation, they all came to me in the middle of the night.

I talked with Jorge for a while and told him all the "preacher stuff" about heaven and how much God loves him and his daddy, that even if his dad died, we'd see him again. Jorge remained sullen and despondent.

"It hurts!" he cried. "It hurts to the core. How could God let my dad die?"

We talked further, and I tried my best to encourage him, but nothing was working. As a last resort, I looked at the young man and said, "Jorge, I've lost everything. You don't really know me, but I've been in prison for five years. I used to have money, cars, houses, and what I thought was a wonderful life. But I lost it all. And right in the middle of it, my wife walked away and divorced me while I was in prison and married my best friend. But Jesus never left me. I know He is real."

I could see a flicker of a light in Jorge's eyes, and his lips showed the slightest hint of a smile. Jorge looked at me and said, "Jim, if you can make it, then I can make it, too."

At that very moment, I knew that Jorge was going to be okay, but beyond that, I knew that I was going to be okay, too. Because, suddenly, when I saw that light return to that boy's eyes, the pain of my prison experience came into focus, and I knew that it had been worth it. The pain that I had been carrying for so long melted away, as I saw good coming out of what the devil had intended for evil.

Jorge's daddy died, but the people of the Dream Center became Jorge's family, took him in, and when I left, Jorge was still there attending school at the Dream Center's academy.

You don't have to have all the answers. All you have to do is care.

Now Is the Time

I'm convinced that as we draw closer to our Lord's return, this world is going to experience gargantuan upheavals. As we have said before, everything that can be shaken will be shaken, including many people's faith. If ever there was a time when we needed the ministry of encouragement, it is now.

The writer to the Hebrews encouraged us:

> Let us hold fast the confession of our hope without wavering, for He who promised is faithful; and let us consider how to stimulate one another to love and good deeds, not forsaking our own assembling together, as is the habit of some, but encouraging one another; and all the more, as you see the day drawing near. (Heb. 10:23–25 NASB)

What day is the writer talking about? The day when Jesus returns. Between now and that day, we need to be encouraging each other as never before. Whether you have a ministry of encouragement or not, we can all stimulate each other to love each other more, to help each other by doing simple, good deeds, and by gathering together to worship and praise the Lord as we see the day of the Lord approaching.

10

CARING FOR ONE ANOTHER

"HAVE YOU EVER LIED in church before?" I asked the startled young man who was carrying his Bible into the main sanctuary of the Los Angeles International Church, or, as it is better known, the Dream Center.

"What do you mean, Jim?" he asked, the hurt clearly evident in his expression. "I don't lie anymore. I used to tell dozens of lies every day. I was a gang member here in Los Angeles, but since I've come to know Jesus, I've been going straight—honestly. I speak the truth."

I smiled at him as I said, "Calm down, Carlos. I know you are a Christian, and I know that you love Jesus with all your heart. But I also know that you just told a lie. When you came in the church this morning, I asked you, 'Carlos, how are you doing?' And you said, 'Fine, Jim.' And that's the answer most Christians would give. But Carlos, I know that you aren't doing fine. I know that you are hurting, that you lost your job because of your uncompromising commitment to Christ, that you are broke, that your wife recently left you, and that, inside, your heart is crushed. Yet when I asked you how you are doing, you told me that you are fine. And Carlos, I really wanted to know. I wanted to share some of the burden you are carrying. I've rejoiced with you when you have rejoiced, and now I hurt with you when you are hurting. Don't rob me of that privilege—and my responsibility as part of the body of Christ—just because you feel that you must give the 'spiritually correct' answer."

Carlos looked back at me in amazement. "Do you really want to know how I'm doing, Jim?"

"Yes, Carlos, I do," I replied, as I put my arm around his shoulder and we walked toward a quiet spot in the sanctuary where we could talk.

"I feel like there is a million-pound weight on my chest, Jim, and if God doesn't do something soon, I'm going to have a heart attack."

Carlos and I talked about the hurt he was presently experiencing, and I shared with him some of the pain I had experienced in my life. Ironically, Carlos had never heard of Heritage USA and knew nothing of my involvement in pioneering Christian television or my nationally televised "disgrace" and subsequent trial and imprisonment. All he knew about Jim Bakker was that I taught a Bible study at the Dream Center and that I loved him as a brother in the Lord. His eyes widened as I told him how I had lost everything I had ever held dearly and had gone to prison for five years, coming out with nothing but the clothes on my back.

I didn't have many answers for Carlos, but answers for his problems or pain weren't necessary. He wasn't looking for answers. All he really needed to know was that somebody else cared, that God had not abandoned him, that he was not alone. He needed to hear that what he was going through was normal for Christians, that with the help of the body of Christ, he could go on, face another day, and take another step into the future that God had for him.

We prayed together and wept together. I promised Carlos that I would keep in touch with him and would link him with other believers with whom he could walk out his Christian commitment, other believers who would help him bear the load he was carrying. To me, that sort of empathy is essential. Beyond that, it is obedience to a basic biblical principle.

Scripture instructs us to "bear one another's burdens, and so fulfill the law of Christ" (Gal. 6:2 NKJV). It isn't enough to pray with hurting people, pat them on the back, and say, "There, there, now; everything is going to work out all right." As fellow followers of Jesus, we have to be there for one another. We must get involved in each other's lives, pitch in where necessary, even when it is inconvenient, costly, or time-consuming. If we cannot remain in regular, long-term contact with someone we help (as I could not with Carlos because of my speaking schedule), we need to hook them up with fellow Christians who can be there for them on a regular basis. When the good Samaritan in Scripture could not necessarily stay with the beaten, battered man he had helped, he made arrangements for the man's care in his absence. We dare not assume that hurting people will be healed all by themselves. We need to care for each other.

ARE WE MISSING THE POINT?

Millions of Christians enter their churches every week spiritually broken, beaten, and battered. Far greater numbers—more than we care to imagine—go to church physically, emotionally, or financially broken. Sadly, most of these believers—fellow members of God's family for whom Christ gave His life—walk out of Christian church services more depressed and discouraged than when they entered. Why? Because they went to church seeking solace and a helping hand, and in many cases, all they found was a greater load of guilt and "the right foot of fellowship."

While we in the church are erecting bigger, more functional buildings, spending an enormous amount of time, money, and energy in promoting our "pet" programs, we are missing some of the basic reasons God has given us the institution of the church: to edify the body, to build each other up in the Lord, to care for one another, to bear one another's burdens, to rejoice with those who are experiencing great victories, and to empathize with those who are struggling through dark times of defeat and discouragement.

While Christians need each other at all times, in every generation, I believe that in the difficult days ahead, the members of the Christian community will be called upon to wrap our arms around each other and care for one another like never before in history. That's why it is so important that we learn how to bear each other's burdens right now, while the opportunities are ripe, while the pressure is less intense, before the chaos commences.

CARE BEGINS AT HOME

This sort of care is another advantage you will find by being a part of a local community of believers. In Galatians 6:10, Paul said, "Therefore, as we have opportunity, let us do good to all, especially to those who are of the household of faith" (NKJV). Paul wasn't saying that we should neglect doing good to those who are not Christians, but he was implying that we ought to make special effort to care for our own family, while we continue to reach out to those who are not part of the body. He was not diminishing our responsibility to society; Paul simply was being a realist: You can't help someone else if you have nothing to share.

In ancient Egypt, for example, Joseph and the Egyptians had grain to spare and to share during the seven years of famine because they had prepared for the lean years ahead of time. No doubt, during the seven years of plenty, while the harvest was overflowing, some people questioned Joseph's hard-line savings plan. "Times are great. The economy is booming. The good times are going to keep rolling along. So why do we need to set aside so much of our grain? Why can't we just eat, drink, and be merry? Save food? For what? That ogre Joseph is just trying to stifle our lifestyle." But when the calamity struck, thanks to Joseph's stringent food storage programs, the people had enough for themselves and for others.

In every community, there are givers and there are takers. But in the Christian community, the givers should outnumber those who are on the receiving end. People who are down and out, who are hurting and in need of help, should be able to turn to the body of Christ for practical assistance, for food, clothing, shelter, and transportation. But as these people are helped and they get back on their feet, they then must become givers. We are not to operate a welfare-type system in which people perpetually keep coming back time after time for freebies.

In Acts 2, the Bible records that when the church was born, people had gathered in Jerusalem from all over the world. On the day of Pentecost, the Holy Spirit was poured out, and a mighty spiritual revival resulted. Though Acts doesn't go into great detail, we can reasonably guess at some of the practical results from this world-changing event. No doubt, some of the visitors to Jerusalem were so thrilled, they did not want to go back home. Many of these Jewish proselytes who had been filled with the Holy Spirit probably decided to stay there in Jerusalem. God was up to something, and they didn't want to miss it! Their attitude was laudable . . . at first.

After a few weeks, though, it is likely that they became more of a problem than a blessing. They remained in Jerusalem without jobs in an economy that was already extremely tight. They were not lazy people who disliked work, but they were people who found themselves out of place for a while. Making matters worse, a severe famine struck that part of the world.

The church must have been faced with the task of feeding and caring for many displaced newcomers, as well as many who had had the rug pulled out from under them economically. Motivated by their love of Jesus, as well as practical necessity, the early church leaders adopted an extreme measure: They decided to share everything they had with each other, and to have all things in common. "Why should one member of the congregation be throwing food away," they considered, "while another member of the congregation can't put food on her children's plates?" They decided that there was no reason for one person to have four coats in the closet—two of which he didn't even wear anymore—when there was a family in the church that had no coats at all. They said, "We are going to pool everything," and they brought their goods to the apostles, and the apostles distributed the items to the church as they found the need.

Now, that is an extremely difficult thing to do. It's not easy to decide who gets food and who does not, who gets a warm coat and who does not, or who gets a warm place to stay while others have to remain out in the cold. In the days ahead, if food, water, and comfortable shelter become scarce, I believe the leaders in the body of Christ are going to be called upon to make precisely such tough decisions. We should decide now how those choices will be made, so when the Tribulation comes, we won't be scrambling around trying to find a way to keep everyone happy.

In the first-century church, as some people began to get better jobs and to prosper, there were some low-life members of the body who selfishly took advantage of the others' kindness. Instead of pitching in and helping to feed, house, and support others, they were not working at all, but were busybodies and acting in a disorderly manner (2 Thess. 3:11). The apostle Paul had little patience for such lazy members of the community. He reminded the Thessalonians that even when he and his coworkers had visited Thessalonica to preach the gospel to them, the missionaries had worked night and day to support themselves, not sponging off the new believers. Although Paul encouraged the fledgling church to care for its members, he also laid down a firm principle: "If anyone will not work, neither shall he eat" (3:10 NKJV). Paul wasn't being mean; he was being practical and fair.

There is a huge difference between a person who will not work and a person who cannot work. The church is called to be responsible for those in its midst who cannot work, and when the tough times come and people are hurting, as the community of believers we must be willing to support those around us who cannot help themselves. Practically, that may involve paying electric bills, providing food supplies, or making car payments for members of the body who are hurting financially. It may mean that the church has to make the house payment or pay the rent this month for some of its members who are temporarily disabled. (Can't you just hear the squawking and squealing among God's people when one person's bills get paid by the Christian community and another's do not?)

It may mean that we can assist groups such as Habitat for Humanity to provide housing for some of our people. Maybe we can work together, as the Amish people are known to do, and have an old-fashioned "barn raising" to help some of the people in our body. In some cases, we may need to open our homes, to take in people who are homeless and destitute, to provide them with a meal or a place to live for a while.

Paul reminded us that we are to "be kindly affectionate to one another with brotherly love, in honor giving preference to one another; not lagging in diligence, fervent in spirit, serving the Lord; rejoicing in hope, patient in tribulation, continuing steadfastly in prayer; distributing to the needs of the saints, given to hospitality" (Rom. 12:10–13 NKJV). Whatever it takes, the Christian community must care for its family members, especially those who are struggling simply to survive.

On the other hand, the church must guard against becoming codependent with lazy sluggards who will not work. At the Dream Center, for example, all able bodies were required to work, to carry their part of the load. If a person is unable to work, the church should be there for him or her, to care for the person's needs as much as possible. But if a person is able to work, and for whatever reason decides that he or she would prefer to leech off the Christian community, the apostle Paul implied that we are under no obligation to feed that person. If you won't work, and we figure it out, you are not going to eat at our expense. Plenty of other people need help; we cannot afford to waste time, food, money, or energy on those selfish individuals who want to take, take, take, but never give. The body of Christ is a mutually caring society, helping people to get on their feet, but it is not a welfare system. We must compassionately care for hurting people, but we must also care enough to look a person in the eye and say, "We love you so much, we want to help you to get a job." The goal is not to have people dependent on the church, but for them to become self-sufficient so they can take care of themselves and help others, as well!

Many churches are doing an excellent job in this area already, providing for the needs of their own people while reaching out to the community, stocking food banks, and providing soup kitchens. One upscale congregation with which I am familiar uses their fellowship hall to house homeless people on cold nights. Compassionate members of the body go around the city in their cars, inviting men (and women on separate nights) to come to the church for a free meal and a warm bed, all in the name of Jesus.

But I Don't Have Time!

Does Christlike caring take time? You bet it does! Is it sometimes inconvenient? Yep. Does caring for others interrupt our plans or disrupt our schedules? Without a doubt.

Unquestionably, this is why many within the Christian community love to talk about caring, but they rarely put their words into action. Some people can become emotionally distraught, they care so much; yet they do very little to actually help meet the needs of the hurting people they supposedly care so much about.

Dietrich Bonhoeffer pointed out that one of the services that we in the Christian community should regularly perform for each other is that of "active helpfulness." By this, he meant "simple assistance in trifling, external matters," or what we might call small, random acts of kindness.

Bonhoeffer bristled at the notion that some of us are too busy to be actively involved in helping others in the body.

> Nobody is too good for the meanest [most common] service. One who worries about the loss of time that such petty, outward acts of helpfulness entail is usually taking the importance of his own career too solemnly.

> We must be ready to allow ourselves to be interrupted by God. God will be constantly crossing our paths and canceling our plans by sending us people with claims and petitions. We may pass them by, preoccupied with our more important tasks, as the priest passed by the man who had fallen among thieves, perhaps—reading the Bible. When we do that, we pass by the visible sign of the Cross raised

athwart our path to show us that, not our way, but God's way must be done. It is a strange fact that Christians and even ministers frequently consider their work so important and urgent that they will allow nothing to disturb them. They think they are doing God a service in this, but actually they are disdaining God's "crooked yet straight path" . . . But it is part of the discipline of humility that we must not spare our hand where it can perform a service and that we do not assume that our schedule is our own to manage, but allow it to be arranged by God.[1]

COMFORTING THE AFFLICTED

The community of believers also comforts those who need comforting. I have experienced that sort of comfort from the body of Christ. When I was in prison, thousands of people wrote to me. Many people took the time and effort to actually go inside the prison walls to visit me, offering prayers and words of encouragement, sometimes just being there with me.

One man who expressed such Christian compassion to me during the several years I was incarcerated in Rochester, Minnesota, was Phil Shaw, an Assemblies of God pastor who watched my highly publicized arrival at prison on television. Phil and I had never before met, but he wrote to me, kindly and compassionately, "Dear Jim, I am a brother in the Lord. How can I help you?" He went on to offer his assistance to my family in any way, whenever they came to visit me at the prison. One night, in desperation, I called Pastor Shaw.

To my surprise, I found him to be soft-spoken, articulate, and most of all, extremely humble and kind. That call began a friendship that continues to this day. Throughout my years of incarceration at Rochester, Phil visited nearly every week. Sometimes, we talked about the Bible; sometimes we talked about events that I had experienced; many times, we hardly talked at all. The wise pastor simply sat with me; he was *there*, that's what mattered. He didn't have to have answers or offer profound advice. The fact that he cared enough about me to be there helped pull me through one of the darkest periods of my life.

Comforting those who are in prison or who are sick or in the hospital is not just the responsibility of pastors. It is incumbent upon all of us who claim to be followers of Jesus. One of the last parables Jesus told His disciples before He went to the cross was about the sheep and the goats (Matt. 25:31–46). It is a poignant story, telling how the Lord will separate those who will inherit His kingdom from those who won't. Interestingly, those whom Jesus said will be rewarded seem to be almost unaware that their acts of kindness in His name have been noticed by the King.

> Then the King will say to those on His right hand, "Come, you blessed of My father, inherit the kingdom prepared for you from the foundation of the world: for I was hungry and you gave Me food; I was thirsty and you gave Me drink; I was a stranger and you took Me in; I was naked and you clothed Me; I was sick and you visited Me; I was in prison and you came to Me."

> Then the righteous will answer Him, saying, "Lord, when did we see You hungry and feed You, or thirsty and give You drink? When did we see You a stranger and take You in, or naked and clothe You? Or when did we see You sick, or in prison, and come to You?" (Matt. 25:34–39 NKJV)

Jesus' answer is both poignant and surprising. He said, "Inasmuch as you did it to one of the least of these My brethren, you did it to Me" (Matt. 25:40 NKJV). This is the standard by which the Christian community must live, and it is also the standard by which we will be judged.

Paul said in Romans 12:15 that we are to "rejoice with those who rejoice, and weep with those who weep" (NKJV). We are family. To the Corinthians, Paul wrote, "And if one member [of the body] suffers, all the members suffer with it; or if one member is honored, all the members rejoice with it" (1 Cor. 12:26 NKJV). In other words, our pains should be divided and our joys should be multiplied by the community of believers.

We understand how this works. Have you ever hit your thumb with a hammer? As pain shoots through that thumb and up through the arm, most of us will grab the thumb, shake our hand violently, stomp our feet, yell, or respond in some other physical way. Why does our body react like that? Because the body is diffusing the pain. If the thumb had to bear alone the full impact of the hammer blow, the pain would be horrendous. But if the other hand can grab that thumb, or you can bite your lip, or in some other fashion distribute some pain, the nerves spread that pain around. As you do so, the body divides the pain so that one member doesn't have to bear it alone.

Paul said that the body of Christ is like that. The church is the place where we say, "How are you doing?" and we mean it from the depths of our hearts. And when we say, "How are you doing?" we are giving the other person the right to break down and lay his or her head on our shoulder, and say, "I am not doing so well; I need help." The church is a place where we are to weep with those who weep. The church is also the place where we can seek out care or comfort if we are the ones in need.

A PLACE OF RESTORATION

The Christian community must also be a place where broken people can find the help and spiritual safety required to put their lives back together—a true sanctuary, a refuge. In Galatians 6:1, Paul said, "Dear brothers, if a Christian is overcome by some sin, you who are godly should gently and humbly help him back onto the right path, remembering that next time it might be one of you who is in the wrong" (TLB).

A young man named Jason Funk, a streetwise, hardened drug addict and alcoholic, became a Christian through the ministry of the Dream Center and came to live with us there. He entered the discipleship training program under the direction of Dominic and Debbie Garcetta, to learn how to live the Christian life and was doing quite well, staying away from drugs, studying the Bible, and helping others find the freedom in Christ that he had found.

One day, Jason was on an outreach mission in L.A., along with a busload of other young men and women from the Dream Center. Somehow Jason and a team of Christian workers from out of town became separated from the others, and at the end of the day, they all were late for the bus. Because the Dream Center deals with many types of former addicts and other aberrant behavior patterns, the rules are extremely strict. It is an iron-clad, "zero tolerance" policy: Anyone who violates a rule is asked to leave the Center for six months, until he or she is willing to live within the strict boundaries.

Because Jason had missed the bus returning to the Dream Center, the rules required that he be ejected from the discipleship program and asked to leave the Dream Center. When my staff and I heard the news, we were appalled. Here was a young man who had been delivered from a horrendous drug addiction, had started a new life with Christ, was doing his best to serve the Lord, and because he had missed the bus, we were going to toss him back out on the streets! It made no sense to me.

Certainly, there is a need for high standards within the Christian community. One of the reasons our Christian community functioned so well in Jesup prison, for instance, was because of the rules and boundaries that governed our lives. We had specific times when we were to get up and go to work, times for recreational activities, times that we could use for personal Bible study, and times when we were permitted to gather in groups. Outside of prison, rules, boundaries, and discipline must be established for any Christian community to function properly. People living together in close proximity cannot simply do whatever they please, whenever the "spirit" moves them.

I respected our need for rules at the Dream Center, especially when dealing with former addicts, but in this particular case, I could not see Jesus tossing Jason back to the streets, to be immediately immersed in his old lifestyle of drugs and violence. My staff and I flew into action. Armando and some of the other guys found Jason, his belongings packed in a knapsack, ready to return to the streets. They brought Jason to the place where Lori and I were living. Dominic was out of town, so we tried to talk Jason into staying until we could address the situation with Dominic.

Jason was understandably angry, hurt, and disillusioned. To him, the one place he had found love and acceptance had turned against him. Our staff members Howard and Leanne Bailey tried to convince him otherwise. While Lori and I raced around with tears in our eyes, trying to find people who could overturn Jason's expulsion from the program, Howard and Leanne enveloped Jason in the love of Jesus. They literally washed his feet, as a gesture of Christ's love to him.

Eventually, we were able to find Dominic and save Jason from being turned back to the streets, but I am convinced that the devil's agents were lurking at the door, waiting for an opportunity to lure the young man back into a life of drugs and debauchery. It was only through the efforts of the body of Christ, leaving the fold and going out after the one "lost sheep" to bring him back and to restore him, that Jason was not lost forever. While to some people, the body of Christ's involvement in this instance might seem trivial, to Jason it was a lifesaver. Lori and I had the privilege of attending Jason Funk's graduation from the discipleship program at the Dream Center. He was one of five who made it through the rigorous training program. Today, Jason is still serving God and helping others find Christ and get free from drugs.

Help Them Up!

However far a brother or sister falls, Paul said that our mission is to set about the purpose of getting him or her back to the place from which they fell. The apostle Paul did not prescribe putting them on probation, nor does he suggest bringing them back partially or conditionally, for a trial run. He said our goal should be to restore the fallen brother or sister in a spirit of meekness, considering ourselves, lest we also be tempted. What he was saying was, Pick them up and do for that erring brother or sister the same thing you would want them to do for you, if you ever are the one who has fallen.

Skeptics may say, "Oh, Jim Bakker is just pushing restoration because his own 'fall from grace' was so widely publicized, and now he is pandering after the Christian community to promote him to the position he once held."

My position is not important to me, but everywhere I go, I meet hurting people who need help. Bill Wilson said that when you lose your own dream, the key to regaining spiritual health is to help other people fulfill their dreams. That's what I want to do.

Yes, I do have a heart for restoration of members of the Christian community who have fallen in battle, well-meaning men and women who have gotten discouraged or disillusioned in their faith. I hurt for those pastors and pastors' wives who, because of some sin or failure in their personal lives, have been cast off, as though they no longer had any value to the body of Christ. I know what it feels like to be regarded as a pariah, to feel disqualified for service, after attempting to serve the Lord all my life. I also know how easily good men and women of God can get burned out trying to do the work of the Lord, trying to meet the needs of their spouses and families, and still trying to function in our hectic, fast-paced society.

But I am not a proponent of restoration so people will applaud me; I am passionate about the reclamation of Christian brothers and sisters because I believe we have direct orders from God to do so. It is not God's plan to condemn His people to the junk heap. If someone chooses to live in open rebellion against God, that is a different case, but when a brother or sister falls and makes a mess of things, it is our spiritual responsibility to help them as much as we can to pick up the pieces and put their lives back together.

Moreover, it is not a coincidence that Paul moves from restoration to the subject of bearing one another's burdens. Look at his profound statement: "Bear one another's burdens, and so fulfill the law of Christ" (Gal. 6:2 NKJV). If the law of Christ is love, we must show that love by helping to ease the load from the shoulders of our brothers and sisters. Certainly, part of our burden bearing is to help meet the practical needs of our brothers and sisters. But Paul is talking about even something beyond that.

The word-picture he uses—bearing one another's burdens—is that of the shepherd bearing on his shoulders the lamb that was lost. Isaiah the prophet used a similar idea when he painted the word picture of the Suffering Servant, "Surely He has borne our griefs / And carried our sorrows; / Yet we esteemed Him stricken, / Smitten by God, and afflicted. / But He was wounded for our transgressions, / He was bruised for our iniquities; / The chastisement for our peace was upon Him, / And by His stripes we are healed" (Isa. 53:4–5 NKJV).

James, the brother of Jesus, put it this way: "Brethren, if anyone among you wanders from the truth, and someone turns him back, let him know that he who turns a sinner from the error of his way will save a soul from death and cover a multitude of sins" (James 5:19–20 NKJV). Here again is a "spiritual safety net" that God gives to us through the community of believers. We can help keep each other on track. Part of bearing one another's burdens involves being willing to confront a brother or sister in love and help them see that they are straying from the truth. Of course, the flip side of that coin is that we must be willing to receive a brother or sister when they approach us about an area where we have gotten off course. I'm not talking about spiritual nitpicking; I'm talking about becoming the body of Christ in reality rather than simply in sermons and songs.

WHERE CAN I FIND SUCH A COMMUNITY?

Unfortunately, we will never find a local church that is doing these things perfectly or completely. Charles Heimsath wryly commented, "The chief trouble with the church is that you and I are in it."[2] And we keep messing it up! But I am not trying to mess it up. I am trying to do my best to serve God and to serve my brothers and sisters. That is most likely your desire as well.

Our realistic goal, then, when we are searching for a local community of believers, should be to find a group with whom we are willing to join our imperfections to theirs. In other words, the *perfect* church does not exist this side of heaven, so seek out the best *imperfect* church that you can find and commit your imperfections to their imperfections and together you can commit yourselves to the purpose of Christ Jesus, who will one day present to Himself a glorious church not having spot, or wrinkle or any such thing, but that she should be holy without blemish (Eph. 5:27).

Maybe what you are expecting is unrealistic, and you aren't going to find a group that is doing any better than the group to which you currently belong. Perhaps, after you have trekked around your circuit of churches, the best you will find is a group of people who are trying their best to serve God and yet are still falling short. (We all fall short, remember?) Maybe you can find a group that recognizes they are not a perfect church, but they are a good group of people, and you can say, "I am going to put down some roots here. I am going to dig in and get involved in the community of believers here. They are trying to do something significant for God, and I want to help; I want to be a part of it."

C. S. Lewis, generally regarded as one of the greatest Christian writers of the twentieth century, reflected on his negative first impressions of the Christian community:

> When I first became a Christian about fourteen years ago, I thought that I could do it on my own. I thought that I could retire to my rooms and read my theology and I wouldn't go to the churches, and I wouldn't go to the gospel halls, because I knew those people. I disliked very much their hymns. I considered their hymns to be fifth rate poems set to sixth rate music. But as I went on trying to make it alone, I saw the merit of the church. I came up against different people of quite different outlooks, different people of different education, and even in the midst of hypocrites, finally, gradually, my conceit began peeling off. I realized that the hymns which were just sixth rate music, yes, were nevertheless being sung with devotion and benefit by an old saint in elastic side boots in the opposite pew, and finally, I realized that I wasn't even fit to clean those boots.[3]

"Join the church," Lewis said. "It will get you out of your solitary conceit."

WE NEED EACH OTHER

The truth is, God does not intend for us to live our spiritual lives in "solitary conceit," as Lewis put it. We need each other, and we need to be interacting with each other closely enough that we can impact each other's lives. We are not meant to be "spiritual butterflies," flitting from place to place with no roots or no accountability.

In his marvelous book *What You Need to Know About the Church*, Max Anders pointed out the "one another" passages in the New Testament. Look at this list, and honestly ask yourself if you can do these things while floating from place to place, participating simply as a spectator.

> Be kindly affectionate to one another . . . giving preference to one another. (Rom. 12:10)
>
> Be of the same mind toward one another. (Rom. 12:16)
>
> Let us not judge one another. (Rom.14:13)
>
> Build up one another. (Rom. 14:19 NASB)
>
> Be of the same mind with one another. (Rom. 15:5 NASB)
>
> Accept one another. (Rom. 15:7 NIV)
>
> Admonish one another. (Rom. 15:14)
>
> Have the same care for one another. (1 Cor. 12:25)
>
> Serve one another. (Gal. 5:13)
>
> Show forbearance to one another in love. (Eph. 4:2 NASB)
>
> Be kind to one another, tenderhearted, forgiving one another, just as God in Christ forgave you. (Eph. 4:32)
>
> Be subject to one another. (Eph. 5:21NASB)[4]

Do you notice the emphasis on taking care of each other, humbling ourselves before each other, and regarding others more highly than we regard ourselves? Here are some more "one anothers" to contemplate:

> Be hospitable to one another. (1 Peter 4:9)
>
> Serve one another. (1 Peter 4:10 NRSV)

Clothe yourselves with humility toward one another. (1 Peter 5:5 NASB)

Love one another. (1 John 3:11)

Regard one another as more important [than yourself]. (Phil. 2:3 NASB)

Bear with one another, and forgive one another. (Col. 3:13)

Comfort one another. (1 Thess. 4:18)

Encourage one another and build up one another. (1 Thess. 5:11)

Live in peace with one another. (1 Thess. 5:13 NASB)

Seek after that which is good for one another. (1 Thess. 5:15 NASB)

Encourage one another. (Heb. 3:13)

Confess your sins to one another, and pray for one another, so that you may be healed. (James 5:16 NASB)[5]

"Wait a minute, James!" someone might protest. "I confess my sins to God. He forgives me, and my sins are washed away. That's enough isn't it? I know I am on my way to heaven, so what else matters?"

If he were alive today, James might say, "I am not talking about the certainty of your future in heaven; I am talking about your life here on earth. Sure, if you have honestly confessed your sins and repented over them, you are forgiven, but you are not healed."

I am convinced that many Christian people are forgiven of their sins, but they have never been healed of that sin's impact in their lives. Why? Because they have never gotten close enough to a group of fellow believers with whom they could be absolutely honest—honest enough to confess their sins to their brothers or sisters in the Lord. They are clean, but they are not whole; forgiven, but not healed. They are still stumbling through life as cripples because they have not found a brother or sister upon whom they could lean long enough to get well.

As the Christian community, we must "be there" for each other. We must be ready to accept another believer when he or she has failed or fallen. And we must be willing to humbly confess our own failures, mistakes, and sins.

Try to find a spiritually mature Christian to whom you can be accountable, in whom you can confide, someone to whom you can confess your sins. Understand that you are not confessing your sins to find eternal, cleansing forgiveness. Only God can grant that, but you are confessing your sins to experience the inner healing that takes place as you bare your soul before another believer. And that sort of honest confession brings freedom, forgiveness, and healing to our hearts and minds, in this life, here and now.

In most cases, you won't experience such times of deep, intimate confession during a public worship time or in a Sunday school class. You need a more private atmosphere, somewhere that you can dare to be vulnerable without fear of what you confess coming back to haunt you. I am not about to do that on Sunday morning, during most church services. But I have some brothers I can talk to, brothers who would go to hell and back for me, who would stand by me even if the whole world turned its back on me.

I experienced something of that kind of brotherly concern when I lost Heritage USA in 1987 and found myself in prison facing forty-five years, practically a life sentence for me. Yet God did not leave me without a witness. He placed people in my life, even in prison, with whom I could be honest—people with the courage to say, "I am going to hold you accountable; I don't condone your sin, that is not right; I expect more of you, but I don't think less of you." That is the community of believers caring for and ministering to one another.

THE SPIRIT OF COMMUNITY

I'VE NEVER BEEN VERY good at sports, although once, when I first found myself in prison, a group of Colombian inmates "drafted" me to play on their soccer team. Later on during my incarceration, I was thrilled when one of my fellow inmates taught me how to catch a baseball.

Ironically, even though I have never been athletically inclined myself, I have enjoyed the friendship of some exceptional athletes. For instance, one of my dear friends is a former NFL superstar who wears a Super Bowl ring. For years, Reggie White led the Green Bay Packers defensive unit in one bone-jarring tackle after another.

A bright, articulate, gentle giant of a man, it must have been frustrating at times for a person with Reggie White's ability to simply knock big men out of the way so he and his teammates could crash through a group of offensive linemen and slam the opposing team's quarterback to the turf. Why would a man of Reggie's caliber be willing to train and discipline his body, mind, and spirit, year after year in such a grueling profession and in such a drudgery-filled position?

Simply this: He was not playing for Reggie White; he was part of a team; he was playing for the Green Bay Packers. Reggie understood that his position was a grunt job; as a defensive lineman, his was not the glamour role of a quarterback or a wide receiver or a running back. Many fans barely noticed that Reggie was on the field, until he burst through the line and gave chase to a wide-eyed quarterback. Reggie knew that he was not the guy who would most likely receive all the awards (although he has received many throughout his career).

No, Reggie White gave everything he had for the good of the team. If it meant pumping iron in the weight room until every muscle in his body screamed for mercy, Reggie did it. If it meant regular, intense physical workouts to keep his body in shape, Reggie did it. If it meant plugging up a hole and hitting a 250-pound fullback head-on, Reggie did it. If it meant ignoring the pain and going to work on a day when he would rather have watched from the sidelines, Reggie gave it his best shot. Why? Because that was the best way Reggie White could help his team.

"Team spirit" can inspire people to do things that they would not ordinarily be prepared to do on their own—things that they might not be willing or able to do if they were operating solely in their own selfish interests.

We see something similar to team spirit in the military corps. One of the terms that is bandied about quite a bit in the armed services is *esprit de corp*, a French term that means "the spirit of a body." The military teaches that individuals can accomplish great feats on their own, but when individuals become part of a group, a body, they can accomplish far more and work more efficiently and effectively than ever before.

It's the old "strength in numbers" concept. Remember the twig that could easily be broken by itself? But if you put that same twig alongside ten or fifteen other twigs—any of which could easily be snapped, cracked, or otherwise destroyed individually—the bundle becomes a strong unit that is not easily broken.

These concepts of unselfish sacrifice and cohesive cooperation are readily apparent in the apostle Paul's discussion of the church as the body of Christ in 1 Corinthians, chapter twelve.

Paul was saying, "Individual Christians can do certain 'Christian' activities on their own; operating unilaterally, they can accomplish much; but when they are involved within the body of Christ, they can do so much more!"

On the other hand, if believers are not involved with the body of Christ, they may be sincere Christians, but they will be lacking in certain areas of their lives. They will be especially deficient in motivation in their Christian journey. Without the support and encouragement of the Christian community, it is tempting to become complacent or lukewarm in our walk with the

Lord, perhaps becoming even callous and cold. God intends for His people to interact as a family, the body of Christ, the community of believers.

DEVELOPING TEAM SPIRIT WITHIN THE BODY

If we truly believe that such body life is important, it raises some questions: How can we develop "team spirit" in the family of God? How can we express it toward each other and demonstrate it to the world? How can we pass it on to others?

Having recently lived in three well-functioning Christian communities—in prison at Jesup, Georgia; at the Dream Center in Los Angeles; and at Morning House in Charlotte—I believe I have gleaned a few insights.

1. WE ARE FAMILY

First, we can develop team spirit in the church by emphasizing our common experience.

In the days ahead, Christians may be forced together by economic circumstances or practical, basic survival needs. If the stock market crashes, or if the world financial markets tumble, millions of people will lose their life savings; others may lose their jobs or their homes. The body of Christ will have no other choice but to help each other in practical ways, possibly even providing basic needs such as food, clothing, and shelter, not just for the "homeless people," or those we have traditionally regarded as destitute, but for some people who formerly "had it all."

Right now, before more calamities strike, we have the opportunity to learn how to cooperate as a community of believers, and one of the easiest ways to do so is to emphasize the things we have in common with each other.

Some people love to emphasize their differences. They tend to talk more about what they disagree over with their fellow "family-members" than the truths they hold in common. They are always looking to pick a fight, trying to instigate some sort of division in the body. After talking to them, you feel as though somebody poured dirt on you. Such flagrant divisiveness is an extremely dangerous habit. If you focus on your differences with someone, it won't be long before your conversation turns sour and negative. Little good will come out of it, and usually quite a lot of evil, destructive, and counterproductive things will be said, conversations that will depress you and grieve the Holy Spirit.

Besides robbing us spiritually, such negative notions are so unnecessary! As Christians, regardless of our denominational leanings, we have far more beliefs and practices in common than points over which we differ. Another part of the body may not say or do things just the way we do, but they are still part of the same body of Christ.

Anyone who has been genuinely born again has God working in his or her life. He may be operating in each of us in a wide variety of ways, but He's still working. Paul reminded the Corinthians, "And there are varieties of effects, but the same God who works all things in all persons" (1 Cor. 12:6 NASB). That's why we need to embrace our commonality with other believers. In truth, we probably have more in common with a believer we do not know than we do with unbelievers to whom we are closely related.

Like many Christians, I have some unsaved loved ones in my extended family. Consequently, I have more in common with you, even though I may not know you personally, than I do with some of my relatives whom I know intimately, but who are not Christians. They are part of my family, but they are not yet part of God's family.

Have you ever been to a family gathering where most of the people are not Christians, where most of your relatives are not interested in becoming Christians, and where most of the conversation focuses on topics of little eternal value? You feel like a square peg in a round hole, with hardly anything to talk about! On the other hand, it's a glorious thing to walk into a room filled with believers and to be able to talk about Jesus. As Christians—as part of the body of Christ—we can share our testimonies, our faith, our trials, our failures and discouragements as well as our victories.

Most of all, we share the Lordship of Christ. Again, Paul wrote, "Therefore I make known to you, that no one speaking by the Spirit of God says, 'Jesus is accursed'; and no one can say, 'Jesus is Lord,' except by the Holy Spirit. Now there are varieties of gifts, but the same Spirit. And there are varieties of ministries, and the same Lord" (1 Cor. 12:3–5 NASB).

2. JUST A LITTLE RESPECT

Another way we can demonstrate our team spirit is by showing respect for every member of the body, despite the person's financial status, intelligence, physical appearance, or other external factors. Our attitude ought to be, "If Jesus can accept him, so can I."

The truth is, some of the people we might ignore or consider to be insignificant, may, in fact, be much more important in God's overall plan than we are. The apostle Paul pointed out:

> But now there are many members, but one body. And the eye cannot say to the hand, "I have no need of you"; or again the head to the feet, "I have no need of you." On the contrary, it is much truer that the members of the body which seem to be weaker are necessary; and those members of the body, which we deem less honorable, on these we bestow more abundant honor. (1 Cor. 12:20–23 NASB)

Paul suggested that those parts of our body that are less visible may be more vital. The parts of the body that nobody notices may be more important than the parts that everybody sees, hears, and knows about. For instance, in every church, there are people who pray. No, I'm not talking about people who simply mouth some spiritual requests by rote. I mean people who really pray, who take prayer seriously, who pray fervently, who touch God with their prayers. Often, these prayer warriors are not the people we see on the church platform, they are not the performers, and often they are not the individuals who are elected to offices. They may be unknown to the masses in the Christian community, but God knows their names. And I am convinced that in heaven, they are going to have a great reward.

One of the most curious spiritual enigmas in recent church history has been the phenomenal impact of Promise Keepers (PK), the ministry geared toward helping men live out their commitments to the Lord and to their families. The question was asked time and again, "What is Promise Keepers doing that is making it so successful, when so many other men's ministries have remained mediocre at best?"

The answer was not the great music, preaching, or stadium events sponsored by PK. The secret to Promise Keepers' success was that at every stadium conference, tucked away in the bowels of the huge sports complexes, a group of men and women spent hours in prayer before, during, and after the conferences. Their slogan was, "If it is going to happen out in the stadium, it must happen here in the prayer room first."

That unknown group of men and women was never seen by the masses of men who attended PK conferences. They were rarely interviewed by members of the press (and when they were, they were usually characterized as spiritual goofs); they received few accolades for a job well done. But in heaven, I believe Jesus was pleased with their efforts. And one day, He will reward them.

For instance, at the Dream Center, I met Billy Soto, a stocky fellow with a big smile and even bigger faith. Almost single-handedly, Billy developed a ministry to feed people who live under the bridges and underpasses in the Los Angeles underbelly. With no financial support and no fanfare, each week he gathered food from the Dream Center and took it to the homeless. Billy had a special place in his heart for people who were dying of AIDS. He spent many hours each week feeding and caring for them and expressing Christ's love to them in practical, tangible ways, helping many to put their trust in Jesus.

Billy sometimes witnessed the death of one of the homeless people to whom he was ministering or stood by the side of an AIDS victim until he or she gasped a final breath. Nobody died alone when Billy was anywhere nearby. Nor did anyone die in vain. Billy used every death as an opportunity to tell other homeless people about Jesus and to encourage AIDS victims, who had little hope of being healed in this life, that they could find eternal life in Christ. While it is unlikely that the world will ever recognize Billy's face, he is well known in heaven.

Plenty of other nondescript positions in the body of Christ are vital to the community, yet they receive little public credit. The custodians who clean the church buildings, the teenagers who visit the widows, the men and women who prepare meals for the homeless people, the self-effacing servants who tend to the babies in the church nursery so the dog-tired parents can enjoy a service unencumbered by diapers, baby bottles, or teething rings—the list could go on and on. And what about the person who clears a path to the church on an icy, cold, snowy morning? Most people in the church don't even think about it as they pull into the church parking lot. But some body member had to get out of bed in the middle of the night and fight through the elements so the rest of the body could get to church in time for the service.

In the days ahead, we will have an even greater need for servant-hearted Christians who will pitch in wherever they see a need. If the commode needs fixing, you don't make a big deal about it or announce it in the next newsletter; you just fix it. If somebody needs food, or a place to sleep, you don't flaunt your willingness to help, you just do it.

So What If You're Up Front?

While Paul clearly stated that there are parts of the body that are less visible, but equally important, he also implied that the converse is true—that there are some members of the body who are more visible than others, but no more important. As I have mentioned, the day of the Christian superstar is over, but that does not mean we will be devoid of leaders. The leadership may just come from circles that we are unaccustomed to seeing.

If we are going to function as the body of Christ, without jealousy or strife, we need to recognize that of course there will be people who get more recognition, more notice, more attention. Certainly, pastors, evangelists, television personalities, musicians, political and business leaders, Christian sports figures, and others in the public eye may get more attention, but that does not mean they are more important. We must understand that the inconspicuous person over in the corner of the community who just does his or her job, never making much noise or getting much attention—that person is just as vital to the overall functioning of the body!

We are not in a popularity contest in the body of Christ. This isn't a "Can you top this?" situation. We are the body of Christ, and every person in the body has equal value, although not necessarily equal visibility or responsibility.

No, not every person will preach, play the piano, teach a class, sing in a choir, or be a guest on a Christian television program, but every one is important, and we need to recognize that. If you are one of those less noticed parts, you need to understand that, too! You need to know that you are valuable to God and that it matters to Him that you render your service effectively and with an attitude of love and gratitude to the Lord.

Regardless of our position in the body, we must have mutual respect, one person for the other. Again, you may not find that attitude in many other aspects of society, but if we are to be a New Testament body, we cannot live without it.

KEEPING IT GOING

How can we pass on this concept of Christian community to others? We must wage war against ignorance and prolonged spiritual immaturity in the body. Paul began his discussion of the body by saying, "Now concerning spiritual gifts, brethren, I do not want you to be unaware" (1 Cor. 12:1 NASB).

Spiritual ignorance is rampant in the church. We have so little knowledge of how God operates, how God has done things in the past, or what He wants to do now. Many Christians have no idea of how the community of believers is to function. By and large, the world looks at the church as a social club, an optional association that one can take or leave as we go through life. And, sadly, we as Christians have done a poor job of informing them otherwise—sometimes because we also see the church as the world does.

When you talk to most people about the church, they immediately begin talking about denominations, buildings, buses, or television evangelists. Either that, or they start comparing pastors or programs. We need to understand that the church isn't somewhere we go, it is something we are!

We need to understand that our main purpose is to love Jesus and to love each other. That is what the apostle Paul explained when he encouraged us to "earnestly desire the greater gifts. And I show you a still more excellent way" (1 Cor. 12:31 NASB). Paul then went on to describe true love in what is often referred to as the "Love Chapter," 1 Corinthians 13.

We need to establish and maintain a loving, concerned atmosphere within the Christian community, so that when people brush shoulders with us, they will sense the love of Christ. By this I mean showing genuine interest in people—caring—and being nothing less than what Jesus wants us to be. Jesus said, "By this all men will know that you are My disciples, if you have love for one another" (John 13:35 NASB).

This sort of love is motivating; it produces and demonstrates a team spirit that pulls us together, gets us going, and will cause us to do greater things together than we ever could accomplish as individual Christians.

Sure, you could do your own thing, and I could do mine, but that is not how God intended for the community of believers to function. When you operate in the Spirit, using the gifts, talents, abilities, and resources that God has given you for His glory, you will find yourself involved in something infinitely bigger than yourself. It gives you a sense that you are contributing, that you are making a difference, that you are a part of all that Jesus is doing in the world!

12

It's a Family Affair

GROWING UP IN MICHIGAN, I attended church services faithfully with my family. Most any time the church doors were open, the Bakkers were there. Every so often, the congregation of my local church observed what we called "Communion Sunday," a day on which the Lord's Supper was served at the end of the service. Some churches in our area celebrated communion services once a month; some participated in the sacrament during every service. Our congregation included communion in our regular Sunday worship service at least once per month.

As a youth, I participated in hundreds of "communion services," yet I am now convinced that not only did I have little understanding of the sacrament, but few others in our congregation—even people who had attended church services for years—truly understood the value and the importance of celebrating communion together.

Every so often, I'd walk into our church and there would be a large wooden table with a white cloth on it at the front of the church. Nobody ever knew exactly why they put a white cloth over the communion elements, except for the fact that we had always done it that way.

All we really knew for sure about Communion Sunday was that church seemed to last longer that morning. We always hoped that the preacher would preach a shorter message on Communion Sunday—but he never did.

WHAT IS COMMUNION ALL ABOUT?

Interestingly, the word *communion* comes from the same Greek word *koinonia* that we often translate as "fellowship." So it would be perfectly acceptable for a church to call itself the "Christian Communion Center," since that is what the church is supposed to be. Unfortunately, fellowship sometimes breaks down; occasionally mutiny breaks out among the members, and communion becomes confusion.

That is what was happening at the church in Corinth, so the apostle Paul sent a letter of correction concerning this matter and numerous other issues that had surfaced in the Corinthian church:

> Now in giving these instructions I do not praise you, since you come together not for the better but for the worse. For first of all, when you come together as a church, I hear that there are divisions among you, and in part I believe it. For there must also be factions among you, that those who are approved may be recognized among you. Therefore when you come together in one place, it is not to eat the Lord's Supper. For in eating, each one takes his own supper ahead of others; and one is hungry and another is drunk. What! Do you not have houses to eat and drink in? Or do you despise the church of God and shame those who have nothing? What shall I say to you? Shall I praise you in this? I do not praise you. (1 Cor. 11:17–22 NKJV)

Whew! Do you get the impression that the apostle was not pleased with the community of believers in Corinth?

WHAT WAS GOING ON HERE?

First of all, we must remember that these Corinthian Christians came out of extremely pagan backgrounds. Many of the early Christians in Corinth had formerly worshiped idols. Often, in their days before meeting Christ, they would regularly hold huge feasts that were associated with their worship of idols. Not surprisingly, when the Corinthians became Christians, they assimilated some of their heathen practices into their ideas of Christianity.

They said, "Hey, this is great! We can get together and have a big party, and then celebrate communion at the end. It will be great!" So that's what they did.

Now, the early Christians already had a celebration they called the "love feast" (the *agape*), a ceremony similar to what we call our modern-day communion services. So the Corinthians simply combined the two. They had a big, carry-in fellowship dinner, with a special time of communion at the close of the meal.

If there is one thing that most Christians can agree on, it is the fact that we do like to fellowship! As the saying goes, we don't drink, smoke, or chew, we just sit around and fellowship, which usually involves food. I think some Christians think that they won't be able to get into heaven without a covered dish!

The theory is that since we don't indulge in those other vices, we have to do something to keep ourselves busy long enough to allow the person next to us to get a word in edgewise, so we eat and we drink a lot of coffee. You've probably noticed that many Christians are either overweight or real jumpy, and many are both!

Unquestionably, fellowship dinners can be fun, and sometimes they can even be funny. For instance, have you ever noticed that the menu is almost always the same? (Don't misunderstand, I'm very grateful for the food, but it seems that we could use a bit of creativity in this area!) I get around to a wide variety of churches, and I have enjoyed many different kinds of worship styles, different styles of preaching, various types of worship centers, new and unusual types of musical expressions, and I've even encountered various theologies and opinions about the Second Coming. But no matter where I go, when it comes to church fellowship dinners, there is always that same *meat loaf!* You know the one—nobody knows what's in it, and nobody is asking, as long as there is enough ketchup to go around! Please don't get me wrong. I love church dinners. In fact, when I was younger, I never missed a fellowship dinner at our church. It was always a perfect opportunity to pig out and not get punished by my parents—sort of "gorging for God"!

Obviously, I'm being facetious about this aspect of fellowship, but something like that was happening in Corinth. They were turning their fellowship into a fiasco! When the apostle Paul wrote to them about the matter, he basically said, "You folks better straighten up!"

Mainly, they were allowing their fellowship to be fractured over foolishness. Paul pinned them to the wall over the issue of the divisions within the body. The word *divisions* comes from *schismate*, which is the Greek root word from which we get our word *schisms*, meaning "splits, sects, cliques, factions," and, some translations even say, "heresies." In the case of the Corinthian communion, Paul did not use the word to imply that they were teaching false doctrine, but that they were fostering a *party spirit*—a "we/they," or "us versus them" attitude.

No Love Lost with This Bunch

The "love feast" or the fellowship dinner was the perfect opportunity for those in the church who were prosperous to help their less fortunate brothers and sisters in a practical sort of way without making a big deal about it. They could do so quite easily and inconspicuously by simply coming in, putting their food on the table, and allowing anyone who was hungry to enjoy it. By the same token, the fellowship dinner was also an opportunity for some of the less fortunate brothers and sisters to have a decent meal.

Here was the church with a perfect opportunity to be the church, to put away class distinctions based on money, position, race, influence, power, and prestige. It was a time when the Christian community could come together as fellow believers under the banner of Jesus Christ, to celebrate His death and resurrection together as "family."

Unfortunately, the Corinthian Christians failed right at that crucial point. Two things happened for sure, and a third is implied.

1. *The rich folks fell into their own cliques.* They came with their fancy covered dishes, placed them on the table, and then gravitated toward their own little group. Their attitude was, "Hey, we brought the food; what's it to you where we sit?" Worse yet, they sometimes brought the food and then selfishly and greedily hoarded it for themselves and their friends, looking after their self-interests first. Sometimes, they wouldn't even wait to see who might have a need; they just started stuffing themselves!

Making matters worse still, some of them started drinking wine before, during, and after the meal, oftentimes ending up at the communion ceremony stone drunk! And all this was going on at a gathering of the church—before communion!

2. *The second issue that irritated the apostle Paul was that the poor among the congregation were standing around still hungry.* While the

wealthy filled their bellies, the less fortunate were left to watch and wait, hoping for a few scraps of leftovers.

3. *Many people were coming only for a big bash.* Paul implied in verse 34 that some of the Christians had come for a "pig-out party" in a spiritual environment. And the text seems to indicate that both the rich and poor people may have adopted this warped attitude toward communion. They were forgetting that their main reason for getting together was to worship the Lord Jesus Christ, to celebrate the Lord's Supper, to praise His name, and to be reminded once again of the price He had paid on Calvary with His body and His blood. They had lost sight of the fact that the sacrament of communion, as instituted by Jesus Himself at "the last supper" before He went to the cross, was an ideal time to thank Him for His sacrificial death, to worship and adore Him, and to fellowship together as His body, the community of believers.

WHAT ABOUT US?

Usually, most modern Christian communities don't have to deal with the pig-out problem, but we still have divisions and factions in the body that fracture and frustrate our fellowship.

What are some of those things that divide us? When do we pull away from each other? When do we allow ourselves to become isolated, cut off from the rest of the body?

I've discovered that there are certain circumstances and situations that the devil often attempts to use to divide us. This is not an exhaustive list, of course, but perhaps it will make you aware of how fragile our fellowship can be and how we need to learn to confess our sins and failures and to forgive each other from our hearts.

1. A Pain That a Pill Won't Help

First, when you are going through sickness, suffering, or satanic attack, it is easy to become cut off from the fellowship.

Given enough pain, most of us will want to be alone. Sometimes it is physical pain, but often it is emotional pain that causes us to retreat into a shell. Sometimes you feel so bruised, beaten, and battered that you want to say, "Aw, who needs the church?"

Do you remember Job and his circumstances? The devil was doing a heavy number on Job—all apparently with the Lord's permission! There was Job with the dreaded disease of boils all over his body, and Scripture calls attention to the fact that he sat "alone" in his misery (Job 2:7–8). Unfortunately, his friends didn't help much, coming around to condemn him. His wife was not much better, whining in an accusatory voice, "Job, why don't you just curse God and die?"

With friends and family members like that, who needs enemies?

Sadly, just when we need a word of encouragement, our friends and family members sometimes let us down. David Wilkerson, the powerfully anointed preacher of *The Cross and the Switchblade* fame, experienced something similar when his wife contracted a serious disease. David later stated publicly that he had received more than 17,000 letters, the tenor of many telling him that if he had just had more faith, his dear wife could be healed. This was a man whose faith in God took him to the New York City ghettos to tell street gang members about Jesus, and 17,000 members of the body of Christ had the audacity to rebuke him for a lack of faith? What gall!

When somebody is sick, or depressed, or suffering, that is not the time to put them down for not being "spiritual" enough. That's the time to reach out in love and compassion, with understanding, tact, and spiritual discernment. That's the time to throw an arm around that person and say, "Come on, you're my brother and I love you. Don't give up. Don't give in; don't fall away from the fellowship of believers. You can make it, and I'm going to help you! I'll stand with you every step of the way."

2. Spiritual Burnout

A second way our fellowship is sometimes fractured is through sheer fatigue.

Spiritual burnout is probably the number one reason why good men and women drop out of a fellowship. I'm certain it is one of the main reasons why so many pastors are getting out, falling out, or being kicked out of the ministry nowadays. We allow our pastors to work themselves into a frenzy, burning the candle at both ends, while it seems that someone else is burning it in the middle.

But pastors aren't the only members of the body who are experiencing spiritual burnout. A lot of Christians are finding themselves weary, dreary, tired, and spent. One guy told me, "I feel like I just don't have another drop of energy left to give to the Lord."

That man was not a pagan sinner. He was a devout, sincerely dedicated believer, but his spiritual vitality had been sapped. The word *weary* surfaced frequently in his conversation with me, and that word sums up how many Christians feel these days.

The great prophet Elijah experienced that sense of awful weariness. After his great spiritual victories, the prophet felt fatigued, famished, and finished. (You can read the account in 1 Kings 19.) Elijah became so depressed that he lamented, "God, take me home!"

Have you ever felt that way?

Yet, it is beautiful to see how the Lord lifted up Elijah and got him going again. The Lord told him that he was not alone, that there were at least seven thousand other men of God in the land. Then God gave Elijah a fresh vision for the work to be done, and, perhaps even more significantly, He gave the prophet a helper and a successor in the person of Elisha.

You may be feeling similar to Elijah, that you are right on the edge of giving up—giving up on the fellowship of believers, giving up on your family, giving up on your marriage or your business, giving up on yourself, or perhaps worst of all, giving up on God.

You don't need somebody badgering you, condemning you, or heaping a bunch of heavy do's and don'ts on you. You need somebody to pray with you and to help lift you up, not to push you down further. Please don't give up on the body of Christ. There really are people in the family who care, and they will care for you if you will just give them a chance.

3. Trouble on the Home Front

A third frequent cause of fellowship fractures is trouble at home, either in your marriage, or with your children.

Remember King David? After his affair with Bathsheba, he was a basket case (read Ps. 32). He was crippled by guilt, his energies were sapped, and he was totally ineffective as a spiritual leader.

If you read David's story carefully, you'll discover that after his sin, he spent an inordinate amount of time *alone*, removed from the fellowship of godly friends.

His family was a wreck, and he was wasting away. It wasn't until he repented of his sin that he was able to have genuine fellowship again with God and with God's people.

4. Friction in the Fellowship

A fourth cause of fractures in our fellowship is friction—between two or more individuals, or between two or more groups.

Friction may take various forms—personality clashes, disagreements, rumors, innuendos, gossip, personal offenses, and more—but the end result is the same: resentment and contention in the body of Christ. Often this sort of friction stems from situations where real, honest forgiveness has never been extended or received. The Scripture says, "A brother offended is harder to be won than a strong city, / And contentions are like the bars of a castle" (Prov. 18:19 NASB).

How easy it is for a person to break fellowship when he or she has been offended. But when a person chooses to walk away from the body of Christ, he or she chooses to live for the rest of his or her life behind big, ugly, hateful, rusty bars of contention.

You can go blind behind those bars—spiritually blind, that is. And you can get mighty bitter behind those bars.

A story is told of two unmarried sisters who had a big fight, so they stopped speaking to each other. They continued to live in the same house; they slept in the same bedroom, but neither one would break through those barriers that separated them. They lived for the remainder of their sad lives, pretending that the other sister did not exist.

Perhaps you think that's weird. But it is no more weird than this: You walk into a church and see someone in the family of God with whom you have had some sort of disagreement or by whom you have been offended somehow. But instead of facing that person, you turn your head and walk the other way. You won't even open your mouth to say hello. Or if you absolutely cannot avoid spending a few moments in the presence of that person, you make it obvious that it sure isn't your preference.

That is *weird!* That is warped.

And that is *sin!*

And it fractures our fellowship.

5. Sin Always Hurts the Body

A fifth cause of fractures in the fellowship is the tolerance of willful sin in your life.

You may say, "My sin is my business," and I would not disagree with you. But let me remind you that your sin will take you to hell if you don't repent, and, in the meantime, it severely damages people all around you.

Have you ever read the story of Achan in Joshua 7? When the Israelites launched their conquest of Canaan, one of the first places they took was the city of Jericho. No doubt, you are familiar with the story of the city walls tumbling down. Prior to the assault, Joshua, the leader of God's people, had declared that the spoils of the city were under a ban—nobody was to take anything; the spoils would belong to God (Josh. 6:18). "All the silver and gold, and vessels of bronze and iron, are consecrated to the LORD; they shall come into the treasury of the LORD" (v. 19 NKJV).

But when Achan found among the spoils a beautiful Babylonian garment, two hundred dollars' worth of silver, and a five-hundred-dollar wedge of gold, he couldn't resist. He took the items for himself and hid them in the ground beneath his tent.

No doubt, Achan must have thought, *What difference does it make if I compromise just a little? This is a perfectly good garment, and we have confiscated plenty of gold and silver. Nobody will miss this small amount, but it's a lot for somebody like me. My family could really use that silver and gold right now. Surely, God understands my need.*

Achan willfully chose to disobey God's clear commands.

When the Israelites went up to battle the small town of Ai, Joshua didn't even bother to send a large assault force. It was a sure victory. But because of Achan's disobedience, the Lord allowed Joshua's troops to be beaten. Achan's crime was brought to light, but not before thirty-six Israelites were slaughtered.

What difference did Achan's private sin make for the community of believers? It brought defeat to the family of God; it brought death to some of Achan's friends, as well as death to his own wife, children, and himself. And worst of all, it brought the name of the Lord into disrepute. All this and more can be traced back to one man's disobedience.

There is no such thing as a private sin. Your sin affects me; my sin affects you; and all sin in the body of Christ fractures our fellowship. In 1980, I willfully sinned sexually in what became—I'm sorry to say—possibly the most publicized moral failure since David and Bathsheba. Although I repented and sought forgiveness from all the appropriate parties, to this day, before I stand and speak to a congregation, I apologize for having hurt them and for the pain I brought to the body of Christ. I do not say these things with any self-effacing motivation, or any attempt to win over the audience by begging their forgiveness. I ask the forgiveness of the body of Christ because I recognize that my sin had repercussions that still ripple throughout the Christian community.

"I forgive you, Jim, but I gotta tell you, I hated you," said one man after I had spoken at his church. He's not alone. To this day, I meet people in churches who approach me and confess that they have hated me for fifteen years or more. I wish they'd learn that not everything that is true needs to be said, but I understand their need to say it! After all, my sin fractured our fellowship; it destroyed our communion together, and whether we like it or not, we are a family, and our spiritual communion with each other and before the Lord is a family affair.

THE DANGERS OF TAKING COMMUNION LIGHTLY

Maybe that's why the apostle Paul cautioned the Corinthian believers against partaking of the communion elements insincerely. The celebration of the Lord's Supper is a symbolic reminder of the price Jesus paid for the community of believers, and to take the elements casually, or with willful sin in our lives, is to mock the cross of Christ. After reminding the Corinthians of the meaning of the bread and the cup, Paul gave the early church a solemn warning:

> For as often as you eat this bread and drink this cup, you proclaim the Lord's death till He comes. Therefore whoever eats this bread or drinks this cup of the Lord in an unworthy manner will be guilty of the body and blood of the Lord. But let a man examine himself, and so let him eat of the bread and drink of the cup. For he who eats and drinks in an unworthy manner eats and drinks judgment to himself, not discerning the Lord's body. For this reason many are weak and sick among you, and many sleep. (1 Cor. 11:26–30 NKJV)

Clearly, Paul correlated a person's physical health with his or her appreciation of, respect for, and proper participation in the sacred things of God, not the least of which is the celebration of the Lord's Supper. Paul said that because they have not discerned the Lord's body, some people are physically weak and sick, and others have even died! I believe we can draw a similar spiritual conclusion today about those who speak the name of Jesus but have never truly understood, appreciated, and rightly participated in the body of Christ, the true Church. They have failed to discern the Lord's body, and the consequences have been devastating—both for them and for the rest of us in the Christian community.

So What Can We Do?

Is your fellowship fractured with the Lord? With your wife, husband, or children? With someone else in the body of Christ?

Please recognize the seriousness of such a condition. Paul said to "let a man examine himself," so you can properly participate in the believers' communion. We should pray with the psalmist, "Search me, O God, and know my heart; / Try me, and know my anxieties; / And see if there is any wicked way in me, / And lead me in the way everlasting" (Ps. 139:23–24 NKJV).

Have you been sick, suffering, or going through a satanic attack? Jesus Christ can bring you through, if you will trust Him.

Are you spiritually weary, tired, or burned out? Reconnecting with the body of Christ and sharing communion with fellow believers may be a step toward renewal and refreshment. Don't back away from the family; instead seek out somebody in the body that you trust, and say, "Would you pray for me? I've really been going through a tough time lately, and I need a fresh touch from God."

Is there trouble in your home? Trouble with your work, your spouse, your children, or your parents? If that trouble is your fault, you need to honestly repent of it right now and seek the forgiveness of those you have hurt.

Is there friction in your relationship with someone else in the body? Please, for your sake and for the sake of the entire body of Christ, don't ignore that fractured relationship. We need to be united in these crucial days. We don't have time for the harboring of grudges or petty resentments from the past. It is a day for coming clean, for seeking and extending forgiveness.

Jesus said, "If you bring your gift to the altar, and there remember that your brother has something against you, leave your gift there before the altar, and go your way. First be reconciled to your brother, and then come and offer your gift" (Matt. 5:23–24 NKJV). Clearly, we need to examine ourselves to see if our communion has been broken. If we discover that we have offended a brother or sister, we must go to that person, seeking forgiveness and reconciliation.

You may say, "What if I'm not sure? How will I know if I have offended a brother or sister?" Ask the Holy Spirit to convict you of sin, righteousness, and judgment. You may be surprised how quickly He answers that prayer. If He convicts you to seek out a brother or sister who has something against you, then obey His instructions.

To attempt to fake our communion without forgiveness and reconciliation where possible would be a farce and would be tantamount to crucifying Jesus afresh (1 Cor. 11:27).

"But the person I go to seeking reconciliation may not understand," you say.

That's their problem.

"They may not accept my apology . . ."

That's between them and God. You are to obey the voice of the Holy Spirit!

If you are living in willful sin, won't you please see that, like Achan of old, your "secret" sin is not just destroying you. It's tearing apart a lot of people who really love and care about you. Most of all, it is grieving the heart of God.

A word of caution: If the Lord has been speaking to you about one of these areas in which your fellowship with someone in the body has been fractured, and you have *not* yet responded in obedience and have not done what He has been prompting you to do, please, do not participate in the Lord's Supper. Simply put, don't take communion until you get things right with God. Otherwise, you will be eating and drinking judgment upon yourself (1 Cor. 11:27–29).

God takes this matter very seriously. It would be foolish enough to know that God is speaking to you and to ignore His voice, but do not make matters worse by making a mockery of the blood and body of Jesus Christ.

On the other hand, if your heart is clean before God, if you know that your sins are forgiven, if you are in good fellowship with His family, then rejoice and be glad. Celebrate the sacred time we have together, uniting our hearts in praise and adoration as we remember His death and look forward to His return!

Admittedly, sometimes you may feel that you have nothing to offer the Lord, that you have no right being at His table. But keep in mind, the key is not what you bring to Him, it's what He brings to us. The late Bob Benson summed up the meaning of our communion together in a down-to-earth but deeply meaningful essay. Benson penned:

Do you remember when they had old fashioned Sunday school picnics? It was before air-conditioning. They said, "We'll meet at Sycamore Lodge in Shelby Park at 4:30 Saturday. You bring your supper and we'll furnish the tea."

But you came home at the last minute and when you got ready to pack your lunch, all you could find in the refrigerator was one dried up piece of baloney and just enough mustard in the bottom of the jar so that you got it all over your knuckles trying to get to it. And there were just two stale pieces of bread. So you made your baloney sandwich and wrapped it in some brown bag and went to the picnic.

When it came time to eat, you sat at the end of a table and spread out your sandwich, but the folks next to you—the lady was a good cook and she had worked all day and she had fried chicken, and baked beans, and potato salad, and homemade rolls, and sliced tomatoes, and pickles, and olives, and celery and topped it off with two big homemade chocolate pies. And they spread it all out beside you and there you were with your baloney sandwich.

But they said to you, "Why don't we put it all together?"

"No, I couldn't do that, I just couldn't even think of it," you murmured embarrassed.

"Oh, come on, there's plenty of chicken and plenty of pie, and plenty of everything—and we just love baloney sandwiches. Let's just put it all together."

And so you did and there you sat—eating like a king when you came like a pauper.

And I get to thinking—I think of me "sharing in the being of God." When I think of how little I bring and how much He brings and that He invites me to "share," I know I should be shouting to the house-tops, but I am so filled with awe and wonder that I can hardly be heard.

I know you don't have enough love and faith, or grace, or mercy or wisdom. But He has—He has all those things in abundance and says, "Let's just put it all together. Everything that I possess is available to you. Everything that I am and can be to a person, I will be to you."

When I think about it like that, it really amuses me to see somebody running along through life hanging on to their dumb bag with that stale baloney sandwich saying, "God's not going to get my sandwich! No sirree, this is mine!"

Did you ever see anybody like that—so needy—just about half-starved to death, hanging on for dear life?

It's not that He needs your sandwich. The fact is, you need His chicken.[1]

That's our Jesus! That is what it means to be a part of His body—it's a family affair! And now in Part II we will look at how we can live successfully as a family by knowing how to hear God's voice, by adopting His vision for our lives, by forgiving each other, and by one day joining His community of saints in heaven.

PART II

LIVING OUT YOUR FAITH IN A COMMUNITY EXPERIENCE

13

HEARING FROM GOD

IF YOU WATCH MOST mainstream television news reports in which a Christian claims to have heard from God, you can almost see the skepticism in the interviewer's face. "Yeah, right, you've heard from God," is the message expressed by the roll of the reporter's eyes. "You and every other wacko cult member who has been deceived into believing that God actually speaks to us today."

Yet hearing from God is not all that unusual . . . or at least it should not be for members of Christ's body. Furthermore, in these exciting times, it is important that we learn to discern the voice of the Lord. As individuals, we need to be accustomed to hearing from God, so that we are ready to start, stop, or change directions on a moment's notice. Similarly, the corporate body of Christ must be ready to respond immediately to specific divine orders, like a highly trained athletic team or a military battalion, as we adjust our tactics and strategies to meet the needs and to deal with the unprecedented problems and opportunities that will be coming our way in the days ahead.

Sometimes God speaks through nature, loudly as through a thunderstorm, an earthquake, or a tornado; at other times He can be heard in the soft, gentle breeze. Sometimes He speaks audibly, literally from on high, as He did at the baptism of Jesus, announcing, "This is My beloved Son, in whom I am well pleased" (Matt. 3:17 NKJV). At other times, He speaks quietly, personally to individuals, in the still, small voice that speaks to our hearts, minds, and consciences.

Hearing from God is not unusual or spooky. It is not strange to talk to God and have God talk to you! Beginning in Genesis 3:9, we find that Adam and Eve walked with God, and they talked with God. They carried on a conversation with Him. Throughout the Old and New Testaments, men and women who had a close relationship with the Lord spent time talking to God and, more important, hearing from God.

Contrary to our human assumptions, a small child can hear the voice of God as well as the most experienced pastor, priest, or prophet, if the child's heart is right with God. Do you remember the story of Samuel? As a boy, living in the home of Eli the priest, God spoke to Samuel three times in the middle of the night. Thinking that it was the aging priest who had called his name, Samuel ran to Eli, and said, "Here I am, for you called for me." Eli told Samuel to go back to bed, that he had not called for him. But after the third wake-up call, Eli finally caught on. He told the boy Samuel, "Go, lie down; and it shall be, if He calls you, that you must say, 'Speak, LORD, for Your servant hears'" (1 Sam. 3:9 NKJV). God did indeed speak to the boy, and Samuel heard His voice and responded. Samuel grew up to be a mighty prophet of God, serving the Lord all his life. It was Samuel who anointed the first two kings of Israel, King Saul, and later, King David.

When I was a little boy, my grandma Irwin gave me a Gideon's New Testament, and I kept it right near my bed. Every night, before crawling beneath the covers, I flipped open my little Testament and allowed my eyes to drop on a verse. Sometimes I'd read more, but never less than one verse.

Once, I flipped open the Testament and my eyes landed on Acts 10:42: "And He commanded us to preach to the people" (NKJV). Now, I don't believe in "Russian roulette" Bible reading, but back then I didn't know any better. Night after night, my Bible kept falling open to the same verse. I said, "This Bible must be stuck! The binding must be bent." So I pulled another Bible off my parents' shelf and let it fall open. Again, the Word fell open to the verse, "And he commanded me to preach." That was the beginning of my hearing God's voice and discerning His will for my life through the Word of God.

WHY IS THIS IMPORTANT?

Why does it matter whether or not I can hear from God? Obviously, if I am to have a relationship with Him, I need to be able to discern His voice. One-way conversations usually get boring before long. Sure, we want to pour out our hearts to God in prayer, knowing that He hears us, but most of us would also like to hear something in return!

Have you ever sent a letter to someone from whom you expected a response? How did you feel when you didn't get a letter back within a reasonable amount of time? Or have you ever called a friend and left an important message on his or her answering machine, and then had to sit back and wait for a return call? We want a response; we need a response.

How much more do we need to hear from God?

Furthermore, in these days, in our personal lives, in our families, and in the body of Christ at large, it is vital that we be able to hear God's directions for our lives. We may need to make some abrupt changes in the way we are doing things. God may move us to another part of the country, or even to another country, with very little notice. He may lead you to bring somebody into your home to live with you, somebody whom you previously had never dreamed of even inviting for lunch! The Lord may lead you to take a new job, so you can spend more time with your family or live closer to the community of believers. He may instruct you to sell some (or all!) of your possessions and give the money to the body of Christ. How will you know God's will if you are not in the habit of hearing from Him?

As calamities occur or new opportunities to minister develop, we will need incredible flexibility to respond. We must be able to hear from God, shift gears, turn around, go a new direction, or stop cold, as He instructs us.

How can you hear from God? First, and foremost, we hear from God through His Word.

THE WORD TAKES PRECEDENCE

Something wonderful happens as we study the Scripture carefully and prayerfully, not looking for sermon material, Sunday school lessons, or examining the texts from an academic perspective, but simply allowing the Spirit of God to speak to us through the Word of God.

Unfortunately, in recent years, the Christian community has been content with a *"Reader's Digest"* mentality in regard to the Word of God. We have been satisfied to hit the high points, to connect the dots from one peak to another without ever exploring the valleys in between. Studying the Word of God has become almost a lost art. Most modern-day believers are "too busy" to get into the Word for themselves, so they rely on their pastor, priest, or favorite television personality to interpret the Word for them. That is extremely dangerous.

I believe that the world is about to enter a horrendous time of difficulty, and many Christians will not survive the tribulations to come if we do not learn how to hear from God on a daily basis. In the days ahead, it will not be sufficient to say, "Well, Pastor Joe says . . ." or, "I heard a preacher on a Christian program teach this principle . . ." Of course, we should appreciate and respect our pastors and teachers. Certainly, we can learn and benefit greatly from gifted Bible teachers, but in the days ahead—more than ever before—it will be crucial for each of us to know the Word for ourselves.

Already today, tragically few ministers, Sunday school teachers, evangelists, and other spiritual "leaders" take time to study the Word of God for themselves. All too often, we simply rely on other sources; we repeat what we have heard other ministers say, assuming that they have done their homework. Sometimes they have . . . but many times they have not. They are merely repeating something they have heard from another source.

This practice both insults the ministry and breeds false doctrine. I know. I was both a victim of, and a perpetrator of, this sort of shoddy handling of the Word of truth. During the 1980s, at Heritage USA, I allowed myself to become so busy building a place for God's people, I slowly but surely got out of the habit of spending adequate time studying the Scriptures for myself. I still loved the Lord, and I did my best to preach and teach His Word, but often I relied on information I had gleaned from other sources, other speakers, books, or magazines, rather than preaching from the overflow of my own relationship with the Lord. Before long, I accepted portions of the "prosperity gospel" message as the truth, and I preached it and lived it. Such lazy lack of study lends itself all too easily to the perpetuation of false doctrine. If we aren't really studying the Word for ourselves but are simply repeating what we hear others espouse, who will notice when the message becomes diluted, tainted, and then subverted completely? Worse yet, who will really care?

A WORD OF WARNING

Through the prophet Jeremiah, God spoke to this issue and rebuked the spiritual leaders of Judah for their spiritual lethargy and laziness. The Lord said:

> Does not my word burn like fire? asks the Lord. Is it not like a mighty hammer that smashed the rock to pieces? So I stand against these "prophets" who get their messages from each other—these smooth-tongued prophets who say, "This message is from God!" Their made-up dreams are flagrant lies that lead my people into sin. I did not send them and they have no message at all for my people, says the Lord. (Jer. 23:29–32 TLB)

Today another generation of false prophets has arisen among God's people, presenting a positive, upbeat message that we all want to hear—but which, in fact, is not what God is saying to His church in these last days. I call them the prophets of the "happy gospel," men and women who teach that everything is fine; in fact, it's never been so fine, and it's getting better.

Historically, we have been blessed by a plethora of godly men and women who have handled the Word correctly, students of Scripture who have interpreted the Scriptures accurately, regarding their responsibility to proclaim biblical truth as a sacred trust. But those days are about to change, if they aren't gone already. Soon, I believe, the Scriptures will be twisted by unscrupulous teachers to support their own perverse actions, similar to the way Adolf Hitler prostituted the pulpits in pre–World War II Germany. The question is, Will we even know the difference? Or will we have become so accustomed to having our ears tickled with upbeat, positive, "happy" messages, purporting that everything is getting better, that we will not even notice when the perverters of the gospel use it, first to draw us into their clutches and then to destroy us.

The true Word of God is mighty like a hammer that smashes rocks to pieces. It hammers at our flesh; it will not comfort us in our lusts or our love of materialism. But not only is the Word a hammer, it is also a beacon that lights our paths. The Holy Spirit uses the Word to shed light on our lives, to convict us of our sin, and to guide us to the truth.

Allowing the Word of God to speak for itself changed my life. While in prison, I studied the words of Jesus. When I found out what He actually said, I was horrified. I discovered that many of the themes I used to preach with fervor and passion were exactly opposite of what Jesus taught! I thank God for my prison experience, because as difficult and as humbling as it was, God used it to bring me into a deeper, stronger, more scripturally based relationship with Him.

I know now that I will be able to survive in the years to come, and I will be able to help "rescue the perishing, and care for the dying," because I have been there. I know what it feels like to lose everything I ever held dear. I know the cold chill that overwhelms a person as he or she struggles through the valley of the shadow of death, and I am not afraid of it anymore, because Jesus held my hand as I went through my valley walk. I was like a lost sheep, lost in that prison, crying out, "Where's God, where's God?"

My material possessions were gone, most of my friends were gone, and all the comfortable things in my life were gone. My spiritual props were gone, too. But in prison, I found Jesus in a fresh way, and He never walked away from me. As I studied the Bible, He began to pour His Word into my heart. I read the Word of God hour after hour, sometimes as many as sixteen hours a day. The more I studied the Scripture, the more I realized that what was popular in the pulpit was not necessarily popular in the Bible.

For instance, I used to refer to Christians at Heritage USA as "King's Kids." It was an endearing term, and I meant it with all love and sincerity. "You are King's Kids," I'd tell them, "so turn around, and tell someone in the audience that your Daddy is a King."

While it is true that we are children of God, and my intention was to encourage Christians to understand how incredibly valuable they are to their heavenly Father, I also mixed in elements of pride and arrogance with that message. I inferred that because we are "King's Kids," we deserve the best that this world has to offer. "Who do you think God made all these things for?" I'd often ask. "The devil's crowd? No way! God wants His children to prosper even as their souls prosper!" It was an encouraging message, designed to puff up the spirits of God's people, and it usually did.

Unfortunately, that is not what the Word says. God said, "Humble yourselves, therefore, under the mighty hand of God, that He may exalt you at the proper time" (1 Peter 5:6 NASB).

How can we be so easily deceived? The Holy Spirit allowed the apostle Paul to see that, in the last days, even Christians can turn away from the true Word and believe lies. Paul warned young Pastor Timothy:

> Preach the word! Be ready in season and out of season. Convince, rebuke, exhort, with all longsuffering and teaching. For the time will come when they will not endure sound doctrine, but according to their own desires, because they have itching ears, they will heap up for themselves teachers; and they will turn their ears away from the truth, and be turned aside to fables. (2 Tim. 4:2–4 NKJV)

We are seeing and hearing a preponderance of such messages today. "God wants you to be rich, to have the best, to own jet airplanes, and fancy cars" and on and on. The "desires" about which Paul warned Timothy are not merely sexual lusts, but strong desires for the material things of the world. Unfortunately, despite Paul's warnings, more and more Christians are becoming enamored with this world. The old saying, "He's so heavenly minded that he is of no earthly good," has been turned upside down. Nowadays, most Christians are so earthly minded, so caught up in their quests to achieve the "American Dream," that few even take heaven seriously, much less feel an urgency to prepare for the soon return of our Lord Jesus. Consequently, we are getting what we deserve from our pulpits. We are inundated nowadays with quasi-biblical messages designed to tickle our ears and lift our spirits.

How can you tell whether a message is on target? The true test of modern teaching, preaching, or what we see or hear on television and radio or find written in books is, How does this line up with the Word of God? If the message is inconsistent with the Word, do not accept it. God will never speak to you or anyone else something that is contrary to His own Word. Those who insist on trying to find exceptions to that rule are dangerous to your spiritual welfare. Avoid them and their false doctrines like the plague.

WITH FRIENDS LIKE THESE . . .

In these last days, we must realize that false doctrine is so enticing that even our friends, family members, and fellow believers may become misguided. When I was teaching the Bible in inner-city Los Angeles, I was constantly amazed and appalled that some of the very poorest of people took offense when they heard me teaching against the love of money. Ironically, many of these people were living on public assistance and food stamps, while they gave their money away to pastors and evangelists who promised them huge returns on their giving to God.

In a bizarre twist on the "Give to God and get out of debt" message that is currently in vogue in many Christian circles, I was shocked to hear a story recounted by a television preacher. Apparently, someone in his viewing audience had incurred a huge debt at a hospital. After sending a "faith" gift to the ministry, the person contacted the hospital to arrange payment terms on his bill. To his amazement, he was told that the computers had malfunctioned and the hospital could no longer find the bill in their system!

Now, here's the disturbing part: The television preacher proclaimed that the computer glitch was God's answer to the person's prayer and His response to the person's faith. According to the TV preacher, God had erased the debt!

Granted, in the Old Testament God's people enjoyed a year of Jubilee every fifty years, when all debts were canceled and people were allowed to return to the property they may have sold off to pay a debt (Lev. 25). But I don't think the hospital had that principle in mind when they couldn't find the person's bill.

We must stay centered on the Word, not on someone's opinion or interpretation of Scriptures. Paul cautioned the Christian community at Galatia, "But even if we, or an angel from heaven, preach any other gospel to you than that what we have preached to you, let him be accursed" (Gal. 1:8 NKJV).

We also need to recognize that some false messages we receive will come from well-meaning, sincere men and women of God. They are sincere, but they are sincerely wrong. Worse still, they may or may not even realize they are propagating false doctrine. After all, that's what they have heard from other spiritual leaders whom they respect.

AN UNPOPULAR MESSAGE

In contrast, the Old Testament prophet Jeremiah knew that he had heard from God, and frankly, the message was not one of peace, prosperity, and pleasure. Jeremiah told the people again and again that God's plan for them included some tough times, some times of captivity, uprooting, and some times of tears. But naturally, the people didn't want to hear that word. They much preferred the more positive messages brought by other prophets, ostensibly sincere men who thought they were encouraging the people by distracting them from the truth. Even when faced with the fact that their lives would indeed be uprooted, the people insisted on believing that the length of time would be much shorter than what God had revealed to Jeremiah.

"Sure, you may have a few bad years," the sincerely wrong prophets declared, "but don't sweat it. In two years or so, you will be right back here on top of the world" (see Jer. 28:3).

As the nation insisted on believing the lies propagated by the false prophets, they slipped ever closer to destruction. All the while, Jeremiah tried repeatedly to warn the people that they were being deceived. But nobody wanted to hear that message.

Imagine the heartache Jeremiah must have felt as he cried out:

> This is what the LORD Almighty says,
> "Do not listen to what the prophets are prophesying to you;
>   they will fill you with false hopes.
> They speak visions from their own minds,
>   not from the mouth of the LORD.
> They keep saying to those who despise me,
>   'The LORD says: You will have peace.'
> And to all who follow the stubbornness of their hearts
>   they say, 'No harm will come to you.'" (Jer. 23:16–17 NIV)

As in Jeremiah's day, we are hearing similar misrepresentations today, messages from so-called men and women of God, proclaiming that "the yoke has been broken," that God is going to deliver us from the difficult circumstances. And yes, He will . . . eventually . . . but not yet. Still the false messengers persist in misleading God's people.

Jeremiah continued:

> But which of them has stood in the council of the LORD
>   to see or to hear his word?
>   Who has listened and heard his word?
> See, the storm of the LORD

will burst out in wrath,
a whirlwind swirling down
    on the heads of the wicked.
The anger of the LORD will not turn back
    until he fully accomplishes
    the purposes of his heart.
In days to come
    you will understand it clearly.
I did not send these prophets,
    yet they have run with their message;
I did not speak to them,
    yet they have prophesied.
But if they had stood in my council,
    they would have proclaimed my words to my people
and would have turned them from their evil ways
    and from their evil deeds. (Jer. 23:18–22 NIV)

A true prophetic word will turn us to the Lord. The true Word of God will turn you toward the love of Jesus, not toward the love of this world. False prophets come in sheep's clothing, with enticing words, hoping to turn you to them, their programs or platforms.

Eventually, of course, Jeremiah proved to be correct. The Jewish people were not sent into captivity for two years, but for *seventy*, just as Jeremiah had predicted. Yet the Lord did not leave His people without hope. He spoke through Jeremiah:

For thus says the LORD, "When seventy years have been completed for Babylon, I will visit you and fulfill My good word to you, to bring you back to this place. For I know the plans that I have for you," declares the LORD, "plans for welfare and not for calamity to give you a future and a hope. Then you will call upon Me and come and pray to Me, and I will listen to you. And you will seek Me and find Me, when you search for Me with all your heart. And I will be found by you," declares the LORD, "and I will restore your fortunes and will gather you from all the nations and from all the places where I have driven you," declares the LORD, "and I will bring you back to the place from where I sent you into exile." (Jer. 29:10–14 NASB)

What a wonderful promise, that God intends to bless His people! But don't miss the other part of the message—that God's people, the people of His pleasure, the ones whom He loves, would not escape the torturous captivity they were facing. They would indeed be destroyed as a nation, swept off to another country (Babylon) to serve as slave labor or in other menial positions. But God would eventually bring them back and bless them again.

God's Word is the most accurate means of hearing from God that most of us experience, and it is an effective means. The writer to the Hebrews reminded us, "For the word of God is living and powerful, and sharper than any two-edged sword, piercing even to the division of soul and spirit, and of joints and marrow, and is a discerner of the thoughts and intents of the heart" (Heb. 4:12 NKJV).

The Word is living; it brings life. It is powerful, profound, and it cuts through the sludge in our lives. It discerns the thoughts and the intents of the heart, which means that it not only reveals the motivations of our inner person, it is the standard against which our thoughts and intentions will be judged.

That's why I get so upset when I hear Christian leaders telling their followers, "Oh, you are okay! Everything is fine, have a little bit of faith. This is our finest hour. Go pick the color of the new car that you want, pick out the seat covers and all that. Just name it and claim it." Although few people are bold enough to admit it, these modern-day false prophets might as well encourage their listeners to "keep lusting for more things; set your eyes and your heart on the things of this world rather than the next"—attitudes that are totally contrary to the teachings of Jesus Christ and His Word!

Oh, God, help us to know Jesus and to fall in love with Him rather than the things of this world! When you fall in love with Jesus, you will be amazed how much easier it is for you to hear from God. Jesus said, "My sheep hear My voice, and I know them, and they follow Me" (John 10:27 NKJV). If you spend time in the Word, you will know His voice. After spending two years studying nothing but the words of Jesus, I suddenly began to see Him and hear His voice in the Old and New Testaments. Now, I can read some of the "types" in the Old Testament, and I understand them. "Oh," I say, "that's Jesus!" I read the book of Revelation, and I can recognize Jesus. I know His voice. I know how He speaks, I know the words He uses, I know the things He likes and dislikes. The reason I know these things is not because I am so special or so intelligent or so devoted to God. I know them because God speaks to me, just as He will to you, through His Word!

SAVED WITHOUT THE WORD?

Nowadays, multitudes of people attend church regularly, yet they know extremely little of God's Word. How can someone know the Lord and have so little desire for His Word? That would be like a newborn baby having no desire for mother's milk. I fear that many we call "babes in Christ" have never truly been born again. They may have made a superficial commitment to the Lord, but they have never gotten grounded in the Word, so they have never truly been able to hear from God.

Many people have made numerous treks to altars, but their lives have remained unchanged. Altar calls, especially in American evangelism, have been used and abused. Granted, in the past 150 years, hundreds of thousands of people have found Christ through the traditional altar call, but all too often, nowadays, the altar call is used to ease the conscience of the preacher and the people alike. People respond to the preacher's message by "going forward," walking down to the front of the church, stadium, or arena. The people feel good because they have taken a step toward God. The preacher feels good because he has completed a successful sermon, meaning he has elicited the desired response from the people. The people pray a halfhearted prayer of repentance, "Dear God, forgive me for my sins. Thank You, God. Amen." Then the preacher tells them, "You are saved now."

Saved? Did anything of eternal significance take place? The people expressed no remorse, no confession of sins, no repentance. They made no commitment to turn away from evil to live for God, to trust Jesus Christ as the only means of salvation. It was just another walk down the aisle. They anticipate no change in their lifestyle, and they experience none. Many of these "believers" show up in Christian communities, and some actually come into a relationship with Christ, take root, and begin to grow in the Word. Others simply attend services, regard the church as a social club, and wonder what all the excitement is about.

Admittedly, many people are offended when they hear the Word of God. They prefer to lust after the things of this world, and when they find out that their desires are opposite from those in the Word of God, they fall away from the faith. In the near future, as times get tougher and we draw closer to our Lord's return, there will be a massive falling away of people who have believed in a "prosperity gospel." Many will realize for the first time that their "happy gospel" just doesn't work in the face of severe trials and tribulations.

Remember, you must spend time in the Word of God to hear the voice of God. Otherwise, you will be susceptible to the subtle lies and half-truths of false teachers, and you may be tragically deceived.

BEFORE IT'S TOO LATE

Now is the time to get grounded in the Word. The Bible indicates that we will soon experience a famine in hearing the Word of God. The prophet Amos wrote, "'Behold, the days are coming,' says the LORD GOD, / 'That I will send a famine on the land, / Not a famine of bread, / Nor a thirst for water, / But of hearing the words of the LORD'" (Amos 8:11 NKJV). There may soon come a time, even in America, when it will be impossible to hear a biblical exposition that is not tainted by evil intentions. Imagine what it will be like when it becomes illegal to own a Bible, much less to read one or preach from one. Impossible, you say? Wake up. We are moving rapidly in that direction.

As you saturate yourself in the Word of God, the Lord will speak to you through the Bible, and you will be amazed at what you begin to understand, including those things that are about to take place on the earth. Throughout much of my Christian life, I must admit, I was never a great student of prophecy. I had read the passages in the Scripture that described the Lord's return and believed them, but I really hadn't paid much attention to them. After all, many of the prophetic passages did not support my happy, "Disneyland" gospel that I enjoyed preaching.

But when I was in prison, God began to show me what was coming: the famines, the earthquakes, pestilence, tribulations, the stars that will fall from the sky, the asteroid that will one day strike the earth, the terrorism that is about to be unleashed, the awful plagues, and the wars that we will experience prior to Christ's return.

The good news is that we will once again be a New Testament church in the last days—or else! The gospel will be preached around the world before the end will come (Matt. 24:14). All of that, I learned by studying the Word. No prophecy teacher clued me in. No television evangelist gave me an insight that I had missed previously. No book like this one alerted me of the things about to come upon the face of the earth. It was simply my study of the Word of God that opened my dull ears so I could hear the voice of God.

I know that what God has done for me, He longs to do for you, too.

14

HOW SHALL WE HEAR?

"THERE MUST BE SOMETHING wrong with me," the petite young woman confessed, while dabbing makeup on my face as I sat backstage waiting to appear on a Christian television program. "I listen to all these great men and women of God come through here, telling stories of how God spoke to them about this, or that God told them that. Jim, to be honest with you, I have never heard God speaking to me, at least not in any audible voice.

"Doesn't God care about me? I'm a Christian. I've lived for the Lord since my teenage years, and I've never once heard God. Oh, sure, I've had spiritual impressions. There have been times when I've had some thoughts that seemed to be inspired by God, but to tell you the truth, I could have dreamed those things up on my own, with or without God speaking to me.

"I pray, I fast . . . occasionally . . . when I'm really desperate. I seek God's face as much as I know how. I work here at a Christian station for pennies compared to what I could make across town at the big station. What more does it take to hear from God?"

That woman expressed what many Christians wonder about: How can I hear from God? The truth is that very few men and women nowadays hear God speaking in an audible voice. Those who do can usually count on one hand the number of times they have heard God speak aloud to them. Frankly, if most of us ever heard God speak out loud to us, we'd be scared out of our wits! Think about it for a moment.

Almighty God, the One who created heaven and earth out of nothing, the awesome Judge of all—what would you do if He spoke to you?

In the Bible, a frequent response of people to whom God spoke aloud was that they fell on their faces—partially out of reverence, and partially out of abject fear.

Maybe that's one reason why God doesn't do much verbalizing these days, at least not out loud. Besides, He's made it quite clear that what He wants us to know is in His Book, the Bible. Perhaps if we ever fully understand and live according to that much of His revelation, we might be ready for more, but not before then.

In the meantime, just because God does not usually speak aloud to His people does not mean that He is silent. He speaks to us in many ways, and if we will attune ourselves to Him, we will have little trouble hearing from God. One of the most obvious ways that God speaks to us is through His ministers.

1. GOD STILL USES PREACHERS

One day, during the first year of our marriage, my wife, Lori, and I were grappling with some heavy issues in our personal lives. As we were leaving for a trip, we received three cassette tapes in the mail from our friend R.T. Kendall, the pastor of Westminster Chapel in London. We popped the first tape in the car's tape deck and sat back to enjoy another stirring message by one of the outstanding Bible teachers of our time. But were we ever in for a surprise!

It was as though R.T. Kendall had been listening in to Lori's and my laments. His preaching seared into our hearts and minds. Lori and I knew the Word, but the spoken word of R.T. Kendall's sermon confirmed the application of the written Word in our hearts.

Despite its shortcomings, preaching is still one of the primary means of hearing God's voice speaking to our hearts and minds. After telling the church at Rome that "whoever calls on the name of the LORD shall be saved" (Rom. 10:13 NKJV), the apostle Paul asked a series of poignant rhetorical questions:

How then shall they call on Him in whom they have not believed?
And how shall they believe in Him of whom they have not heard?

And how shall they hear without a preacher? And how shall they preach unless they are sent? (Rom. 10:14–15 NKJV)

God calls preachers to proclaim His Word; He anoints preachers with supernatural power to expound the Scriptures and to teach and edify the body of Christ. If we will listen carefully, we will often hear God's instructions for our lives coming through the mouth of an anointed preacher. Next time you are tempted to doze off during a sermon, remind yourself that God may be speaking to you through the message. We dare not ignore the fact that God has chosen to use preaching to speak to us.

Sometimes God uses Scripture, along with preaching and the confirmation of His Word through a prophet, to speak to our hearts and minds.

2. DON'T DESPISE PROPHETIC VOICES

In recent years, we have seen a resurgence of the prophetic ministry within the body of Christ. Prophets should not be considered weird or abnormal human beings. Admittedly, many of the prophets I have met seem to focus their attention more on matters of eternal significance than on this transient world. I suppose that puts them out of sync with most people. Nevertheless, prophets who properly exercise their gifts should be welcomed by the Christian community. They have a valid ministry and we need them! The Scripture says that the Lord "gave some to be apostles, some prophets, some evangelists, and some pastors and teachers, for the equipping of the saints for the work of ministry, for the edifying of the body of Christ" (Eph. 4:11–12 NKJV). Clearly, the apostle Paul implied that the various ministries are all important in the community of believers, including the ministry of prophets.

It is important to understand that in the Bible, the prophet's ministry was not always predictive. In fact, some prophets spent as much time "*forth*telling," doing what we might call preaching, as they did "*fore*telling" future events. The same is true today. To some prophets, God gives predictive words, often warnings of things to come. At other times, He uses the prophet to speak a word of confirmation, emphasizing a Scripture or a biblical truth through a spoken or written word.

It is an awesome experience to have a word confirmed by a prophet, but it is not unusual. During the winter of 1999, I attended a prophets conference in the mountains of North Carolina. Just prior to the conference, the mountains were struck with a terrible winter storm, making it almost impossible to ascend the heights to the conference center. Nevertheless, I felt strongly that I needed to be there, so I geared down my Jeep and inched my way up the mountain. Finally, I made it to the top.

Cindy Jacobs, one of the conference speakers, was delayed in Detroit because of the storm, but God still spoke to us on the mountaintop. All of us had prophetic dreams that first night. I was reminded that during my last week in prison, a man of God came from Los Angeles to visit me in Jesup, Georgia. This man did not know me; he was not a close personal friend, he had never been a guest on my television program—we had no real connection at all, except for the Lord. Yet God had instructed him to travel all the way across the United States to give me a message.

The man came to the prison, and after exchanging brief pleasantries, he said, "Jim, God wants me to give you Isaiah 40:1–3." It was a prophetic word from God to His people after a time of extreme trouble and despair. Sitting in prison, my life having been devastated by the events that led to my being there, I could relate to the message. But my visitor was not content to let me hear an ambiguous word that could be applied in a general way to a large variety of circumstances. He said, "God had me come from Los Angeles to Georgia to give you this message." The man then read the passage, and as he did, he inserted my name: "'Comfort Jim, comfort Jim,' saith your God. 'Speak ye comfortably to Jim and cry unto him, that his warfare is accomplished, that his iniquity is pardoned: for he hath received of the LORD's hand double for all his sins.'"

The man and I talked briefly, and then he left.

Nearly six years later, Cindy Jacobs arrived at this prophets conference with no knowledge of the prophetic word I had received in prison. As a group of prophets ministered to each other, Cindy suddenly said to me, "Jim, I've got a Scripture for you. God wants me to give you Isaiah 40:1–3." Then she went on to tell me the dream that I had had the night before, describing exactly everything that God had said about it. Then she did the same thing for my wife.

What was happening there? Simply this: While all Scripture is inspired by God and is profitable for doctrine, reproof, correction, and instruction in righteousness, that we may be thoroughly equipped for every good work (see 2 Tim. 3:16–17), not every Scripture is applicable to every person in every situation. It is often by the preached word, and sometimes by the prophetic word, that the written Word is confirmed to us, making it a *personal* word applicable to a specific situation.

Some people say, "Well, I just believe the Bible, and I don't trust any other so-called 'words' from the Lord." I understand that. I can't even begin to estimate how many kooks and crackpots have claimed to have divine messages for me over the years. I have rejected almost all of these so-called "prophecies." At times, when I have failed to discern whether someone was truly speaking on behalf of the Lord, I have paid a high price.

Not surprisingly, today I do not readily receive so-called "prophetic words" from people whose spiritual authority I don't trust. I recommend that you be equally cautious. But be careful that in your skepticism you don't miss an opportunity to hear from God. Make sure that you are not imposing your own limitations on the "packaging" in which you will accept His message. Not only does that attitude reveal a haughty spirit, it also disregards the clear teaching of Scripture that we should indeed seek confirmation of what we believe to be God's direction in our lives based upon His Word. Could not God's direction for His family members be confirmed through the prophets He has assigned to function within His body?

Seek Confirmation

For example, in His instructions concerning how we should approach a brother who has sinned, Jesus quoted Deuteronomy 19:15, "that by the mouth of two or three witnesses every fact may be confirmed" (Matt. 18:16 NASB). A few verses later, He promised the disciples that if two of them agreed on anything for which they prayed, it would be done. Moreover, Jesus said, "For where two or three have gathered together in My name, there I am in their midst" (Matt. 18:20 NASB).

Throughout the Bible, the "plurality of confirmation principle" can be clearly seen. For instance, the apostle Paul instructed:

If anyone speaks in a tongue, let there be two or at the most three, each in turn, and let one interpret. But if there is no interpreter, let him keep silent in church, and let him speak to himself and to God. Let two or three prophets speak, and let the others judge. (1 Cor. 14:27–29 NKJV)

Certainly God can and does confirm His Word privately and personally to our hearts every day, but in a public setting, He has built in a safety net for us, to help us avoid mistakes and errors in our understanding of His message. That safety net is the plurality of confirmations. We ignore such protections, cautions, and boundaries to our own peril.

The apostle Paul continued, "If anything is revealed to another who sits by, let the first keep silent. For you can all prophesy one by one, that all may learn and all may be encouraged. And the spirits of the prophets are subject to the prophets" (1 Cor. 14:30–32 NKJV).

Understand, prophets are not spiritual superstars. They do not have a divine right to direct your life—only the Holy Spirit can do that. Prophets are fallible human beings just like the rest of us. When they prophesy, they are merely using the spiritual gift that God has given to them, to help edify the entire body of Christ. Their prophecies are to be weighed by the other prophets, to make sure that they are on target with their messages.

I get really nervous when I hear about "spiritual superstars." Besides the fact that I have seen too many Christian stars crash and burn, I am convinced that the day of the big-name Christian personality is over. Arrogance in the pulpit is over. I am not a prophet, but I do recognize and appreciate the prophetic ministry when I see it operating biblically, which means that the prophets are subject to one another, that they are accountable to the other prophets in the local body and to the body of Christ at large. This same principle is true of Christian musicians, traveling evangelists, seminar leaders, Christian television and radio personalities, and others who are "speaking into" the Christian community messages that supposedly have God's stamp of approval.

Notice that there should be a mutual accountability among those who speak for God. No human being has a unique, inside track with God concerning the message God wants to say to His church. None of us have a handle on the entire Word that God is revealing. Most of us have only bits and pieces of the message. That's why we need each other. We have His Word, the Bible, and the messages spoken by prophets or others who claim to speak for God can be easily tested against Scripture. No human being has the right to arbitrarily speak into your life and declare that this is the unequivocal word of God for you. Sadly, we have experienced awful tragedies in the body of Christ when individuals and sometimes even couples and families have allowed another person to become a demagogue in their lives. Prophetic words should always be "tested" to see if they really are from God.

For instance, I am aware of a Christian woman who married a man solely on the basis of a "prophecy" she received at a Christian meeting. Unfortunately, her new husband was a charlatan who abused her, stole her money, and disappeared.

Paul was not bashful about reminding the early Christians to seek confirmation of what they believed God was saying to them. Quoting Deuteronomy 19:15, he wrote to the church at Corinth, "This will be the third time I am coming to you. 'By the mouth of two or three witnesses every word shall be established'" (2 Cor. 13:1 NKJV). He advised Timothy to make use of this principle in deciding issues of church discipline. Paul wrote, "Do not receive an accusation against an elder except from two or three witnesses" (1 Tim. 5:19 NKJV).

Why all this concern about accurately hearing from God?

Confusion Is Not of God

Paul reminded us, "For God is not the author of confusion but of peace, as in all the churches of the saints" (1 Cor. 14:33 NKJV). I have been in some segments of the body of Christ where it seems as though mass confusion is reigning. That is not of God. On the other hand, some groups deliberately design their worship services so they can control what goes on; that's not of God, either. What if God wants to do something that is not included on the church bulletin?

By the same token, we should not get upset when things that are out of order are rebuked by the proper spiritual leadership, preferably a pastor, elder, or ministry head. Many churches nowadays are too afraid of legal or other consequences to rebuke anyone about anything. But clearly the New Testament church was designed to function in an orderly fashion while fostering a freedom of expression and creating an environment conducive to worship, praise, and prayer—no small challenge these days.

3. HEARING FROM GOD THROUGH SPIRITUAL GIFTS

A healthy Christian community will have various gifts of the Holy Spirit operating on a regular basis. Ideally, all the gifts of the Holy Spirit should be apparent in every community of believers, but in reality, that is not always the case, especially in smaller congregations. The gifts of the Holy Spirit are intended to edify the entire body of Christ. When a variety of spiritual gifts are operative in the community of believers and used according to clear, biblical directions, we should learn to listen for the Lord speaking through them.

One of the first times I relied on the gifts of the Spirit for direction and discernment took place when I was working at the Christian Broadcasting Network in 1960. I was hosting *The 700 Club* when suddenly, as I sat at the desk in our studio in Portsmouth, Virginia, I could "see" into a living room. In my mind, I could see the room in which a person had some special need. I could describe the room in detail and tell the person what disease they were suffering from, and amazingly, they were often healed on the spot.

It was an awesome, yet frightening, gift, because I recognized the enormous responsibility that went along with it. I also recognized the potential for abuse of such a gift, even in my own heart. Before long, other people were operating on Christian television with a similar gift, some of whom seemed quite sincere, and others whom I am now convinced were charlatans. Sadly, I saw so much abuse of the genuine gift that I suppressed it in my own life.

Now, nearly forty years later, the Holy Spirit has been nudging me back to actively using His gifts in my life. As the Scripture says, "For the gifts and the calling of God are irrevocable" (Rom. 11:29). God does not withdraw His gifts and callings from us, but we must be willing to allow Him to use those gifts for His glory. Recently, God has been showing me some things, and He has encouraged me to "stir up the gift that is within me."

When I was twenty-one years old, a prophet in my local body of believers prophesied over me. Some of the prophet's words had immediate ramifications and provided specific direction for my life; other portions of his word have been fulfilled over time.

For instance, he told me, "You are going to have two decisions to make immediately. Regarding the first one, say no; to the second one say yes." About that time I was offered a job in Chicago setting up a restaurant business, financed by my brother. I desperately needed the money that the employment would bring, but I recalled the words of the prophet. "Say no to the first decision." With a quivering voice, I told my brother that I appreciated his offer but I must decline.

Not long after that, I received an invitation from Pastor Aubrey Sara, inviting me to Burlington, North Carolina, to conduct a series of "revival" meetings. I had never preached a revival before. My preaching experience was limited to sermonettes for kids, which I had presented as a teenager. But again, I recalled the words of the prophet, "Say yes to the second decision." Without hesitating, I told Pastor Aubrey that I would be glad to come and preach for him. I have been preaching ever since. I have no doubt in my mind that I would be in the restaurant business today if that prophet hadn't spoken to me and if I had not trusted God and obeyed His word.

That same man of God told me that, as a twenty-one-year-old, wet-behind-the-ears young man, I would go where no other ministry had gone before. In a real way, through my involvement with Christian television, that prophecy, too, came to pass. The prophet also predicted that that I would help usher in the coming of the Lord. Now, that's a staggering thought! Perhaps my role in that respect has been fulfilled, or is yet to come, but I believe that it will indeed be fulfilled to the letter.

Numerous contemporary prophets have spoken into my life, and I have taken their words seriously. All have boldly and often unabashedly spoken specific words of prophecy concerning my life, not always what I have wanted to hear, but often what I needed to hear, confirmed from God.

The Direct Approach
Sometimes, of course, God speaks to us directly through our hearts and minds. For example, I believe God spoke to me in prison, giving me the message I have been preaching for the past few years. Since then, He has confirmed to me that even though perilous times are coming and evil leaders will dominate the world, including the United States, God's Spirit will continue to be active. Many world leaders are going to call for the prophets of God to come to them. Whether the leaders will accept what the true prophets have to say is doubtful, but in the midst of the turmoil that is to come, we can be confident that God will still be at work in the world. It is the hour of the harvest, it is the hour of victory and the coming of the Lord; we must not be dismayed.

While God often speaks to us through His preachers, prophets, and the proper employment of spiritual gifts, we should not be surprised when God speaks to us through more "unusual" methods.

4. DREAM ON!

God also sometimes speaks to us in our dreams. Scripture is replete with instances in which God has spoken to His people through their dreams. He spoke to Joseph in a dream (Gen. 37:5), as well as to Pharaoh (Gen. 41:25), the ruler of Egypt. The Lord spoke to Gideon in a dream (Judg. 7:13); the Lord appeared unto Solomon in a dream by night (1 Kings 3:5). God spoke similarly to Daniel and to King Nebuchadnezzar (Dan. 4:18). The Lord spoke to others in their dreams, as well. Perhaps the most familiar instance to us is the message to Joseph in a dream, announcing the birth of Jesus Christ (Matt. 1:20).

Clearly, God often provides direction through dreams, although not every dream contains a message from God. On the other hand, some dreams should be carefully analyzed because they may well be God's means of communicating a special message to us. I once had a dream in which I saw my parents down over a cliff, in a car wreck. When I awakened, I was flustered at what I had dreamed, but I shook it off and I didn't do anything about it. *It's just a bad nightmare,* I told myself.

Within forty-eight hours my father and mother had a wreck in Pennsylvania, plunging their automobile down over a cliff, just as I had seen in my dream. Thankfully, they were not seriously hurt, but I couldn't help wondering if somehow I could have warned them or even prevented the accident, had I paid attention to what God had shown me in my dream. The very least I could have done would have been to pray for them and bound the devilish thing that caused the accident. But I was young in my faith and not at all used to hearing from God in my dreams, so I ignored the message, and my parents suffered the consequences.

Years later, when I was in prison, my dreams frequently had spiritual significance. One of my dreams impacted me so profoundly, I will never be the same. In that dream, I was sitting next to Jesus, and He instructed me to put a piece of His eye into my eye. He told me, "I want you to see everyone and everything through My eyes." (For the complete story, see my book *I Was Wrong,* Chap. 22.) That dream changed my life. As a result of it, I began to study the Bible to learn more about Jesus, and that began my new adventures and finding the truth of God and His Word.

5. VISIONS

In the Bible, numerous individuals received messages from God in visions. For instance, in Genesis 15:1, we find, "After these things the word of the LORD came to Abram in a vision" (NKJV). Similarly, the Lord told Moses in Numbers 12:6, "Hear now My words: / If there is a prophet among you, / I, the LORD, make Myself known to him in a vision; / I speak to him in a dream" (NKJV). In the New Testament, God spoke several times through visions. Peter had a vision (Acts 10). Paul had a vision in the night (Acts 16:10). Much of the book of Revelation was given to John in the form of a vision. For example, "And thus I saw the horses in the vision" (Rev. 9:17 NKJV).

On the day of Pentecost, the apostle Peter quoted the prophet Joel and predicted that "it shall come to pass in the last days, says God, / That I will pour out of My Spirit on all flesh; / Your sons and your daughters shall prophesy, / Your young men shall see visions, / Your old men shall dream dreams" (Acts 2:17 NKJV). I believe we are living right smack-dab in the fulfillment of that prophecy today.

I've had a few visions in my lifetime, but none have been so vivid as the one I had in 1997, as I was being driven to the Larry King show in Los Angeles. I told the story in my book *Prosperity and the Coming Apocalypse*, but it bears repeating here.

> California, of course, is under the constant threat of a major earthquake. Hundreds of minor tremors shake Southern California every day. Californians have become so accustomed to these minor seismic motions, most of the population does not even flinch when the ground groans beneath their feet. Nevertheless, both scientists and preachers predict the "Big One" is coming.

> At the risk of sounding like an alarmist, I feel compelled to report an unusual personal experience that causes me to believe a major earthquake will soon shake Los Angeles to its foundations. In 1997 I traveled to L.A. to appear on the CNN broadcast of *Larry King Live* and to speak at several churches in California. I arrived at night and a chauffeured limousine picked me up. I was thankful for the ride, but a little uneasy about getting into the limo. In the years since I lost PTL, I had become much more comfortable riding in my Jeep.

Nevertheless, the Larry King show had provided the transportation, so I gratefully climbed in the back seat of the limo and settled in for the ride to my hotel. As we drove from the airport toward the bright lights in the heart of L.A., I experienced one of the strangest sensations of my life. It was as though my body became a human Geiger counter; I started resonating with the earth deep below Los Angeles. I began to shake and suddenly, in the Spirit, it was as if I could see down into the earth. I saw huge boulders, bowed upward and grinding against each other, like one fist pushing against another.

The Lord began to speak to my heart and mind as clearly as if He had called me on the limo's car phone. "This is the pressure of the ages," the Lord revealed to me. "And it's about to let go." Trembling, I looked out the car window, just as the limo whisked past the beautiful, statuesque skyscrapers in downtown L.A. It was then that I sensed God speaking to me, words I am reluctant to actually put in print, yet words that have been seared for eternity into my spirit.

As I stared at the tall buildings, the Lord said to me, "Not one of these buildings will be left standing. There is going to be an earthquake unlike any other earthquake this area has experienced. There will be nothing left."[1]

I allowed those words to go into print with a great measure of trepidation. After all, I've made a new start in life and have been warmly accepted by most of the Christian community. I have established a new ministry of restoration, and I am back working with Christian television, a ministry I have always loved. Why should I risk it all by telling this story and having people laugh at me and call me a fanatic? I could easily have kept the vision to myself; everyone knows how unstable the earth is below California. The world did not need me to remind them that California is a prime possibility for a major earthquake. Yet I could not shake the vision that the Lord had given to me, and I decided that I would rather warn people and have them laugh, than to remain mum and have them dead. Sometimes the burden of foreknowledge can be a heavy weight to bear.

On Friday, March 5, 1999, I picked up a Los Angeles newspaper and the headline nearly floored me. "Massive Hidden Fault Threatens

Downtown," it said in bold, inch-high letters on the front page. The article stated:

> Scientists have found solid proof of a massive thrust fault under downtown Los Angeles capable of producing devastating earthquakes across a broad area.
>
> After years of speculation, the discovery . . . is the first to decisively map a "blind thrust fault under the city, similar to the previously unknown fault that caused the catastrophic Northridge Earthquake on Jan. 17, 1994."
>
> Called the Puente Hills Fault, the newly identified fracture lies two miles or more below the surface and stretches 25 miles south of downtown.[2]

The article reported that scientists put together reports from the oil and gas companies in the area—exploratory data not previously available—and discovered that "one of the fault's three segments tends to rupture about every 250 to 1,000 years, causing a Northridge-size quake of a magnitude 6.6 or greater. A simultaneous rupture of the three segments occurs between every 500 to 2,000 years, resulting in a magnitude 7.0 temblor."[3]

The article went on to say that the scientists were able to create a clear picture of the seismic activity beneath Los Angeles for the first time in history. They said they had known that something was lurking in the bushes, but this was the first time they saw it for certain.

"Because it's so close to a populated area the fault has to be considered a serious potential hazard," said Peter M. Shearer, a seismologist at Scripps Institute of Oceanography in La Jolla, who conducted the study with geologist John H. Shaw of Harvard University.[4] Even more compelling to me was the scientists' explanation of a blind thrust fault: "Such faults cause the ground to drop at angles or almost vertically, as compared to slip-strike faults [such as the more commonly known San Andreas fault] that move the earth horizontally."[5]

"A 6.6 to 6.7 earthquake would be just terrible underneath downtown Los Angeles," said Paul Davis, a professor of seismology at UCLA. "It obviously would be much more devastating than a similar earthquake in a less populated area."[6] Accompanying the shocking article was a map, showing the location of the fault and an artist's sketch showing how a blind thrust fault slides the earth vertically. The sketch showed two blocks of earth, split down the middle, one pushing upward and the other pushing downward. They looked like two fists pushing against each other . . . just as I had seen in the vision I had while traveling through the heart of Los Angeles!

How could I have seen in 1997 something below the surface of the earth, something that the scientists discovered two years later? There is only one explanation: the vision I saw was a genuine word from the Lord.

Hotel California

A few months after our wedding, Lori and I drove from Los Angeles to San Diego to pick up our wedding photos. Originally, we had planned to stay at a hotel along the beach, but we got a late start and by the time we arrived, we decided to check in to the first hotel we could find. We stopped at an inexpensive motel, collapsed in the bed, and quickly fell fast asleep. I was holding Lori when suddenly my body lapsed into what I can only describe as a trance. Lori felt my body stiffen and knew instantly that something strange was happening.

"Jim, what's wrong?" I heard her calling me. For a long time, I didn't say a word. I didn't want to scare her. Finally, I said, "Honey, I better tell you something; I just feel like I am supposed to go on record telling you this."

"What is it, Jim?"

I said, "Something terrible is about to happen. People are suffocating; there is a terrible tragedy, and they are suffocating to death. They are down under a mass of mud, and they are being inundated, and they are dying and screaming."

Lori and I prayed concerning the vision and tried as best we could to go back to sleep. My racing thoughts kept bringing back pictures of people buried beneath the mud. Sleep was impossible that night. Two days later, I learned that as part of the aftermath of a hurricane in South America, thousands of people had been killed—not by the high winds or the water or by falling debris, but by the immense mass of mud that surged over the area as a result of the storm.

I can't explain it, but somehow I connected with that event—two days before it happened! I'm not a psychic, and I don't have a hot line for you to call on me for advice about your future. I don't understand all these things that are happening to me, but I believe that God is trying to warn us as to what is going to happen in the days ahead. He wants to connect with you, too, but we won't hear His voice if we spend most of our time and energy running through the shopping malls, or the flea markets, or the sporting events that all bid for our time. We will not likely hear from God if our attention is glued to a television set for hours on end.

God is trying to work in between our busy schedules—think of that: The Almighty, majestic King of all creation is deigning to speak to us whenever we can find a few spare moments to listen to Him! But many of us can't even find a few minutes to focus our hearts and minds long enough to hear His voice!

We need to take time to listen for the voice of God.

Timing Is Key

An interesting and important factor to understand about dreams or visions is that sometimes a dream or vision may not be for this exact moment. Joseph waited thirty years before his vision came about. Daniel had a vision of end-time events that is yet to be fulfilled in its entirety. The angel Michael told Daniel, "Now I have come to make you understand what will happen to your people in the latter days, for the vision refers to many days yet to come" (Dan. 10:14 NKJV). So don't worry if God has spoken to you and His word to you has not yet been fulfilled. If the word was truly from God, you can be absolutely certain that it will come to pass. In the meantime, remain faithful and obedient to the Scriptures. If possible, submit what God has spoken to you to your spiritual leaders who have a track record of accurate discernment in such matters.

One word of caution: It is useless to seek confirmation of what you believe to be a word from the Lord if the person from whom you are seeking the confirmation does not believe that God speaks to us in such a manner today. Seek wise counsel, and ask the Lord to lead you to the people whose spiritual insight you can respect.

6. ANGELS WATCHING OVER YOU

God recently spoke to me saying that He is going to anoint the children in these last days. God is going to use children to speak to this generation, so don't despise the little ones. Moreover, the Lord revealed to me that children's angels will visit them. So don't get upset if one of your children or grandchildren comes up to you and says, "An angel came and talked to me."

Angelic visitations, of course, will not be restricted to children. Down through the ages, God has used angels to send messages to His children. That's what angels are—*messengers* of God. They are not part of the godhead; they are not to be worshiped (though it seems to be okay to be in awe of them); they are simply created beings, made to do God's bidding in ministering to and helping His people.

Angelic appearances can be found throughout the Bible, from Genesis to Revelation. For instance, in Genesis 22:11, an angel of the Lord spoke to Abraham. In Numbers 22:3–5, an angel of the Lord spoke to Balaam. Gideon, Elijah, David, and others in the Scripture also received heavenly messages from angelic beings. Beyond that, the Bible hints that you and I may have hosted angels without our knowledge, since we are reminded, "Do not forget to entertain strangers, for so by doing some have unwittingly entertained angels" (Heb. 13:2 NKJV). I wonder how many of us have driven off angels without knowing it, as well!

One underemphasized aspect of angelic visitations is that angels often speak to us in our dreams. For example, in Matthew 1:20, "An angel of the Lord appeared to him [Joseph] in a dream."

God is no respecter of persons. He speaks to adults and to children, to men and to women. My wife recently experienced an angel visitation in a dream, and in a most unusual manner, I got to enjoy the experience with her!

Lori often talks in her sleep, usually uttering only a few words, phrases, or a sentence or two, but it is enough to wake me up. I tease her, telling her that I always listen carefully when she is talking in her sleep, because I want to make sure she is talking about me!

On this occasion, however, she spoke much more than a phrase or a simple sentence. As I listened to her, it became obvious that she was *living* in a dream, and she was talking about it as she experienced it. I quickly realized that this was no ordinary dream, so I tried to pay close attention.

In her dream, she was in a large, barnlike building with rugged ceiling beams. A large group of young people in their late teens to early twenties was gathered around Lori, and she was telling the young men and women about Jesus. Her Bible was opened to the words of Jesus; she could see the red letters in the gospel accounts.

As I listened to Lori describe her dream, she said, "The kids are on their faces before God!" Soon other people came into the building and began doing other things, such as dramatic plays and other fun activities, but Lori stopped them. "Listen," she said, "those play things are all right, but the Spirit of God is here." The kids who had been doing the plays fell on their faces before God.

I listened even more intently as Lori cried out, "Oh, my! Oh, my! The angels of God are coming through the auditorium. It's a host of angels!" Suddenly, Lori's voice rose ecstatically, "Oh, my! One of them is coming to me!" The angel swept close to Lori and nodded approval, as if to say, "Yes, this is pleasing to God."

After a few minutes, Lori woke up, blinking her eyes as though she were coming out of a deep sleep. She looked at me and said, "Honey, I just had the most wonderful dream!"

"I know!" I said. "I was with you, listening to you describing it word for word."

THE MESSAGE IS WHAT MATTERS

Whether through the written Word, the spoken word, prophetic utterances and confirmations, spiritual gifts, or through dreams, visions, or angels, the medium God uses to communicate with us is secondary. It is His message that matters. God wants us to "hear His heart"; He wants to communicate with us. The only question is whether we will hear what He is saying to His church in these last days.

It is easy to get so caught up working for God and talking about God that we miss spending quality, intimate time with Him. When we allow that to happen, God's voice seems almost inaudible. For us to hear from God, we must be in close relationship with Him.

After I had the dream in prison, in which Jesus showed me that He wanted me to see everybody and everything through His eyes, I was both encouraged and exasperated. There I was in a federal prison in Rochester, Minnesota, with hurting, angry, lost men all around me, and I felt powerless to help them. I prayed, "God, why are there so many dying people here, and why can't I help them? I'm not allowed to preach [by orders of the warden]. I don't even feel welcome in chapel. What can I do?"

If I was expecting God to pat me on the head and comfort me, I was in for a big surprise. He did nothing of the sort. God said, "You are arrogant. You think that you are the only person I have in this prison. I have many others here. I am God."

And then God spoke to me the words that eventually put my entire prison experience into perspective. He said, "I did not bring you to prison to minister. I brought you here to get to know Me."

God fervently desires that we get to know Him, that we learn how to have intimate fellowship with Him, that we be able to recognize His voice when He speaks to us. Only as we hear His voice will we truly be able to enjoy being in His presence.

SPIRITUAL VISION OR SPIRITUAL BLINDNESS?

ONE OF THE HOT buzzwords at the end of the twentieth century and the beginning of the twenty-first century is the word *vision*. If you want to impress your boss or your teacher or your spouse, you can describe that person by saying, "You are a real *visionary*." Nowadays, that's a high compliment.

A few years ago, to call someone a visionary was merely a nice way of saying, "He's a real daydreamer!" But today, everybody is looking for someone with vision. Companies crave it. Leaders lust after it. Pastors and churches that have vision thrive, and those that don't, die.

What is this strange stuff known as vision? Where does it come from? How do you get it?

Vision, in the truest biblical sense, is "the revelation of God's will in the world." In other words, it is what God wants done here on earth, the way God wants it to be done. Vision often implies the ability to see what God wants done when others do not, to perceive His presence in a situation, to focus on His power to get the job done, in spite of the obstacles.

It is important that we understand this because, in the tumultuous times ahead, many voices will be declaring that they have a fresh "vision," and that we should follow them. Some of these voices may come from merely misguided members within the body of Christ, but others may be deliberate distractions, sent by the devil himself to deceive the Christian community. Unfortunately, our lack of godly vision, and the confusion within the body of Christ over what true godly vision is, how it should be developed, and how we should pursue it, may make the adversary's task all too easy.

Nowadays, we have a tendency to equate vision with buildings, budgets, new projects, and bringing in more money. Those are totally inaccurate means of measuring vision. After all, who had the greater vision—Andrew Carnegie or Mother Teresa? They both were visionaries, weren't they?

Many of our ideas of vision center around a person—a man or a woman who has a big idea, a big dream of doing something great for God and for the body of Christ. And that can be dangerous. Dietrich Bonhoeffer referred to this sort of human-centered dream of an idyllic Christian community as a "wish dream." In his book *Life Together*, Bonhoeffer sternly warned against confusing our own dreams of a Christian community with the divine reality of genuine Christian fellowship. Bonhoeffer said:

> Every human wish or dream that is injected into the Christian community is a hindrance to genuine community and must be banished if genuine community is to survive. He who loves his dream of a community more than the Christian community itself becomes a destroyer of the latter, even though his personal intentions may be ever so honest and earnest and sacrificial.[1]

I fell headlong into this trap when I attempted to build a Christian "oasis" known as Heritage USA. I envisioned a place where Christians could come year-round to hear the Word of God, to fellowship together, to enjoy a spiritual retreat in a "safe" environment that was as nice or nicer than anything the world had to offer. I truly wanted to build a place where the body of Christ could find rest and refreshment.

Ironically, even back in the 1970s I began to see in the Scriptures that difficult times were about to come on the earth, that the signs of the times were being fulfilled, and that the return of the Lord Jesus was imminent. Unfortunately, I believed and preached that true believers had nothing to worry about, that we would never experience the end-time cataclysmic events described in the Bible, because Jesus would take us out of this world, that we would be caught up in the "Rapture" before the tough times started happening. I formed that opinion not after intense study of the Scripture, but because it was the prevailing view at the time among ease-loving, evangelical Christians, and by far the most acceptable doctrine within the Christian community at large; beyond that, it just felt good. Besides, who wants to be here during the nasty stuff that we read about in the book of Revelation? Not me!

I didn't understand everything the Bible had to say about the end times (and I still don't), but looking back, I can now see that God was leading me even when I was unaware of it to prepare a place where His people could find refuge, a place that was not dependent upon the government to function, a place that was self-sufficient as much as possible in our modern age. For instance, we installed our own water and sewage system at Heritage USA, we maintained our own roads, we were beginning to grow our own food, we established affordable retirement homes and apartments for senior citizens; we provided homes for the homeless and were taking in unwed mothers, handicapped children, nonambulatory senior citizens, and others who could not care for themselves. All of these things and more we did in an effort to be the body of Christ in deed, as well as in word.

Unfortunately, the vision got out of control. Soon my lofty dreams began to take on a life of their own. As I often relate to friends now, I had a tiger by the tail. Four days out of every five, my job was to get up, go on television, and raise a million dollars—not to establish some new ministry or mission, but simply to maintain everything that we had initiated already. By 1987, my original vision was careening out of control. A short time after that, it crashed, and the repercussions continue to ripple through Christian as well as non-Christian circles to this day.

Several years later, while I was languishing in federal prison, still trying to figure it all out, God used Dietrich Bonhoeffer's book *Life Together* to help me understand why my vision, which was originally an "Isaac," meant to be a blessing to the world, became an "Ishmael," a self-manipulated method of trying to help God accomplish His work through my human efforts rather than His. Bonhoeffer wrote, "By sheer grace, God will not permit us to live even for a brief period in a dream world. He does not abandon us to those rapturous experiences and lofty moods that come over us like a dream. God is not a God of the emotions but the God of the truth."[2]

We certainly had our share of rapturous experiences and lofty moods at Heritage. I preached a "happy" gospel, with few insurmountable obstacles, few sacrifices, and little or extremely short-term pain. On a daily basis we lived out my melding of positive thinking and a prosperity gospel. It was a message that people wanted to hear and believe.

Critics of Heritage USA often castigated me for building what they called a "Christian Disney World," but I didn't see Heritage that way at all. Sure, it was a Christian environment, but it wasn't heaven on earth. We had just about every problem that you might find in any American town or city at that time. But we believed that God can and does forgive sin, so our unwillingness to give up on people was often meshed with our fervent desire to perpetuate the dream. Unfortunately, in doing so, we fostered the image that despite our problems, everything was fine. We gave the impression that it would only be a matter of time, over the next hill, after the next building was erected, until our dreams could come true. That, said Bonhoeffer, is a "wish dream," and "innumerable times a whole Christian community has broken down because it had sprung from a wish dream . . . But God's grace speedily shatters such dreams."[3]

In prison, Bonhoeffer's words pummeled me. "God hates visionary dreaming," Bonhoeffer said. "It makes the dreamer proud and pretentious."[4] I reeled at the realization of the painful truth. For most of my adult life, I had been hailed as a visionary, someone who saw things as they could be rather than as they were, someone who saw the potentially great things we could do for God and for the body of Christ, someone who often saw what even other believers could not see. Other ministers applauded me and, I'm told, even emulated me. "Oh, Jim Bakker, he's a great visionary. He knows how to get things done!" they'd say. And there was some truth to their words. Where other people saw an empty field or a cow pasture, I saw a "Crystal Palace." And yes, I had learned how to motivate men and women to do things for the cause of Christ that they might not have undertaken on their own. But now, Bonhoeffer's insightful comments shredded my wish dream.

He not only pulled the veneer off my vision, he ripped into my unspoken frustrations. Bonhoeffer explained, "The man who fashions a visionary ideal of community demands that it be realized by God, by others, and by himself . . . He acts as if he is the creator of the Christian community, as if his dream binds men together. When things do not go his way, he calls the effort a failure. When his ideal picture is destroyed, he sees the community going to smash. So he becomes, first an accuser of his brethren, then an accuser of God, and finally the despairing accuser of himself."[5]

Ouch! Bonhoeffer slugged me right in the pit of my stomach. I had unwittingly stepped into all of those traps in my desire to create a Christian community at Heritage USA. My intentions had been good, but my vision had veered off course, especially when I had allowed the work to overshadow the Lord and His people. In one sense, the vision had been marred from the start since my ideas of Christian community had been so idealistic.

For instance, for many of my years as president of PTL, I resisted implementing security cameras and accountability procedures among our mail room personnel as they opened the thousands of envelopes containing checks and cash from our donors. "Why do we need watchdogs?" I reasoned. "After all, we're Christians! If we can't trust these people to handle the money honestly, then who can we trust?"

Imagine my shock and disillusionment when internal auditors later estimated that we may have lost hundreds of thousands of dollars due to simple theft by our own employees. Besides the loss of money, I also bore the responsibility for exposing our workers to unnecessary temptation. Not many people can avoid compromise if allowed to handle large amounts of cash over time, with no real supervision or accountability. But in my wish dream, Christians didn't steal.

That's what I mean when I say the vision was misguided from the start, and that's why in these last days, we need to get real. We need to recognize that even the most well-intentioned Christians sin and fail, and rather than sweeping those mistakes under the carpet as though they never happen in our circles, we need to learn how to lovingly confront the sinner, encourage confession in a confidential environment, and then restore the repentant sinner and continue our communion with God and each other. To do that, however, we need to understand the true nature of a biblically based vision.

WHAT BIBLICALLY BASED VISION IS NOT

The concept of vision often gets confusing, even in Christian circles, so before we examine what biblically based vision entails, perhaps it may help to recall what biblically based vision is *not*.

Vision Versus Visions

First, having vision is not necessarily the same as *having visions*. All sorts of people in the Bible had visions. Most of the visions you read about in the Bible came from God, although Scripture also records sorcerers, magicians, seers, and even a few false prophets who either had visions, said they had visions, or tried to explain someone else's vision. All of these fake visionaries are condemned in Scripture.

Consider, for instance, Pharaoh's magicians, or the prophets of Baal, or Balaam, the conniving prophet. Recall also Nebuchadnezzar's magicians, his conjurors and diviners and others. All of these people provided false information based upon "visions," their own or someone else's.

On the other hand, many of God's people had bona fide, divinely inspired visions: Joseph, Daniel, Ezekiel, Isaiah, the apostle Paul (who was instructed in a vision to "Come over to Macedonia"), Peter (who was instructed through a vision to take the gospel to Cornelius, a Gentile centurion), and the apostle John, whose visions are recorded in the book of Revelation.

Vision is a very biblical word. It is used eighty-six times in the Old Testament (twenty-two times in the book of Daniel alone). The term is used fifteen times in the New Testament, with eleven occurrences in the book of Acts.

Many people today have had visions from God. That should not strike us as unusual since on the day of Pentecost, following the birth of the New Testament church, Peter stood and declared that in the last days such a phenomenon would occur. Quoting the prophet Joel (Joel 2:28), Peter preached God's message to the people:

"And it shall be in the last days," God says,
"That I will pour forth of My Spirit upon all mankind;
And your sons and your daughters shall prophesy,
And your young men shall see visions,
And your old men shall dream dreams;
Even upon My bondslaves, both men and women,
I will in those days pour forth of My Spirit,
And they shall prophesy." (Acts 2:17–18 NASB)

It is interesting to note the timing of biblical visions. When do visions come? You won't find them on every page of the Bible. But fresh visions frequently are found in Scripture when God wants to do something new, or when He wants His people to change directions.

To whom do visions come? Normally, to men and women who are already sold out to the Lord or at least seeking Him with all their hearts.

For example, Cornelius was a non-Jewish man, but he was a "god-fearing" fellow. He truly believed in the Lord, and was doing his best to know Him, when God gave him a vision (Acts 10).

Divine visions happen. But having visions and having vision are not necessarily the same.

Vision Versus Hype

Nor is vision the same as hype and hoopla. It is not "working the crowd," trying to get people to see things your way or mine. It is not trying to get people to sign up for something or to give money or to join our cause, whether good or bad.

Furthermore, biblically based vision is not Madison Avenue imagery. To the advertising community, vision means getting us to buy something that they are trying to sell us. Often the "vision" they are selling and the actual product are nowhere near the same.

For instance, Kent, a friend of mine, enjoys trying new colognes, so several years ago, I wasn't surprised when Kent's interest was piqued by a television commercial advertising a new fragrance. The commercial, however, was rather provocative. In the commercial, there was a half-naked fellow crashing through a jungle, following a black panther. Every now and then, the guy stopped and growled, "Grrrrrrr!"

Quickly, the camera switched to the panther, and the panther growled, "Grrrrrrrr!"

Meanwhile, insets of the cologne that they were advertising flashed on and off the screen, almost as though the advertiser was attempting to insert a subliminal message.

For a full thirty seconds, the guy chased the panther all through the jungle—both man and panther periodically growling as they went. The commercial climaxed when a beautiful woman, dressed in one of those "Me Tarzan, you Jane" outfits, stepped out of the jungle. She sensuously walked over to the heavily breathing fellow, placed her head on his chest . . . and then *she* growled! "Grrrrrrrrr!"

Kent later told me, "Watching that commercial, I thought, *Wow! That must be pretty amazing cologne!*"

So the next time Kent was at a fancy department store, he spied some of the powerhouse panther stuff. He bought some, slapped on way more than necessary, and headed home, practicing his growling as he drove.

When he got home, he pulled in the driveway and hurried to the door. His new cologne 'got there before he did. As he walked in the house, his wife curled up her nose and cried, "Oooooh! What's that awful smell?"

So much for the new panther aroma.

Kent had bought the image the cologne advertisers were selling. He hadn't purchased a cologne; he had purchased a fantasy. It was sheer imagery; he wanted to look, sound, and, yes, smell successful—just like the guy on television. So he set aside his brain for a while and laid his money on the counter. Who cared that the stuff smelled like a cross between a skunk and a gorilla?

Can you see the correlation between such hype and what frequently happens in the body of Christ? Nowadays, there are all too many people who claim to be speaking for the Lord, who are trying to sell us on imagery rather than a godly vision. Don't be deceived; there is a world of difference between a God-authored vision, and a humanly manipulated image of spiritual success.

WHAT VISION IS

With those qualifiers in mind, what then is this thing called *vision?* What good is it, and how do we find it? Let's start with a simple definition.

In the Scriptures, sometimes vision comes through a dream. Sometimes it is something that is revealed to the heart and mind of God's prophet. Sometimes it is an unusual insight into a situation, or an unusual foresight, or an unusual discernment about a matter. Sometimes it comes through a time of concentrated prayer, but godly vision may come just as easily through a sermon, song, or a genuine "word"—a message from the Lord spoken through a person. Sometimes a divine vision may be linked with an angelic visitation.

Certainly in our day, most of God's revelation has already been given through His Word, and He does not contradict Himself.

That's why when somebody says, "I've received a fresh vision from the Lord," we must immediately ask, "Is the vision consistent with the Word?" If not, forget it!

Remember, "In the beginning was the Word, and the Word was with God, and the Word was God" (John 1:1 NKJV). Any vision that God gives will always be consistent with His Word. If somebody tells you that he or she has a revelation from the Lord, and it is in opposition to, or out of sync with, God's Word, then forget you ever heard that word!

The apostle Paul said in Galatians 1:8, "But even if we, or an angel from heaven, preach any other gospel to you than what we have preached to you, let him be accursed" (NKJV). The word Paul used here for "accursed" is *anathema*, which means "given over to destruction." The apostle was warning that if anyone attempts to pawn off a new "vision" or another message as if it were from God, we should not simply avoid that person and that doctrine, but also know that person and message are doomed to divine destruction.

Vision, when it is of God, will be what God wants done in this world, and it will be consistent with God's Word. Now, we know from our examination of the biblical data in previous chapters that God has committed Himself to working in and through the community of believers. What He wants done in this world He wants to do in and through the church of Jesus Christ. Certainly, God could dispatch a battalion of angels to do His work on earth, but in some respects, at least, God has chosen to limit Himself to working through us. Certainly, He works through nature. Have you ever noticed how people suddenly get "spiritual" when they are faced with an impending hurricane? And clearly, God works through everyday circumstances. But the spreading of His message has been placed in our hands.

No wonder the Scripture declares, "Where there is no vision, the people perish" (Prov. 29:18 KJV).

WHEN GOD'S PEOPLE LACK GODLY VISION

That word translated "perish" has some interesting connotations. It means that the people are naked, bare, unprotected, stripped of their armor, exposed to danger.

The word can also be translated to mean that the people are "without restraint." They are ungovernable. They cannot be directed. And as a result, *they perish*. They become disorderly. The people are dispersed, rebellious, confused, easily deceived, uncontrollable.

They are easily drawn away from their duty. They fall into spiritual decay. They open themselves to personal and spiritual calamity and, eventually, disaster.

Without a *vision*, which is a revelation from God, they lose their desire for the Word of God, the will of God, and the work of God. Before long, hope and love vanish from their lives. Their dedication and devotion to God become compromised.

In many cases, even their day-to-day energy levels decline, because for those who ignore the Lord, it is easy to assume that life is meaningless and without real purpose.

Look at the people who have recently lost a loved one or gone through a divorce, or people whose dreams have been dashed or who have lost a job at which they have worked for years. If they don't have a strong relationship with Jesus Christ and a vision of what He is doing in their lives, when tragedies or difficult circumstances strike them they can easily slide downhill. Frequently, they get physically sick as depression sets in; they just want to lie in bed and not even get up.

Their attitude often is, "Who cares? What's the use?" Or else they become "users," selfishly sucking as much concern and compassion out of as many people as possible. All of this is implied when the Scripture warns us that without a vision, the people perish.

Thousands of sermons and motivational speeches have been based on this scriptural truth: "Without a vision, the people perish." And unfortunately, that is where we usually stop.

But read the rest of the verse: "Happy is he who keeps the law" (Prov. 29:18 NKJV). Happy is he who keeps God's Word!

Without the Word of God in our lives, we perish. But with the Word, there is life! Happy is he who walks in the fear of the Lord, and in the love and service of Jesus Christ!

WHEN GOD'S PEOPLE HAVE GODLY VISION

What will this kind of vision do for you? Why is it important to us? The body of Christ and each of us as individuals benefit in at least five ways when we have a sense of God's vision.

1. We Really Are One Family

First, godly vision unites us. A godly vision brings together people from all sorts of backgrounds to work for the Lord Jesus Christ. It causes us to lay aside our differences and work together for His glory, to see souls saved, to see lives changed, to see people empowered by the Holy Spirit, to live the way God wants us to live.

During every disaster, whether an earthquake, tornado, hurricane, or flood, we see instances of people in the general public laying aside their differences, pitching in toward the common goals of saving lives, and helping people to put their homes and lives back together. How much more should our vision of being the body of Christ and doing what God wants us to do cause us to lay aside our differences and work together to see people saved and homes and lives put back together!

2. It's Catching!

Another benefit of godly vision is that it is contagious! When people know where they are going, what they are supposed to be doing, and they are excited about doing it, that rubs off!

Something deep down inside of us admires a person who stretches out and starts living a life with vision. You want to be around that sort of person. Maybe at first you might think that he or she is half "nuts," or that some of his or her actions based on faith in God are a bit outlandish, or possibly even foolish. This is especially true if you don't understand the truth that his or her faith is founded upon. But faced with real vision, even jaded skeptics, after a while, turn into grudging admirers.

Noted author Chuck Swindoll tells a story about two nuns who worked as nurse's aides in a hospital. While driving to work one morning, they ran out of gas.

A gas station was nearby, but the women didn't have a container in which they could retrieve some gas and bring it back to the car. Then one of the nuns remembered that she had put a bedpan in the car's trunk.

They walked to the gas station, filled the bedpan with gasoline, and then carefully carried it back to the car. As the two nuns poured the gasoline from the bedpan into the car's gas tank, two guys drove by in a pickup truck. They gawked in amazement at the habit-clad women. Finally, one guy just shook his head and said, "Man, that's what I call faith!"

To those guys, the actions of the nuns must have looked like utter nonsense! Silly! Stupid, foolish, and naive.

But those guys didn't have the facts. They didn't know what the nuns knew. The nuns knew that there was explosive power in that pan! Imagine the surprised expressions on those guys' faces when the nuns zoomed by them on the freeway!

Something similar happens every day in the body of Christ. Some people may laugh at you when you tell them what you believe God is leading you to do. "Go get a real job," they may scoff. Others may chide you for wasting your time. "Why don't you do something significant with your life?" they may ask when you tell them that you are pouring your life into helping to build up the body of Christ. They simply don't understand the facts.

We are not working according to our own vision or our own efforts. Nor are we working for our own self-fulfillment or our own prosperity. We are depending upon our heavenly Father's resources, to do what He wants done in these exciting last days . . . and we are trying as best we know how to allow Him to use us to do His will in His way, rather than ours. Practically, that means as we attempt to feed, clothe, and house people in these days, we are not depending on our own resources. As we attempt to carry the gospel to the world, we are not attempting to fulfill our own selfish ambitions. We must rely on God's power and His provisions, and as we do, the work will get done efficiently and effectively. Scripture says that His work is done "'not by might nor by power, but by My Spirit,' says the LORD of hosts" (Zech. 4:6 NKJV). Most of us are familiar with the verse; perhaps the real question is, Do we really believe it?

The real issue. This is a vital question during these last days: Who are you going to believe? What are you going to believe? Will you believe and act upon what God says He wants you to do, or will you compromise and succumb to the so-called "voices of reason"? Will you trust God to supply your needs, or will you fall prey to the hysteria around you? Will you do what God has spoken to you about doing, or will you listen to the scoffers and the doubters and those who say you can't do what God has called you to do?

Have no illusions; we don't have time for any more "wish dreams," and the period of tribulation we are entering will not be easy. But those who will dare to trust and believe God will see genuine miracles as we participate in His vision—the community of believers, His church.

3. God Breathing into Us

A third benefit of godly vision is that it inspires us. The word *inspire* comes from a word in Latin that means "to breathe in"; you could say that to be inspired is to be "in-Spirited."

As you are filled with the Holy Spirit and begin to catch a glimpse of what God wants to do in and through your life, you get inspired and you become a source of inspiration to somebody else.

What is your vision? What kind of role is God calling you to take within the Christian community? Are you living a dull, drab, mundane existence, merely going through religious motions, keeping up the facade of being part of the body of Christ? God wants us to be "in-Spirited" by the Spirit of Jesus Christ.

What kind of life do you want to live? One that is routine—get up, go to work, come home, watch TV till you're tired, go to bed, get up, do it all over again? Or do you want to start living a life that is inspired by a vision—the revelation of Jesus Christ and what God wants to do in and through you?

What about your career? Would you rather have a boring, lackluster career, or one that is in-Spirited by the person of Jesus Christ?

And here is the icing on the cake! The Lord Jesus wants to give each of us one or more spiritual gifts that we can use to help us function in our particular place within the body, and to help us get His work done in the world. Are you willing to receive what He has for you and are you willing to use whatever gifts the Spirit gives you to honor Jesus?

4. Godly Vision Lasts

A fourth benefit of having a godly vision is that it will see you through the tough times in this life. Certainly, it will help you during the difficult times that come to every believer. I know some Christians don't believe it, and frankly, I dislike having to be the one to tell you this, but you are not going to escape some pain and suffering in this life. If you haven't had a severe crisis—I mean the kind of experience that truly tests your faith—just wait. You will. I don't mean that to be a negative statement; it is merely a fact, and all the "positive confessions" you can make will not keep life from happening to you and to those you love.

Beyond that, as I have mentioned numerous times in this book, I believe that the church of Jesus Christ is about to enter a period of extremely troublesome times. Whether or not you will be here for the Great Tribulation period, I do not know. Nevertheless, keeping the vision that God has given us will help us to remain faithful during the transitions that will be taking place.

When you know why you are here and what you are supposed to be doing, you'll find that you don't sweat the little things. A godly vision will help you to overcome the little hurts of life, and sometimes, if you can't overcome them, a godly vision will help you to overlook them.

A story is told about the great football coach Vince Lombardi, when he was trying to pep up his Green Bay Packers at halftime. As Lombardi came in and looked around the locker room, he heard several of his players complaining about bumps, cuts, and bruises that they had received during the first half of the game. Although the coach cared deeply for each of his players, he was not about to let their complaints deter them from their goal.

Lombardi said, "Look, boys; I know you're hurting; I see your bumps, your scrapes, your cuts, your bruises, and your blood. But every great game in life is won by those who have learned to play in spite of a lot of little hurts. Now get back out there and win this game!"

And they did. Was Lombardi's speech motivational hype? Sure. But was Lombardi right? Absolutely. If we are to function as the body of Christ in the days ahead, helping each other, encouraging each other, and yes, banging into each other, too, we must learn to overlook our trivial, minor scrapes and bumps—not because they don't hurt, but because the pain is not worth mentioning as we pursue the goal of being the body of Christ in these final moments of the game.

History is replete with illustrations of men and women who have overcome huge obstacles and have impacted the world, making a difference in the lives of others.

Milton wrote his beautiful and colorful descriptions of paradise—and Milton was blind.

Beethoven wrote fabulous, intricate symphonies, even after he became deaf.

Fanny Crosby wrote those great hymns of the church, songs with lyrics such as "Blessed assurance, Jesus is mine. Oh, what a foretaste of glory divine!" And, the classic, "And I shall see Him face to face." Many of us have grown up singing Fanny Crosby songs in church, and we often forget that she was blind.

Once, when a well-meaning friend was lamenting over Fanny's blindness, Fanny Crosby interrupted and said, "Oh, don't feel sorry for me. Don't you realize that the first face I'll see will be that of Jesus?"

And what of contemporary heroes such as Joni Eareckson Tada, who for most of her adult life has not been able to move her hands or her legs, due to a diving accident? Yet she writes books and paints pictures with a pen or a brush in her teeth. And I've heard her singing, too. Joni has inspired thousands of people to trust Jesus despite their circumstances in life.

In my own life, often people come to me and express their sorrow for what I've been through. I tell them, "Please don't feel sorry for me. I wouldn't be the person I am today, and able to minister to hurting people, had I not experienced the trials in my life. The trial of my faith has been more precious than gold."

If you want to do something great for God, you will find a way! And God will help you, if you will trust Him.

GOD'S VISION FOR YOU

Have you ever truly considered God's vision for your life? If you haven't, I suggest that you take some time to pray specifically about it. Ask the Lord to let you peek behind the curtain just long enough to get an idea of what it is He wants to do in and through you, and your life will never be the same!

Moreover, I suggest that you write down what the Lord shows you. God told the prophet Habakkuk, "Write the vision" (Hab. 2:2 NKJV). Something amazing happens as we see God's vision, His "mission statement" written down. I suggest that you not only write it, but that you display the vision in prominent places where you will be constantly reminded that God has revealed a portion of His plan for your life. Post it on the refrigerator, on your computer, in the car, on your desk at work, anywhere you can!

I'm convinced that in the days ahead it will be vital that the Christian community get a fresh vision of what we are to be and how we are to operate. It is absolutely essential for survival! Such godly vision comes by trusting Jesus Christ as Lord, not simply as your Savior, and allowing Him to fill you with His Holy Spirit—to in-Spirit you. Such godly vision usually comes to those who are already sold out to Him. It goes far beyond anything we can imagine in our minds. It's much deeper than a dream, much bigger and broader than merely a good idea or a new gimmick.

5. Godly Vision Is Creative

God's vision moves us out of the safe, comfortable, routine, expected areas of life and into the realm of trusting, believing, and depending upon the Lord. Sure it may be risky at times. But godly vision says, "Go out on a limb, because that's where the fruit is located."

You may not need to ask God to give you vision. He has already given His Word to you. He has already done everything that is necessary and said everything that you need to hear. But perhaps you need to ask the Lord for eyes to see, ears to hear, and faith to take that next step of obedience. Perhaps you need to ask the Lord to stretch your horizons, to stretch your understanding of His vision for your life. Maybe you need to say, "Lord, I know that people are perishing all around me. I want to get in on what You want done in my town, in my church, in my family, and in me."

In these exciting days, our prayer should be that of the old hymn writer, "Take my life and let it be consecrated, Lord to Thee."

God has given us no mandate to build buildings, buy carpet, sell books or tapes, or conduct conferences. But He has instructed us in how we ought to function as the community of believers, as we care for one another, and as we take the gospel to the world. That is His vision for us.

16

FORGIVENESS
IS THE KEY

ONE OF THE MOST incredible examples of forgiveness I've ever seen was when Pope John Paul II traveled to the prison cell of Ali Ajga, the man who had attempted to gun down the pope in the streets. The world reeled in confusion. "What is this?" people asked. A publicity stunt? Some superpious action on behalf of the pontiff? Was the pope just being an especially nice guy?

No, Pope John Paul demonstrated something most of us have ignored. He understood Jesus' words in Matthew 6:14–15:

> For if you forgive men their trespasses, your heavenly Father will also forgive you. But if you do not forgive men their trespasses, neither will your Father forgive your trespasses. (NKJV)

This is a serious statement, especially when we consider that it came directly from Jesus Himself. That's why the pope visited the man who attempted to assassinate him, to express his forgiveness to Ali Ajga. Certainly, the pope knew Ajga needed God's forgiveness and that the assassin might appreciate the pope's forgiveness, as well. But Pope John Paul II also knew that if *he* refused to forgive the gunman from his heart, if he held animosity toward the man who had tried to destroy him, then the heavenly Father would not forgive the pope for his own sins. And we all need to be forgiven by God . . . even popes.

A willingness to forgive those who have hurt us or who have tried to hurt us is a key element within the Christian community. Although most of us have never tried to murder a man, as Ali Ajga did, the truth is that even devout Christians sometimes "murder" each other in their hearts, and the consequences for such feelings of misplaced anger can be severe. In the Sermon on the Mount, Jesus taught:

> You have heard that it was said to those of old, "You shall not murder, and whoever murders will be in danger of the judgment." But I say to you that whoever is angry with his brother without a cause shall be in danger of the judgment. (Matt. 5:21–22 NKJV)

Yet if we are going to live and work together in close proximity, Christians will grate against each other from time to time. We are not in heaven yet! We do things differently. Sometimes our differences irritate each other. We have various personalities, various preferences, and various needs. It only makes sense that sooner or later, even sincere believers will have differences that can lead to sin, which can lead to division and possibly destruction if not dealt with promptly and completely.

The discovery of sin in the body of Christ, though not condoned, is not unusual. Only those Christians who wish to live in a dream world will refuse to admit that sin happens in our good, Bible-believing families and churches. As Dietrich Bonhoeffer wrote:

> The pious fellowship permits no one to be a sinner. So everybody must conceal his sin from himself and from the fellowship. We dare not be sinners. Many Christians are unthinkably horrified when a real sinner is suddenly discovered among the righteous. So we remain alone with our sin, living in lies and hypocrisy. The fact is that we *are* sinners![1]

WHEN YOU ARE THE OFFENDER

Admitting that we all are suffering from the same disease does not excuse us of our responsibility to avail ourselves of the cure, especially when one is so readily available and was purchased at such a dear price. The apostle Peter wrote:

You were not redeemed with perishable things like silver or gold from your futile way of life inherited from your forefathers, but with precious blood, as of a lamb unblemished and spotless, the blood of Christ." (1 Peter 1:18–19 NASB)

Nor does the fact that we all are in the same boat mean that we do not have to repent and seek forgiveness when we sin, when we are the offenders, rather than the ones who have been sinned against. You are aware, most likely, that when you sin, you must seek God's forgiveness. Scripture clearly says:

If we say that we have no sin, we deceive ourselves, and the truth is not in us. If we confess our sins, He is faithful and just to forgive us our sins and to cleanse us from all unrighteousness. (1 John 1:8–9 NKJV)

You also must seek the forgiveness of the person you hurt by your sin, and if possible, make restitution for it. Go to the person you have wronged, and, in an open but discreet manner, admit that you have erred and ask for that person's forgiveness. It isn't enough simply to say, "I'm sorry." That is merely a statement of fact. If you have sinned against another person, or if your sin has impacted another person negatively or brought the Lord's name into disrepute with another person, you must ask for the person's forgiveness. Tell that person, "I apologize. I was wrong. Would you please forgive me?"

Keep in mind that you can ask for forgiveness, but you cannot demand it. If the other person refuses to forgive, that is his or her problem; you can do nothing about it if you have sincerely repented—which means to turn around 180 degrees from your sin—and sought forgiveness.

Perhaps the most difficult person to forgive when you sin is yourself. Yet you must. To do otherwise is not a humble sense of unworthiness; it is the height of arrogance. It is like saying to Jesus, "What You did on the cross is insufficient, Lord. Your shed blood may have purchased everyone else's salvation, but my sins are too bad. It will take more than Your crucifixion to deliver me."

What an insult! If you have honestly repented and sought the forgiveness of God and those people whom you have hurt by your sin, you owe it to Jesus to forgive yourself.

Another often overlooked aspect of forgiveness is the confession of our sins to one another. James said:

> Therefore, confess your sins to one another, and pray for one another, so that you may be healed. The effective prayer of a righteous man can accomplish much. (James 5:16 NASB)

James was not talking about confessing to a human being to find salvation; he was talking about confessing our sins to one another to find healing and spiritual health. Bonhoeffer pointed out that in this sort of honest, open confession, we take a major step toward being an accountable Christian community. He noted:

> In confession the break-through to community takes place. Sin demands to have a man by himself. It withdraws him from the community. The more isolated a person is, the more destructive will be the power of sin over him, and the more deeply he becomes involved in it, the more disastrous is his isolation. Sin wants to remain unknown. it shuns the light. In the darkness of the unexpressed it poisons the whole being of a person . . . The sin must be brought into the light . . . Since the confession of sin is made in the presence of a Christian brother, the last stronghold of self-justification is abandoned.[2]

Something incredibly powerful and liberating takes place as we honestly admit our sin to a brother or a sister in the Lord. Wisdom strongly suggests that such confessions be kept within the sexes—men confessing to men, women confessing to women. But any true believer can hear the confession of another believer and not only identify with the sin, but know that it is only the grace of God that has delivered him or her from committing that same sin. As Bonhoeffer said, "Anybody who has once been horrified by the dreadfulness of his own sin that nailed Jesus to the Cross will no longer be horrified by even the rankest sins of a brother."[3]

WHEN SOMEONE SINS AGAINST YOU

Sometimes even dedicated Christians say or do nasty things to each other, things that are downright wrong, that are blatant, flagrant sins. These things do not catch God by surprise. Jesus recognized that such sin happens, and He told us in advance how to deal with it when it occurs. Jesus said:

> Moreover, if your brother sins against you, go and tell him his fault between you and him alone. If he hears you, you have gained your brother. But if he will not hear, take with you one or two more, that "by the mouth of two or three witnesses every word may be established." And if he refuses to hear them, tell it to the church. But if he refuses even to hear the church, let him be to you like a heathen and a tax collector. (Matt. 18:15–17 NKJV)

Notice that our primary purpose in seeking to deal with someone who sins against us is not to make the person feel like dirt. It is not to humiliate the sinner or exact an apology, although repentance and acknowledgment of the sin are implied in Jesus' words "if he hears you," or *listens* to you—if he accepts your assessment of the situation and agrees that he has sinned. The goal is correction, reconciliation, and restoration of a brother or sister in the body of Christ.

GOD'S FOUR-STEP PROGRAM IN CONFRONTING

Jesus gave us four simple steps to take when we must do the tough job of confronting a fellow believer about sin in his or her life. The order in which we take these steps is not arbitrary; it's not up to us which of the steps we will take first. Jesus specifically laid out the plan, and we dare not deviate from it. The number of people involved and the way in which the situation is handled changes only if the person who is confronted refuses to listen and continues to live with unforgiven sin.

1. Take the direct approach. If your brother (or sister) in the family of God sins (most modern versions of the Bible translate Matt. 18:15 as "sins against you"), you are to go to that person alone for a one-to-one conversation about the matter. Your attitude should not be accusatory, but redemptive. In other words, you don't want to approach the person with the attitude, "Hey, buddy! You sinned against me, and I'm here to call you on it." Your goal, remember, is reconciliation, not further alienation from each other.

At the same time, don't be reluctant to let the other person know that your fellowship has been fractured and is in need of repair. As in most confrontational situations, it is always wisest to couch your approach in terms of how the sin has impacted you. "I feel that what you have done is wrong. You have hurt me. I expected better of you."

If the person acknowledges the sin, repents of it, and asks God for forgiveness, as well as you (or others if the sin involves other people), the matter is over and done. It should go no further. In fact, if you do disclose the matter to others, you become a gossip, which is a sin for which you will then need to repent!

"If he hears you," Jesus said, "you have gained your brother." You are reconciled. The fracture in the body has been forgiven, and the healing process must be allowed to begin. Although you may never be able to forget it, you do not have any reason to keep bringing the sin up in your heart or mind, mulling it over, or seeking any further action. It is forgiven. Done.

Only if the person refuses to acknowledge and deal with the sin should you proceed to the second step that Jesus directs.

2. Take one or two witness with you (preferably fellow believers) and confront the offending person again. Notice, you are not to take a group of people; you are not to embarrass or attempt to trap the person in a public forum. At the most, you are to take only two trusted advisers to witness the confrontation. The two people you take with you need not know everything about the sin that has occurred, only that the situation is still festering and needs to be fixed. While the two witnesses may offer insights and suggestions, don't try to get them to do your dirty work. The breach in the body is between the person who has sinned and you.

Again, if the offending party hears you out, agrees that he or she has sinned, and seeks forgiveness, the matter is closed. Both you and your witnesses can let the issue drop.

3. If the person who has sinned refuses to admit the sin or refuses to repent and be reconciled, you are to take the matter to the church.

Many Bible scholars believe that "the church" in this context can be a representative body, such as a group of elders, deacons, or pastors. It does not necessarily mean that someone should get up in front of the full body that gathers for worship and announce that a sin has been committed and that the offender refuses to deal with it. Only in extreme cases should such a public comment be made. Remember, everyone attending our worship services is not necessarily "born again." In most cases, the offender can be confronted by the group that represents the church, and the matter can be handled discreetly.

Again, Bonhoeffer offered wise counsel:

> A confession of sin in the presence of all the members of the congre-
> gation is not required to restore one to fellowship with the whole
> congregation. I meet the whole congregation in the one brother to
> whom I confess my sins and who forgives my sins. In the fellowship
> I find with this one brother I have already found fellowship with the
> whole congregation.[4]

*4. If the person continues in willful sin and refuses to deal with it, he or she
is to be excluded from the fellowship.* That is the meaning of the phrase "let
him be to you like a heathen and a tax collector" (Matt 18:17).

But proceed with great caution. Before you start running around trying
to see who should be kicked out of the fellowship, remember that it is
God's heart to bring people *in* to His family, not to exclude them.

Only in one extremely rare case in the New Testament do we see a
member of the body of Christ being cast out of the fellowship because of a
refusal to deal with overt sin (although in Acts 5, Ananias and Sapphira
were struck dead for their sin). In Corinth, a young man was committing
sexual immorality with his father's wife. Some commentators believe that
the father had married again, and the young man had a relationship with
the father's second wife. Other commentators hint that the sin involved an
incestuous relationship with the son's own mother.

Regardless, the apostle Paul instructed the church to "deliver such a one
to Satan for the destruction of the flesh, that his spirit may be saved in the
day of the Lord Jesus" (1 Cor. 5:5). Even in this extreme situation, however, Paul's intent was not simply to punish the offending parties by excom-
munication. Paul's drastic steps were disciplinary in nature, intended to
bring the fellow to a place of repentance so his soul could be saved. Later,
in 2 Corinthians 2:5–11, Paul reminded the fellowship that it was time to
restore the brother who was under church discipline. (See also Gal. 6:1.)

BINDING AND LOOSING WHAT?

Interestingly, it is immediately following Jesus' instructions concerning how to confront and seek reconciliation with a fellow believer who

has sinned, that we find His instructions concerning "binding and loosing."

> Assuredly, I say to you, whatever you bind on earth will be bound in heaven, and whatever you loose on earth will be loosed in heaven. (Matt. 18:18 NKJV)

In recent years, many believers have applied Jesus' words here, as well as His promise to Peter and the disciples in Matthew 16:19, to the supernatural realm of spiritual warfare, claiming that as believers we can "bind" the demonic powers that assail us, and "loose" people who have been bound by demonic oppression and possession. Still others claim that as believers we can "loose" God's blessings upon people. Unquestionably, Satan, the enemy, attempts to tie believers up in knots, and many need to be released from the bondage in which they have lived for far too long.

But don't let it escape your notice that in Matthew 18, at least, Jesus' comments about binding and loosing are in the context of *forgiveness!* Whatever disciplinary actions we as the body of Christ choose to bind or loose on earth will be ratified in heaven. If a person refuses to repent after the Christian community has exhausted all reasonable efforts to reason with him or her, the discipline imposed or rescinded by the church will be regarded in the same manner in heaven! Talk about serious clout. We in the body of Christ frequently do not realize just how seriously God takes us.

PETER'S QUESTION

No doubt, as Jesus described how a fellow believer who has sinned against another believer should be confronted, the wheels in Peter's mind were already turning. Living and working together with eleven other disciples, Peter knew all too well how easily one or more of them could get bent out of shape. The Scripture records:

> Then Peter came to Him and said, "Lord, how often shall my brother sin against me, and I forgive him? Up to seven times?" (18:21 NKJV)

Peter probably thought of himself as quite magnanimous in his offer to forgive an offending brother seven times, since Jewish tradition said to forgive a person only three times, or at most, four. After that, if the person offended again, forget him! Perhaps Peter was expecting Jesus to pat him on his self-righteous back, but instead, Jesus' answer must have made Peter's head snap back. Jesus said to him, "I do not say to you, up to seven times, but up to seventy times seven" (18:22).

Jesus was not telling us, "Forgive that person 490 times, but on the 491st offense, say, 'That's it. I've had it with you. I'm out of here!'" The number 490 was irrelevant. The point that Jesus wanted Peter (and us) to catch is that forgiveness does not have a stopping place. We don't ever stop forgiving! And notice, our forgiveness is not contingent upon the person's confessing and repenting of their sin against us. Jesus commands us to forgive no matter what. God will deal with the offending party. Our job is to forgive when we have been offended.

To illustrate this point, Jesus told the disciples a story that explains why we must forgive and keep on forgiving, why we can never withhold forgiveness, and why we must learn to live daily in forgiveness if we are going to be a Christlike community. This simple story that Jesus told is loaded with profound insights concerning spiritual and emotional healing.

AND YOU THOUGHT *YOU* WERE IN DEBT!

You can read the story in its entirety in Matthew 18:23–35, but let's look at a few highlights. When a king decided to settle accounts with his servants, he discovered that one servant owed him the enormous sum of ten thousand talents, roughly the equivalent of $10 million today, although the buying power of ten thousand talents in biblical times would have been exponentially greater. To give you an idea of what a huge amount of money this was, consider this: the annual taxes for the provinces of Judea, Idumea, Samaria, Galilee, and Perea all totaled only came to about $800,000. And here was a fellow who owed $10 million!

To further put this debt in perspective, consider this: The normal daily wage in New Testament times was one denarius for an average day's work. Ten thousand talents equaled sixty million denarii, so working every day for the average wage, it would take this guy 1,099,044 *lifetimes* to earn enough money to pay off his debt (assuming that he didn't spend any of his earnings on anything other than debt reduction)!

Do you get the picture? This guy owed more than he could possibly ever repay. Now, Jesus purposely chose this enormous amount of debt to drive home a crucial point: namely, that our debt of sin and our need for forgiveness are so enormous that we can never truly pay God back, no matter what we do—no more than this servant could have saved up enough money to pay off his $10 million bill.

In Jesus' story, the king commanded that since the servant couldn't repay his debt, he should pay with his life. He was to be sold as a slave, along with his wife and children, and everything they possessed (18:25). That's when things really got interesting!

The servant fell down on his knees, probably with his face to the ground, and begged the king for mercy. "Master, have patience with me, and I will repay you all," the man groveled. "Just give me a little more time, Lord, and I'll get it together; honestly, I will! Give me an extension on my taxes, a little more interest on my credit card."

Then comes the most beautiful part of the story:

> Then the master of that servant was moved with compassion, released him, and forgave him the debt. (18:27 NKJV)

More than $10 million! The king just wrote it off! He said, "Forget it. It's over and done. It's gone." He didn't even ask for an IRS tax-deductible receipt—he just said, "I forgive you. The debt is erased; let's forget it."

What would you have done? If somebody came along and had the power to cancel all your debts—your car payment, mortgage payment, and anything else that you owed—wouldn't you respond with a tremendous sense of gratitude? Similarly, wouldn't you expect the fellow in our story to fall at his king's feet and cry out, "Oh, Master! Thank you! You have forgiven me so much! Thank you for taking this heavy load off my shoulders. Thank you for setting me free!" Wouldn't you think that the guy would sing "Amazing Grace" or something?

But he didn't. Instead that servant went out and found one of his fellow servants who owed him one hundred denarii—about eighteen to twenty dollars. He grabbed his fellow servant and started choking him, saying, "Pay me what you owe me!"

When the coworker couldn't pay up, the first servant showed no mercy. He had his buddy thrown into debtors' prison until he could pay back the debt in full (18:28–30). It's difficult for modern-day inmates to pay back debts while in prison, where they earn eleven to fifteen cents an hour, but in biblical times it was even worse. Furthermore, the debtors were not allowed out of prison until the debt was paid, so the crunch usually fell upon family members and friends, or else the debtor remained in prison. It was like a death sentence with no appeal, no way out, and no hope.

Fortunately, the fellow who owed the twenty bucks had some good friends. "So when his fellow servants saw what had been done, they were very grieved, and came and told their master all that had been done" (18:31). When the king got wind of it, he summoned the first servant and said, "You wicked servant! Look, I forgave you all your debts, because you begged me, and now you treat your *fellow servant* this way? How can you do this? When I've forgiven you so much? Do you mean to tell me that you won't forgive your friend such a relatively small thing? Shouldn't you have had mercy and compassion on your fellow servant, as I had on you?"

So in raging anger, the king turned the servant over to debtors' prison—some translations of the Bible say that the king turned the servant over to "the torturers"—until he could pay back the original $10 million debt! Notice this: The unmerciful servant's unwillingness to forgive was not only selfish and stupid, it also destroyed the offer of forgiveness from the king! It blew the whole deal! Now, that's bad enough, but Jesus' next statement is the real zinger.

I can see Jesus turning and looking at His listeners as He summed up the point of His story: "So My heavenly Father also will do to you if each of you, from his heart, does not forgive his brother his trespasses" (18:35 NKJV.)

Jesus made it extremely clear that He will not tolerate unforgiveness in the hearts and minds of His people. He will not stand by idly, while we hold grudges from the past—whether it be the past week or the past decade—or while we continue to harbor bitterness and resentment against our fellow servants. Such unforgiveness on our parts is especially appalling since He has forgiven each of us so very much!

EMOTIONAL AND SPIRITUAL PROBLEMS IN THE BODY

Many emotional and spiritual maladies in the Christian community today (not to mention many physical ailments) can be traced to two main causes: (1) the failure to understand God's forgiveness of us, including the failure to understand, receive, and live out God's unconditional grace; and (2) our failure to give out that unconditional love, forgiveness, and grace to people who have offended us or have hurt us in some way. Let's look at these two causes individually.

1. Failure to Receive God's Forgiveness

Many of us are like the first servant in Jesus' story. He didn't really grasp the fantastic gift the king gave to him. The king didn't merely give him an extension of time, he gave him far more! He forgave the debt entirely. He released the servant from bondage that he had been living under for years!

Sadly, the servant never truly caught on. He probably never really heard a word that his master had said to him. Quite possibly, the servant thought that the king had granted his request for more time.

"Please, Lord, just have a little more patience with me."

"Don't foreclose on my debt yet! Please, just extend my credit a bit further, and I promise that I will pay you everything that I owe!"

This foolish servant was so proud and arrogant, he may have actually thought that he could repay the king the entire $10 million, if given enough time.

But the master, in his mercy and compassion, knew better. He didn't extend the note. He tore it up! He canceled the debt and set the man free from his debts, free from condemnation, free from the threat of a hellish life in prison!

And that is what Jesus has done for us! He canceled our debt of sin; He set us free, so "there is therefore now no condemnation to those who are in Christ Jesus, who do not walk according to the flesh, but according to the Spirit" (Rom. 8:1 NKJV). That is good news!

But the fellow in Jesus' story couldn't or wouldn't accept the good news. He couldn't believe it, receive it, or enjoy it. He thought that he was still under condemnation as a debtor—and a big debtor, at that! He thought that he had merely been given a little more time to work things out, to get his life together, to work harder, scrimp and save more diligently, and to pinch pennies more tightly.

And because he *thought* he was still living in bondage, he was! All the guilt, resentment, anxiety, fear, stress, and striving were still there in his life, as far as he was concerned. Moreover, because he thought he still owed, he thought he still had to pay; and because he thought that he still had to pay, it was then necessary that he collect from everyone and anyone who owed him anything, large debts or small.

Furthermore, he felt that he had a *right* to extract payment from others, no matter how badly they were hurting already, or how badly he hurt them by demanding either payment or imprisonment. Many of us are like that in the way we deal with our immediate family members as well as our "extended" family members in the body of Christ. We need to realize that Jesus bought and paid for our salvation and for our daily forgiveness. He paid the price for our sins, so we might be free—free to live in heaven one of these days, but also free to enjoy living in close relationship to His family here on earth.

Recently, my wife, Lori, and I enjoyed having lunch at a local restaurant with some friends, one of whom picked up the tab. On the way out the door, the cashier growled after us, as though we were trying to abscond with the silverware, "Come back here! You need to pay for your meal!"

"That man back there paid for our meals," I said, pointing to our benefactor in the back of the restaurant. The cashier acquiesced and smiled sweetly. She knew that she had no right to ask me to pay for something that had already been paid for by my friend. I returned the cashier's smile, as we walked past her register and out the door. I had no guilt or fear of condemnation because the bill had been paid.

Jesus paid! He paid the price for our sinfulness; He paid the price for our freedom; and He paid the price for our fullness, that we can live life abundantly now and enjoy heaven throughout eternity, as well.

We need to understand that grace is not only God's undeserved mercy and favor (it is that, of course), but grace is also *unearned.* God's grace is not like airline frequent-flyer programs in which you can accumulate so many points to be used for a later free trip. No, there is no way we can earn God's grace, not with money, not with good works, not with spiritual exercises or rituals. We can't earn God's grace, and it cannot be *repaid!* All we can do is live in His forgiveness and extend it to others.

We can never "pay God back" for loving us, for having compassion on us, and for forgiving us. We can't work a little harder and hope to even the score with God. "Hey, God, You pat my back, and I'll pat Yours!"

How ludicrous! Yet many Christians have not understood how great God's forgiveness is, and they remain on a spiritual treadmill, constantly trying to show God that they can make it, that given enough time, they can build something or do something that will cause God to be impressed, that they could somehow get rid of their own guilt, cancel their own sins, and square their debts with God.

I recall a preacher's wife who was one of the most diligent workers in the church. But she was constantly critical of other people, including her husband. She was a harsh, demanding, sarcastic woman, who frequently said things that cut and hurt other believers in the body of Christ. In the home, she was even worse! She was nasty to her husband and withdrew from any of his advances toward intimacy. She didn't want him to touch her, and she never touched him, at least not on purpose. She rejected his love and affection for years. It is a testimony of his commitment to God and to his wife that he did not leave her.

Finally, the woman came to her senses and realized that she was destroying their marriage. She went for help and found a competent Christian counselor to help her work through her problems. At first, she blamed everybody and everything else. The place where she lived was too small. The church work was too much for her. Other people in town had it in for her. Her husband was a jerk. On and on she went.

But eventually the truth came out. Several years before she and her husband had married, she had been on a vacation to a foreign country, where she had succumbed to sexual temptation. Though she knew better, she had compromised her values, let down her guard, and given in to the sexual advances of a man she had known only briefly, someone she had met during the trip. That incident was bad enough, but in the years to follow, she continued to have numerous affairs.

Then she met the man she wanted to marry. She asked God for forgiveness and told her fiancé about her sordid past. His response was full of compassion and forgiveness. "It's okay," he said, "you didn't even need to tell me. It's over and done; it's forgiven; it's in the past."

The couple married, but the woman could not forgive herself. In her head, she knew that she had asked God for His forgiveness, and intellectually, she felt that He had forgiven her. But in her heart of hearts, the guilt still plagued her. She began to hate herself. Every time she looked in the mirror, she became nauseated. She couldn't stand to see the person who was staring back at her.

She became less and less concerned about her appearance, health, or hygiene. She sometimes went weeks without brushing her hair, and wore the same clothes again and again until her husband could talk her into allowing him to wash them. She put on weight, which only added to her revulsion at herself.

Her emotional conflicts spilled over into every area of the couple's marriage and into the ministry that God had given them. She could not accept complete forgiveness, and she refused to forgive herself for what she had done. Consequently, she would not accept her husband's love, affection, or forgiveness, either.

She felt that she had no right to be happy. "I have no right to enjoy my husband," she told the counselor. "I have no right to enjoy my life. I've got to pay back this debt to God."

So she poured herself into working in the church and making everyone else miserable. She was trying to punish herself, to suffer, and to somehow atone for her own sins, to pay for her own salvation. And it was an impossible debt.

How beautiful it was when, with the help of the Christian counselor over an extended period of time, the pastor's wife finally allowed the truth to set her free, the truth that Jesus had truly paid the price for her sins. She realized that, in the words of the old song, "Calvary covers it all." Jesus paid. She no longer had to, nor could she. The woman finally received full and free forgiveness from God, from her husband, from others in the Christian community whom she had hurt or offended, and most of all, from herself.

2. Failure to Extend Forgiveness

The second main cause for many of our emotional and spiritual problems is our reluctance to extend God's forgiveness to others, especially to those who have hurt or offended us. Oh, yes, we want God to forgive them (in most cases). We don't even mind if they forgive themselves (usually). But don't ask me to forgive somebody who has hurt me!

Yet when we refuse to forgive those who have offended us, we perpetuate a tragic cycle. The *unforgiven* become the *unforgivers!* The hurt then hurts others. And the cycle of pain, bitterness, and resentment continues—yes, even among Christians.

If we don't understand that we are forgiven, and if we don't accept that forgiveness, how can we ever extend that forgiveness to anyone else? On the other hand, when we do understand that God forgives us, we must forgive our fellow servants!

Notice again, in the story Jesus told, the folly, futility, and frustration that were foisted upon others when the cycle of unforgiveness was perpetuated by the man who failed to grasp the true meaning of his own forgiveness.

> But that servant went out and found one of his fellow servants who owed him a hundred denarii; and he laid hands on him and took him by the throat, saying, "Pay me what you owe!" (Matt. 18:28 NKJV)

How ludicrous! If it wasn't so painful—and if it didn't happen over and over in our churches yet today—this story would almost be funny! Because the first servant did not realize that he had been forgiven, he figured that he had to go around collecting debts from people who owed him, so he could pay a debt to the king—a debt that had been canceled! Forgiven!

He said, "I've got to get all this money back because I've got to pay!" So he grabbed one of his fellow servants who apparently wasn't doing so well himself, and the first servant started strangling the fellow, demanding, "Pay me what you owe me! Give me that eighteen bucks!" When the fellow servant was too poor to pay, his creditor had him thrown into prison! The unforgiven became the unforgiver. The unaccepted became the unaccepting. "If I don't feel accepted, I'm not going to accept you." The unloved become the unlovely.

It happens again and again in the body of Christ. Your parents may have hurt you in some way, perhaps during your childhood, or possibly as recently as last week. The pain is just as real. Or perhaps you have brothers or sisters who let you down, who turned away just when you needed them most. Maybe your friends or other family members teased you or put you down, made fun of you, or humiliated or embarrassed you in some way that causes your face to flush with color every time you think of it to this day. Maybe your friend used you or betrayed you, or possibly a sweetheart rejected you. Perhaps you've known the pain of a marriage partner who was untrue to you. Possibly your pastor or other spiritual leaders have let you down.

And even as you read these words, something wells in your heart and mind that wants to cry out, "These people *owe* me!"

You may not say much aloud, but your stomach churns every time you think of how that person offended you, and you want to scream, "I have a *right* to feel hurt! I have a right to feel bitter, angry, and yes, I have a right to withhold forgiveness. You owe me a debt!"

Can I tell you something in all love? Will you accept it from one who has experienced all of the above disappointments, feelings of rejection, and more?

No, you do not have a right to hold on to that bitterness. If Jesus forgave us, we have no right to withhold forgiveness from anyone else. Worse yet, if you continue to clutch your hurt so tenaciously, refusing to let go of it and to forgive, you are killing yourself emotionally, harming yourself physically, and placing yourself in extreme peril eternally.

GET OVER IT!

Many Christians harbor resentments due to unresolved anger, disappointments, and disagreements with fellow believers; others allow bitterness due to disillusionment with the church, spiritual leaders, or disappointment with God to eat away at their spiritual and emotional vitality. Some Christian husbands and wives feel that they were sold a bill of goods in their marriage partners.

One Christian couple with whom I am familiar seem destined for divorce unless they learn to forgive each other for not being perfect. They are so disappointed in their marriage, they have gotten to the point where they are saying, "Aw, let's just forget it. You go your way, and I'll go mine."

Part of their problem is that they had been given such a high ideal of marriage in their church. They had grown up in the church, met, fell in love at a youth function, dated through college, and then attended premarital counseling with their pastor. Throughout all of that time, the picture of Christian marriage was one of a happy couple living in perfect harmony and continual ecstasy. They received the false impression that Christian couples never have the problems that plague other people. But shortly after they returned from their honeymoon, the young couple woke up one morning to the awareness that the person to whom they were now married was not the person they had known all those years! Before long, their relationship began to disintegrate. Each marriage partner was disillusioned with the other.

She had married him for his spiritual leadership capabilities. He seemed so disciplined, intensely focused, firmly grounded in the Word, hardworking—a guy who was really going places for the Lord. Imagine how shocked she was when within the first year of their marriage, she discovered that he was actually quite indecisive, undisciplined, a procrastinator at best, and, frequently, downright lazy! In her anger, much like the unmerciful servant, she figuratively clutched his throat in her hands, while she screamed, "You cheated me! You owe me all the good qualities I saw in you while we were dating. That was the person I married . . . not . . . not . . . *YOU!* Pay me what you owe!"

For his part, he had married her for her attractive physical appearance, her neatness, orderliness, and organizational qualities. Imagine his disappointment when within the first year, her hourglass figure began to bulge. He soon found that she was sloppy in her personal life at home, leaving clothes, makeup, hair-care paraphernalia and other intimate items all over the bathroom. She hated housework (who doesn't?) and was content to let the mess lie until he decided to hire a weekly maid service. She was disorganized, constantly frazzled, going from one crisis mode to the next, and frequently forgetting important names, dates, or events that they were obliged to attend.

In his own way—which is through sarcasm and deeply cutting remarks—he seized her by the throat and screamed, "Pay up, woman! You owe me. You didn't come through on your promise!"

Can this marriage be saved? Yes, but only if the couple adopt a realistic attitude toward marriage, and more important, if they learn to forgive each other from the heart.

WITHHOLDING FORGIVENESS IS DANGEROUS

Many parents unwittingly withhold forgiveness from their children, especially their teenagers. Rather than forgiving them for their wrong actions and continuing to pour unconditional love on them, many Christian parents are figuratively strangling their offspring. Their hands are around the kids' throats as they yell, "Pay up, kid! I've been good to you! You owe me. You are in debt to me, and you are going to pay!"

You can find this same attitude growing like a bad fungus in many parts of the body of Christ. Another brother or sister in the family of God said or did something that offended you, and rather than forgiving that person, you are still hanging on to it. You refuse to let go, and continue to hold onto deep-seated anger. Oh, you may not express it verbally, but it's still there, seething below the surface like a volcano ready to erupt with just the least bit of jostling. You won't go to that person to attempt to resolve the matter, but every time you see him or her, you want to start choking that person again. "You hurt me! You offended me! You owe me! I have a right to be angry. I have a right to withhold forgiveness."

And all the while, Jesus says, "Who do you think you are?"

The King of kings and Lord of lords looks at you and asks, "What right do *you* have to withhold forgiveness from anyone? After all I have done for you? After the sins you have committed, and I have forgiven you of so much. Will you not forgive your brother or your sister? Who do you think you are to be demanding your eighteen dollars, when I have had compassion on you and have forgiven you of more than $10 million?" How dare we say, "I won't forgive that person!" when Jesus has forgiven us of so much?

But let's be honest. Most of us know that we are on thin ice when we withhold forgiveness, but sometimes we want to say, "Okay, Lord. I know I have to forgive him or her, but can't I just compromise a little? Can't I just make him pay a little longer before I forgive? Can't I make her suffer the way she has made me suffer? Can't I rub it in just a bit? Can't I hurt him the way he hurt me? Please, let me hold it over their heads just a little longer. Yes, yes, I am going to let go of it, but God, I'm enjoying this. I like watching that person squirm; it feels so good. Can't I just withhold forgiveness a little longer?"

And King Jesus says, "*NO!* Not if you expect Me to cancel your debt and forgive you. If you want forgiveness, you must forgive those who have hurt you."

Forgiveness is sometimes easier said than done. It took me nearly five years in prison to fully forgive the people who seemed so obsessed with putting me behind bars and hurting my family and me. It took even longer to forgive myself for my sin and the negative impact the events that toppled me from the presidency of PTL brought on the body of Christ. But God clearly showed me that I would never get out of prison until I forgave everyone involved in the demise of Heritage USA and my subsequent imprisonment. God seared into my heart and mind the Scripture, "And when you stand praying, if you hold anything against anyone, forgive him, so that your Father in heaven may forgive you your sins" (Mark 11:25–26 NIV).

R.T. Kendall's book on the life of Joseph, *God Meant It for Good,* helped me to work through the process of forgiveness. Dr. Kendall wrote:

Sometimes . . . we are called upon to forgive people who refuse to acknowledge that they have done anything wrong . . . But you have to forgive them, too—they are the hardest people to forgive . . . It is one thing to say, "I have forgiven him for what he did"—we can say it and think we mean it—but it is another thing to truly and totally forgive.[5]

No Fish Story

You probably know well the story of Jonah, the reluctant Old Testament prophet who didn't want to go to Ninevah and who became the focus of a huge fish story as a result. But did you ever notice *why* Jonah had been reticent about preaching in Ninevah?

When Jonah finally struggled onto shore after an unexpected three-day sea excursion in accommodations somewhat less than those offered by "Royal Mediterranean Cruise Lines," he preached the message of God's judgment to the city. And the people of Ninevah repented! They said, "This is a scary message; we'd better get right with God!" So the Lord did not destroy Ninevah.

At the close of the story, then, we find Jonah, God's prophet, outside the city, sitting under a tree, sulking. In an astonishingly honest confession, he says, "See, God! That's why I didn't want to come here in the first place. I knew that You are a gracious and compassionate God, and if these people repented, you'd have mercy on them and forgive them!" (see Jonah 4:1–3)

Can you believe the audacity of this guy? After he had disobeyed God and had run away from what he knew was God's plan for his life? After God had literally saved Jonah from the deep?

Yet Jonah sounds a lot like us. "I know You loved those people, too, Lord. And I know You want to save them and forgive them, too. And Lord, they don't deserve it! They owe me, God! They've hurt us!"

But God says, "You let Me take care of them. Your responsibility is to forgive."

Forgive or Forget It

Is there resentment still stirring in you? Is there someone you have never let off the hook because that person offended you, sinned against you? A parent perhaps? A child, your brother, sister, sweetheart, marriage part-ner, or coworker? Is there someone against whom you still hold a grudge, someone who perhaps hurt you back in your childhood? Someone who may have used you or abused you?

God says, "I want you to forgive that person—from your heart. Make a conscious choice of your will, and say, 'I forgive him' or 'I for-give her.'"

Are you ready to take responsibility for your own faults, failures, and sins? Or will you continue to try to pass the buck by blaming somebody else or something else? Yes, you were hurt. Perhaps you were taken advan-tage of or even sucked into sin . . . the first time. What about all the other times? Who is responsible for those incidents in your life?

Maybe you do have reason to recoil at even the thought of the person who hurt you. But until you consciously forgive that person and move on, the ball and chain of unforgiveness that you are dragging around will eventually pull you down to destruction unless you allow God to break that bondage and set you free.

Some people foolishly say, "Oh, if only that person would have given me what they promised or paid what they owed me, I wouldn't be in this mess! I wouldn't have all these problems. They made me what I am! He did it! She did it to me!"

Please believe me! It doesn't matter anymore. No matter what some-body else has done to us, we must forgive!

How Can We Deal with the Hurt?

Three things are necessary if you want to be free from the hurts of the past.

1. *You must choose to forgive.* We say it so often, yet few of us truly believe it: Forgiveness is a choice! Forgiveness does not mean mushy, emotional feelings. It is a matter of the will. We choose to forgive, or we choose not to forgive.

2. *You must surrender any resentments that you know you are holding on to.* You're probably familiar with the story of Corrie ten Boom, who was arrested along with her father and her sister Betsey, for sheltering Jews from the Nazis during Hitler's attempt to rid his empire of anyone with Jewish blood in their veins. Corrie's account of the atrocities that

she and her sister endured during their imprisonment in Nazi prison camps is included in her book *The Hiding Place.* Following the war, Corrie dealt successfully with many issues of forgiveness toward the men and women who had humiliated her in the camp. She forgave each one as the Lord brought the person to mind. But when Corrie first saw the nurse who had so viciously mistreated her sister Betsey in the camp, resentment overwhelmed her. Eventually, though, Corrie ten Boom not only found God's strength to forgive the nurse, but she even led the nurse to a relationship with Christ. It's not always easy to forgive those who have hurt people we love, but it is possible, and it is essential to our spiritual and emotional well-being.

3. *Allow God to change those hurts into means of healing.* One of my favorite accounts in the Old Testament is the life of Joseph. You may recall that his jealous brothers threw Joseph into a pit, a cistern. Then they sold him into slavery. Years later, after Joseph had risen to the number two position in all of Egypt, when his brothers bowed down before him, Joseph didn't say, "Guys, do you remember how you treated me? Now it's my turn!"

No, Joseph forgave them from his heart. He said, "Do not be afraid . . . you meant evil against me; but God meant it for good" (Gen. 50:19–20 NKJV).

NO GUARANTEES

I wish I could tell you that other members of the body of Christ will not sin against you. But they might. I don't understand how some people who claim to love God can be so mean. But we all have encountered Christians who offend, hurt, and even violate us.

When the offenses come, we must remember that we have been forgiven. We have seen the Master tear up the charge card! The debt is paid. It is canceled. And because the King has set us free, because He has forgiven us, we can now forgive others. Because of the price Jesus paid on Calvary's cross, we can say from the heart, "I forgive," and mean it.

17

WE'RE GOING TO
A WEDDING!

I LOOKED OUT THE window and saw the crowd of friends and family members talking excitedly among themselves on the afternoon of September 4, 1998, at John and Joyce Caruso's beautiful backyard, high in the hills, overlooking the city of Burbank, California. The Carusos' house and yard were splendidly decorated with candles, flowers, and ribbons, all witnessing to the sheer joy of the occasion. The soft music wafting through the air reminded me that it was time to go. Clad in a black tuxedo, I walked outside the house, through the crowd, toward the gazebo at the back of the yard. Accompanying me were my son, Jamie Charles, Tommy Barnett, R. T. Kendall, Matthew Barnett, Lloyd Zeigler, Phil Shaw, Paul Olsen, and B. J. Brown, a young man Lori had met in her "bus ministry" in Phoenix and to whom I had become a godfather and a spiritual mentor at the Dream Center. I stepped up into the gazebo and turned around to face the crowd of smiling faces. What a great day!

The music stopped, then began again, this time slightly louder and with a slight swing as all eyes turned back toward the house. A procession of beautifully bedecked bridesmaids gracefully made their way through the yard toward the gazebo. Everything was now in place. The ministers, the groomsmen, the bridal attendants, and, of course, I could barely stand the excitement as our anticipation heightened toward the crowning moment—the appearance of the bride.

Suddenly, the music swelled, every head in the crowd turned, and there she was! *Here comes the bride!* The bride! *My* bride! Lori Beth

Graham. And she was radiantly beautiful, dressed in a fabulous white wedding gown, her face that of an angel!

Instinctively, the crowd of well-wishers rose to its feet. Fathers of young daughters went weak-kneed. Tears welled in the eyes of mothers and grandmothers. Single guys and young women looked on with delightful envy, dreaming of their own future wedding day.

As the bride walked slowly down the aisle, on the arm of her father, the entire gathering turned slowly to follow her path. Many in the crowd caught her eye and waved politely, and the bride nodded with her sparkling eyes that no veil could conceal.

This was the day Lori and I had been waiting for—our wedding day! It was only fitting that the ceremony should begin with young B. J. Brown reading from 1 Corinthians 13, the "Love Chapter" in the Bible.

It was a marvelous wedding. Andraé Crouch sang a song he had written years earlier, which had become Lori's and my theme song, "To God Be the Glory." My daughter, Tammy Sue, sang "Amazing Grace." The pastors all spoke kind, glowing words. Lloyd Zeigler, Lori's pastor and director of Master's Commission, presented her with a pair of old-fashioned, high-button shoes, symbolizing her self-effacing service of shining shoes, which she had done to support herself while working in the ministry in Phoenix. Then he gave her glass slippers as a reminder that some "Cinderella" stories really do come true! (You can read all the wonderfully mushy details of our romance and wedding day in Lori's book!)

As much as I savored every part of the ceremony, my anticipation intensified with each passing moment. Lori and I committed ourselves to each other in our wedding vows, and finally, the distinguished pastor of Westminster Chapel in London, R.T. Kendall, declared us to be . . . *husband and wife!* In an instant, the bride and the groom were united; the two became one!

WE ARE THE BRIDE!

It is no accident that one of the word-pictures used for the Christian community in Scripture is "the Bride of Christ." That is who we are. We are His bride, in waiting. We are not merely "good friends"; we are much more than lovers; we are destined to have the intimacy with Jesus that can only be known as, and compared to, that of a husband and a wife. Throughout the

Bible, the relationship between God and His people is spoken of as a husband and wife. This is why, in the Old Testament, when God's people went astray, He referred to them as a harlot. In the New Testament, He was equally possessive of His people. For instance, in 2 Corinthians 11:2, Paul wrote, "For I am jealous for you with godly jealousy. For I have betrothed you to one husband, that I may present you as a chaste virgin to Christ."

Interestingly, one of the most familiar passages describing the husband-wife relationship in the New Testament has a dual meaning that applies also to the church.

> Husbands, love your wives, just as Christ also loved the church and gave Himself for her, that He might sanctify and cleanse her with the washing of water by the word, that He might present her to Himself a glorious church, not having spot or wrinkle or any such thing, but that she should be holy and without blemish. (Eph. 5:25–27 NKJV)

Following some practical applications of this truth, Paul concluded his discussion of the husband-wife relationship by saying, "This is a great mystery, but I speak concerning Christ and the church. Nevertheless let each one of you in particular so love his own wife as himself, and let the wife see that she respects her husband" (Eph. 5:32–33 NKJV). Did you catch that? After talking about wives submitting to their husbands (yes, this is *that* passage!) and husbands loving their wives enough to die for them, as Christ gave Himself up for the church, Paul turned around and said, "Well, we've been talking about the husband and wife relationship here, but, really, we're talking about the relationship between Jesus and the community of believers." Clearly, Paul is using marriage as a symbol of our relationship with the Lord. Perhaps the most intriguing issue in Paul's discussion is, Which is real and which is the symbol? We may never know . . . until the marriage has taken place.

Moreover, we are not simply meandering meaninglessly through life, biding our time until we die. We are not merely preparing for the tough times of tribulation. We are getting ready for the Wedding! Soon, the groom, King Jesus, will be united with His bride, the church.

In these turbulent times, we may be tempted to get our focus off the Lord Jesus and succumb to worry about how we are going to survive the coming days of difficulty. Some people are worried about the economy collapsing. Others are frightened about the crime in our streets and the "killing fields" that used to be known as our schools and churches. Still others worry about the natural disasters descending on the earth with ever-increasing frequency and intensity. Many Bible teachers and preachers warn that the Antichrist and the one-world economic system are upon us. The mark of the beast cannot be far off. Armageddon looms largely.

All of these things may be worthy of our attention, but they should not cause us to worry or lose hope. In fact, Jesus instructed us, "Now when these things begin to happen, look up and lift up your heads, because your redemption draws near" (Luke 21:28 NKJV).

"What are we going to do? What's going to happen to us?" many lament. "Where's it all going to end?"

I don't know about you, but *I'm going to a wedding!* The marriage of the Lamb, the Lord Jesus, to His bride, the church, is soon to take place! And, oh! What a celebration it is going to be! People from every nation, every tribe, and every tongue will be there, all gathered to give honor and praise to the King of kings and Lord of lords. The apostle John wrote of this event: "Hallelujah! For the Lord our God, the Almighty, reigns. Let us rejoice and be glad and give the glory to Him, for the marriage of the Lamb has come and His bride has made herself ready . . . 'Blessed are those who are invited to the marriage supper of the Lamb'" (Rev. 19:6–7, 9 NASB).

Now, here's where it really gets good. With all of creation gathered to honor King Jesus, the Groom will honor *His bride.* Jesus Christ will honor *us,* His church, the community of believers, in a marriage ceremony like no other ever conducted. Think of it! We are the bride of Christ, to be honored, extolled, and glorified by Him! Is that a Cinderella story or what?

We will be His and He will be ours, in intimate fellowship, forever! We are His chosen ones, the ones He died to redeem and save, the ones He wants to live with, not just for a lifetime, but for eternity in heaven. Talk about "someday my Prince will come!"

But what do we know about heaven and our future life with the King?

WHAT IS HEAVEN LIKE?

The Bible mentions *heaven* quite frequently, fifty-two times in Revelation alone! Hundreds of other references to heaven are sprinkled throughout the Scripture. Granted, the biblical writers were not always referring to eternal bliss. Many times the term was used merely to describe the atmospheric conditions and the skies above us. Jesus sometimes used the phrase "kingdom of heaven" synonymously with His spiritual kingdom (Matt. 5:3; 10:7; 16:19). But the Bible also pictures a *place* called heaven, which is the abode of God and the future home of the bride of Christ— our future home!

Most important, we know that heaven is the home of our Lord Jesus. Certainly, His Spirit resides within the hearts of all true believers, but in heaven, we will see Jesus, alive and in person! What an astounding thought: We are going to see the King! Not only will we see Him at a royal ceremony, we are going to live with Him forever.

In my lifetime, I have occasionally been privileged to be in the presence of presidents. I have been a guest of the president of the United States aboard his plane, *Air Force One.* I have met with leaders of foreign countries and dignitaries of every sort. Many of these great leaders have inspired a measure of awe within me. But I cannot imagine the feelings that will rush through me when I see Jesus Christ, King of kings and Lord of lords. I have no doubt that, like the apostle John, I will fall at His feet when I first see Him (Rev. 1:17). You probably will, too!

Yet, amazingly, He wants us to be with Him! He is preparing a place for us right now, our eternal home. The night before His crucifixion, Jesus told His disciples, "I go to prepare a place for you. And if I go and prepare a place for you, I will come again, and receive you to Myself; that where I am, there you may be also" (John 14:2–3 NASB). Can your mind conceive of the kind of place that the regnant, all-powerful King is creating for those whom He loves? For us! His church!

John attempted to describe heaven (sometimes referred to as the "New Jerusalem" or the "Holy City") as a huge cube, approximately fifteen hundred miles in each direction (Rev. 21:16). The predominant building material of the Holy City seems to be pure gold (21:18). The New Jerusalem has walls of jasper (21:18) and has twelve gates, three entrances on each side (21:21). An unusual river is there, "a river of the water of life, clear as crystal, coming from the throne of God and of the Lamb, in the middle of its street. And on either side of the river was the tree of life" (Rev. 22:1–2 NASB). It's difficult to determine how much of John's vision is to be interpreted literally and how much should be interpreted symbolically, but there is no question that he is picturing a magnificently gorgeous place, far beyond anything that our minds can imagine.

In heaven there will be no sea (Rev. 21:1), which leads some Bible scholars to believe that there will no longer be any separation between loved ones in the body of Christ. No tears are in heaven, either, because our God will wipe them all away (Rev. 21:4). Nor will there be any death, mourning, crying, or pain in heaven (21:4). Neither will there be any temple (21:22); no sun, and no moon. We won't *need* the sun, moon, or stars in heaven, because Jesus will be the light of that city! John wrote, "The glory of God illuminated it. The Lamb is its light" (21:23 NKJV).

Interestingly, night will be a thing of the past in heaven. Nor will the gates ever need to be closed (21:25). Why? Because nothing unclean, or we could say, unholy, will be there (21:27). The curse of sin and its effects will have been broken and destroyed forever (22:3), and Jesus Christ will be Lord of all.

God Himself will dwell in our midst; we will be His people and He will be our God forever! (Rev. 21:3). We will have complete and unrestricted fellowship with our Lord. The Bride and the Groom will be one.

What Will We Do There?

Apparently, one of the paramount and most exciting activities of heaven will be an opportunity to enjoy a dimension of true praise and worship unlike anything we have previously experienced here on earth. We will join the four living creatures of Revelation 4:8 who "do not cease to say, 'Holy, holy, holy, is the Lord God, the Almighty, who was and who is and who is to come'" (NASB). We will sing along with heaven's twenty-four elders who "will fall down before Him who sits on the throne, and will worship Him who lives forever and ever, and will cast their crowns before the throne, saying, 'Worthy art Thou, our Lord and our God, to receive glory and honor and power; for Thou didst create all things, and because of Thy will they existed, and were created'" (Rev. 4:10–11 NASB).

Whew! Sometimes we think we have fabulous music here on earth. Can you imagine the singing in heaven? *Praise* is going to be the predominating language of heaven. *Worship* will no longer be "worked up," but will flow naturally from the hearts of God's people to the heart of their holy God.

Besides having intimate fellowship with Jesus, some Bible scholars speculate that we also will rule over certain parts of God's creation. After all, we are joint heirs with Jesus (Rom. 8:17), so what He rules, the bride of Christ will rule also. Billy Graham has often said that he thinks we may even have work to do in heaven, although it will be without the drudgery and stress that accompany much of this life's work. Maybe so. I don't pretend to understand all about these things.

All I know is that I want to be there. I want to be with Jesus, the One I have fallen in love with! He has promised that it will be good; it will be beautiful; it will be worth the wait. That's all I need to know.

I also want to spend eternity with the body of Christ, the community of believers. What delights we will enjoy together in the eternal kingdom of God. No more worries about time, money, or reputations. No more attacks from the devil. Heaven will be a safe place, a place of unfathomable security—the ultimate refuge—because wherever Jesus is, that is our refuge. We will be home—home with Him, home at last. And we will no doubt discover that Jesus is, was, and forever will be, our Refuge.

NOTES

Chapter 3
1. Flavius Josephus, "The Jewish War" from *The New Complete Works of Josephus,* translated by William Whiston with commentary by Paul L. Maier, © 1999 by Kregel Publications, 898. Used by permission.
2. Ibid.
3. Ibid.

Chapter 6
1. Max Anders, *What You Need to Know About the Church* (Nashville: Thomas Nelson, 1997), 7.
2. Harold Kushner, in an interview with Peter Lowe; *Peter Lowe's Success Talk,* © 1998 Peter Lowe International, 8405 Benjamin Road, Tampa, FL 33634. Used by permission.
3. Anders, *What You Need to Know About the Church,* 7–10.
4. K. P. Yohannan, *The Road to Reality* (Lake Mary, FL: Creation House, 1988), 51–52.
5. Rick Warren, *The Purpose Driven Church* (Grand Rapids: Zondervan, 1995), 79.

Chapter 7
1. Chad Walsh, *Early Christians of the Twenty-first Century* (New York: The Seabury Press, Inc., 1985), 19.
2. Anders, *What You Need to Know About the Church,* 56.

3. Ibid.

4. Ibid., 59.

5. Richard Neuhaus, *Freedom for Ministry* (New York: Harper & Row, 1979), 126, cited in Charles Colson, *The Body* (Dallas: Word, 1992), 142.

6. Colson, *The Body*, 143.

7. Adapted from: Kefa Sempangi, *A Distant Grief* (Glendale, CA: Regal Books, 1979), 149.

Chapter 8

1. Dietrich Bonhoeffer, *Life Together*, trans. John W. Doberstein (New York: Harper & Row, 1954), 20.

Chapter 10

1. Bonhoeffer, *Life Together*, 99.

2. Quoted in Anders, *What You Need to Know About the Church*, 40.

3. From *God in the Dock* by C. S. Lewis. Copyright © C. S. Lewis Pte. Ltd. 1970. Extract reprinted by permission.

4. Anders, *What You Need to Know About the Church*, 10–11.

5. Ibid.

6. Ibid.

Chapter 12

1. Bob Benson, "Sunday School Picnic," *Laughter in the Walls*, ed. Gloria Gaither (Alexandria, IN: Gaither Family Resources, 1996), 42.

Chapter 14

1. Jim Bakker, *Prosperity and the Coming Apocalypse* (Nashville: Thomas Nelson, 1998), 110–11.

2. Greg Gittrich, "Massive Hidden Fault Threatens Downtown," *Daily News*, © *Los Angeles Daily News*, 5 March 1999, 1.

3. Ibid.

4. Ibid.

5. Ibid., 15.

6. Ibid.

Chapter 15

1. Bonhoeffer, *Life Together*, 27.

2. Ibid.
3. Ibid., 26.
4. Ibid.
5. Ibid., 27–28.

Chapter 16
1. Bonhoeffer, *Life Together*, 110.
2. Ibid., 112.
3. Ibid., 118.
4. Ibid., 113.
5. R.T. Kendall, *God Meant It for Good* (Charlotte, NC: Morningstar Publications, 1988), 249.